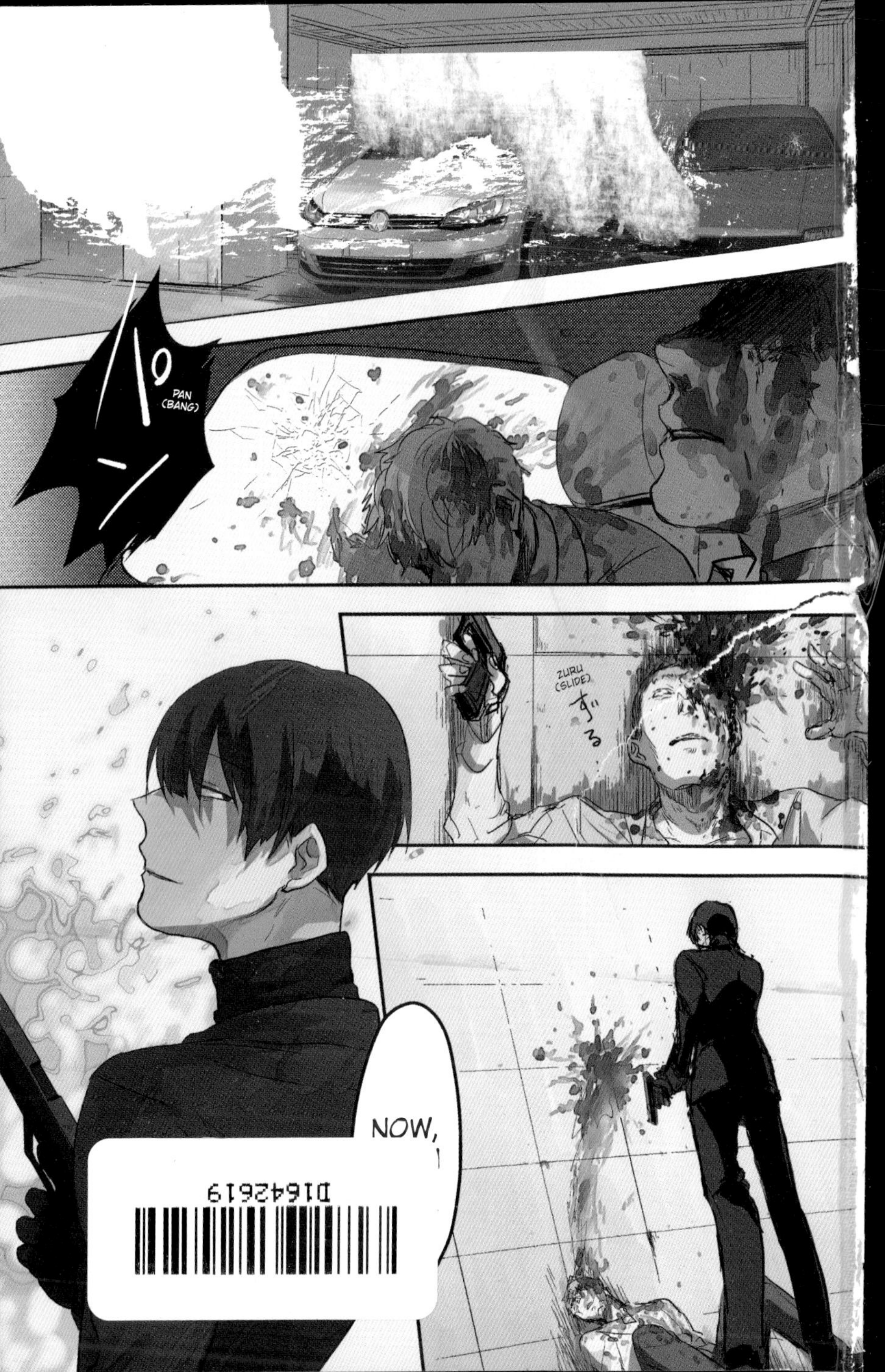
PAN
(BANG)
ZURU
(SLIDE)
ずる
NOW,
I

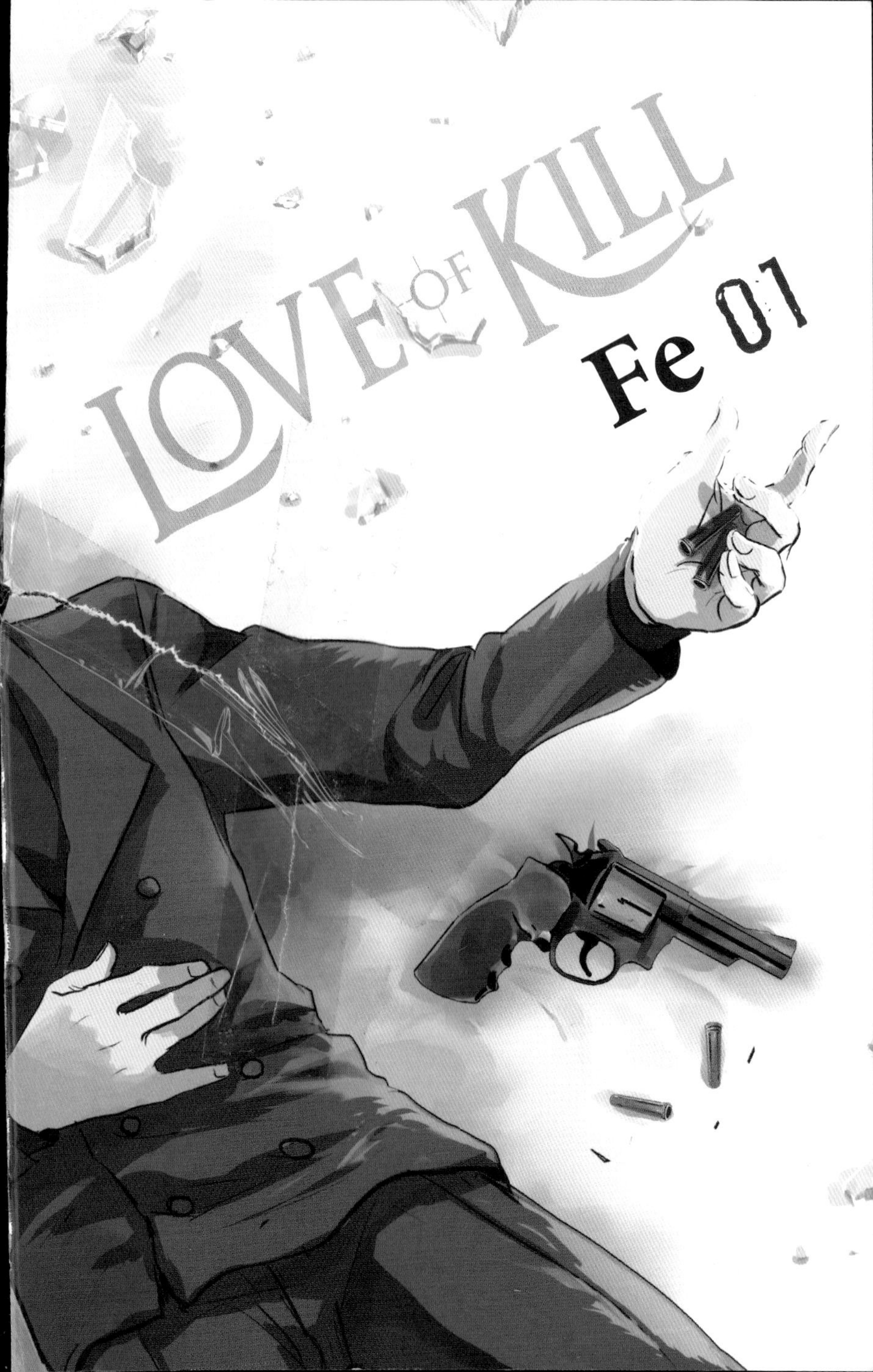
LOVE OF KILL
Fe 01

C
O
N
T
E
N
T
S

FILE 01 **WHAT'S YOUR NAME?** 001

FILE 02 **TRADE** 031

FILE 03 **WITNESS** 057

FILE 04 **TARGET** 085

FILE 05 **CAR CHASE** 107

FILE 06 **FATE** 129

SPECIAL FILE 155

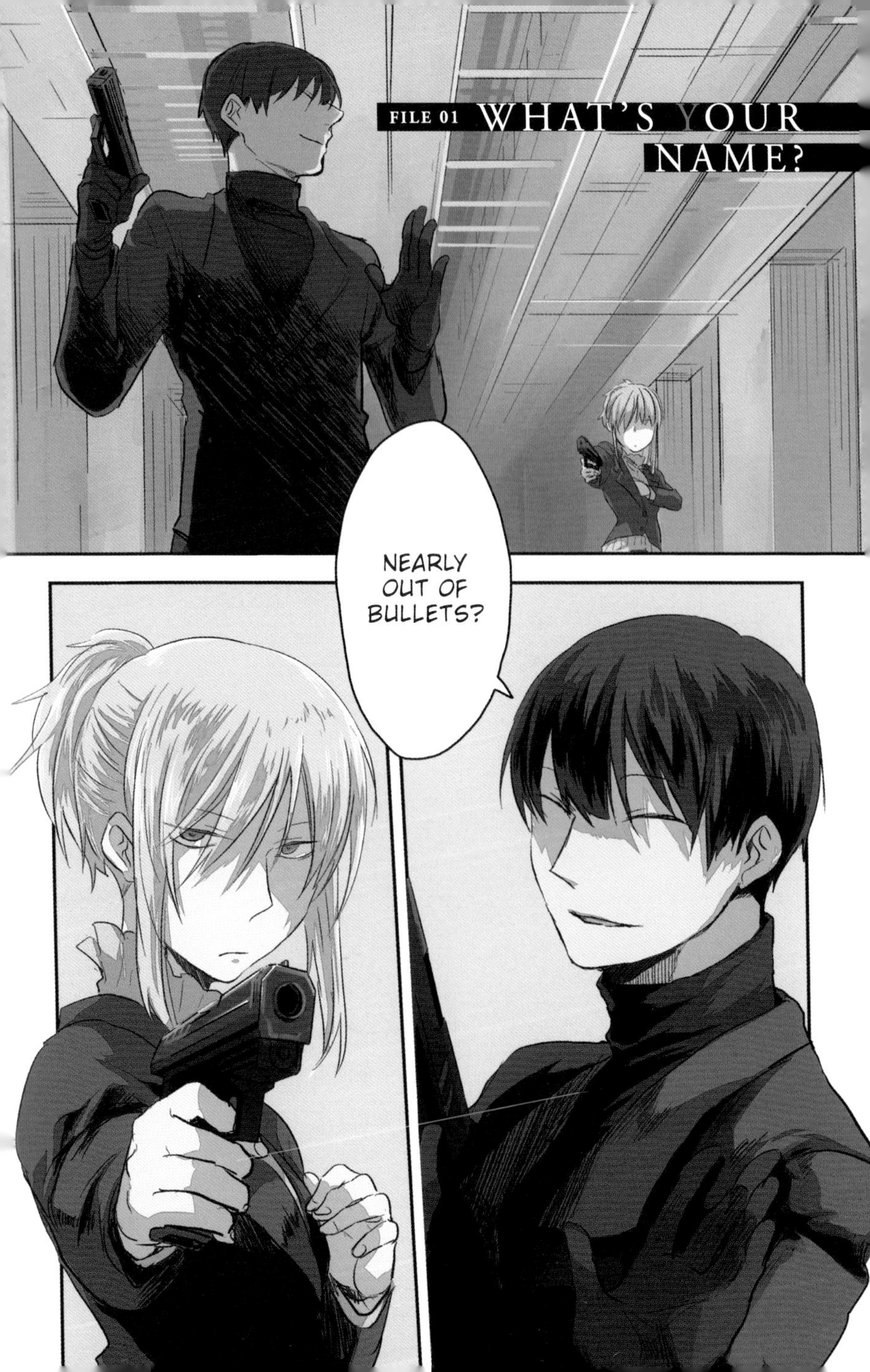
FILE 01 WHAT'S YOUR NAME?
NEARLY OUT OF BULLETS?

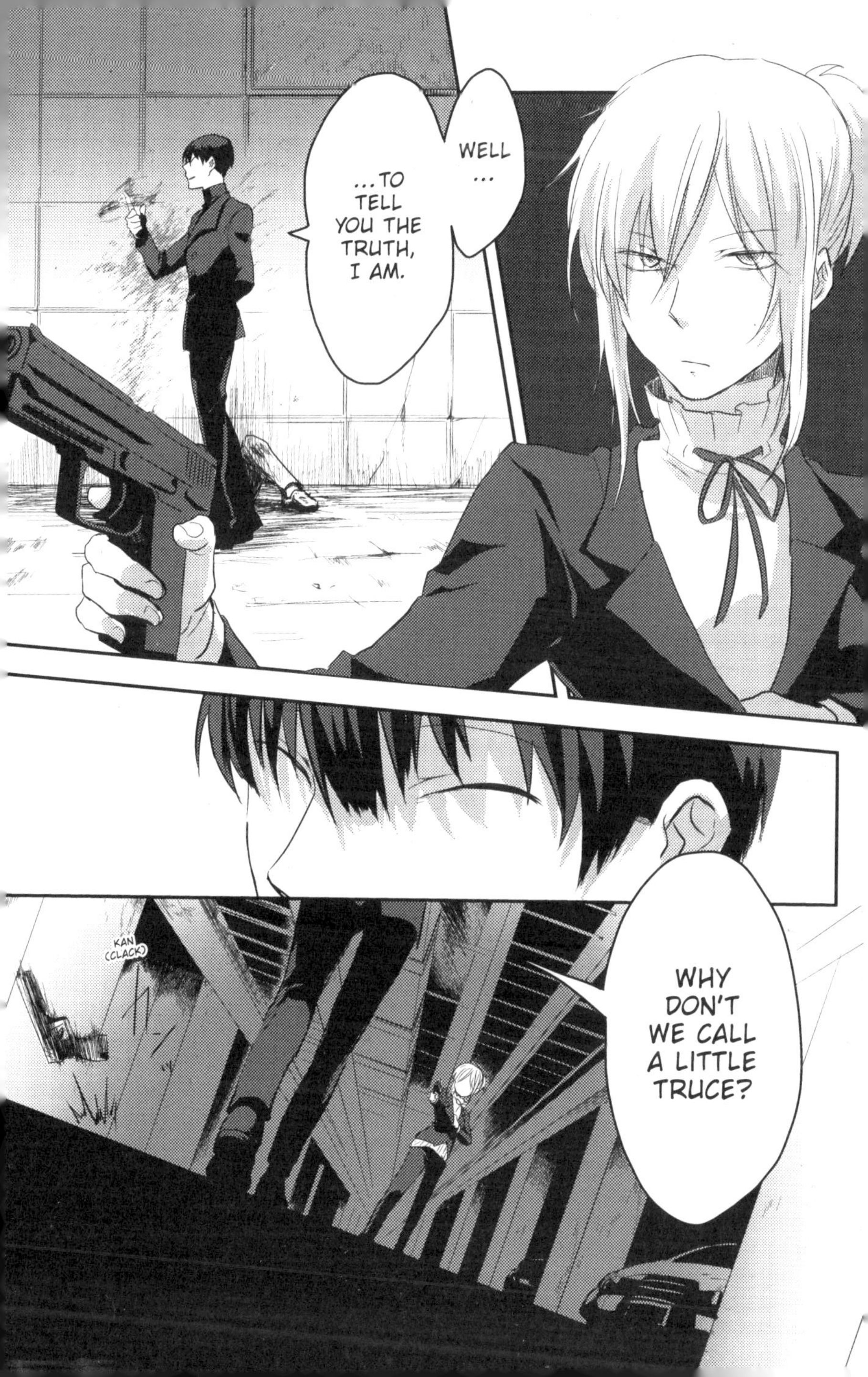
WELL ...
...TO TELL YOU THE TRUTH, I AM.
WHY DON'T WE CALL A LITTLE TRUCE?
KAN (CLACK)

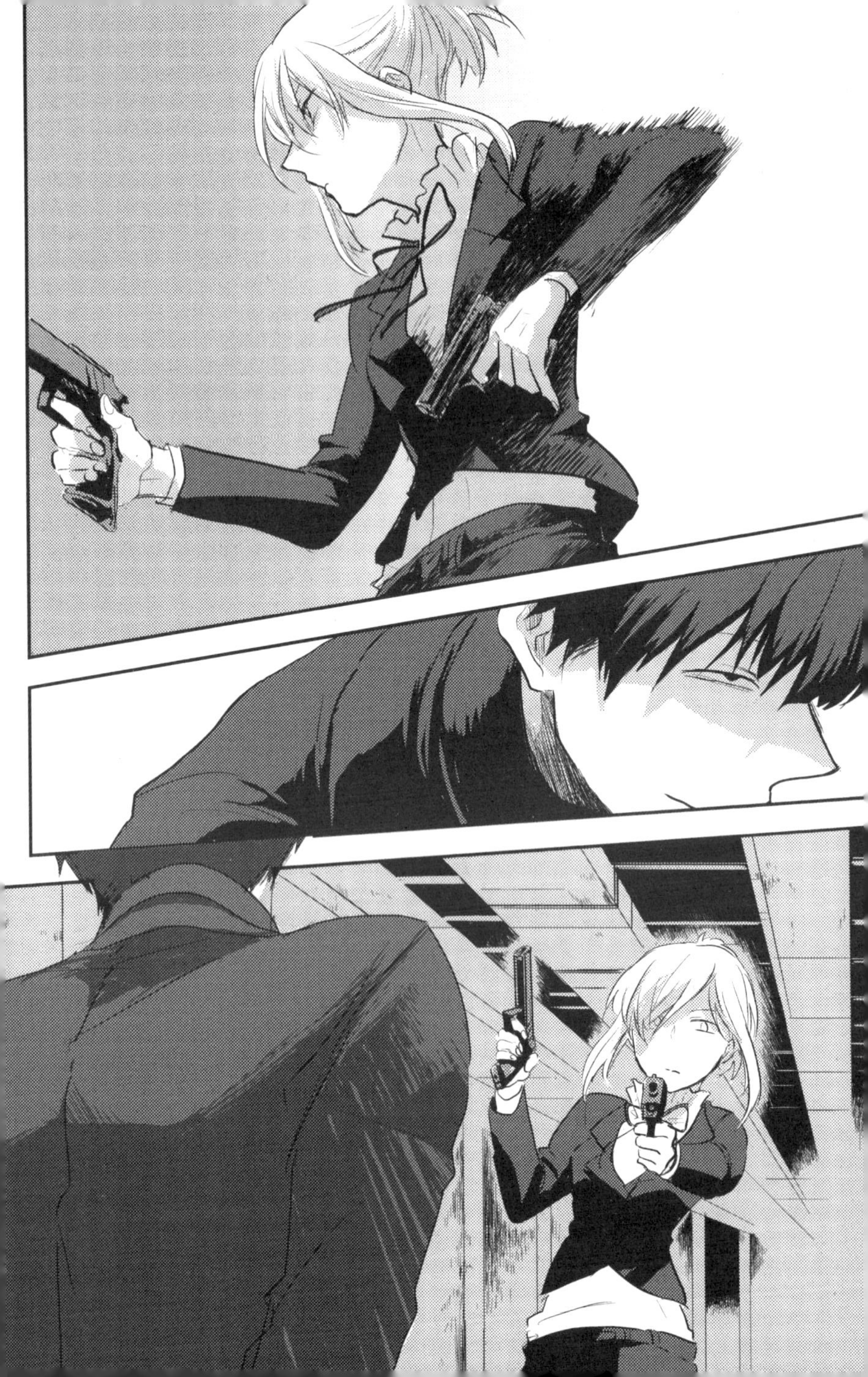

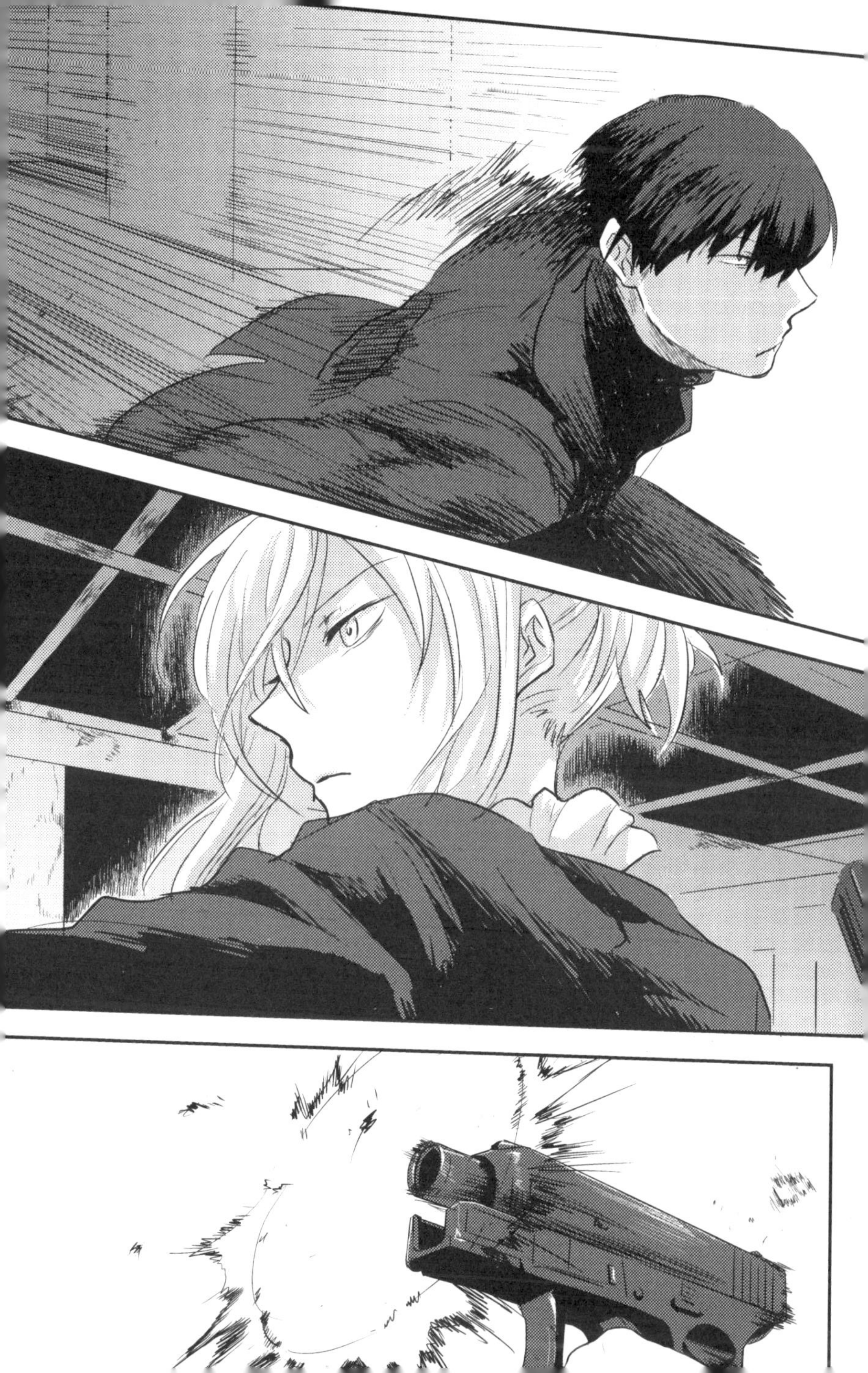

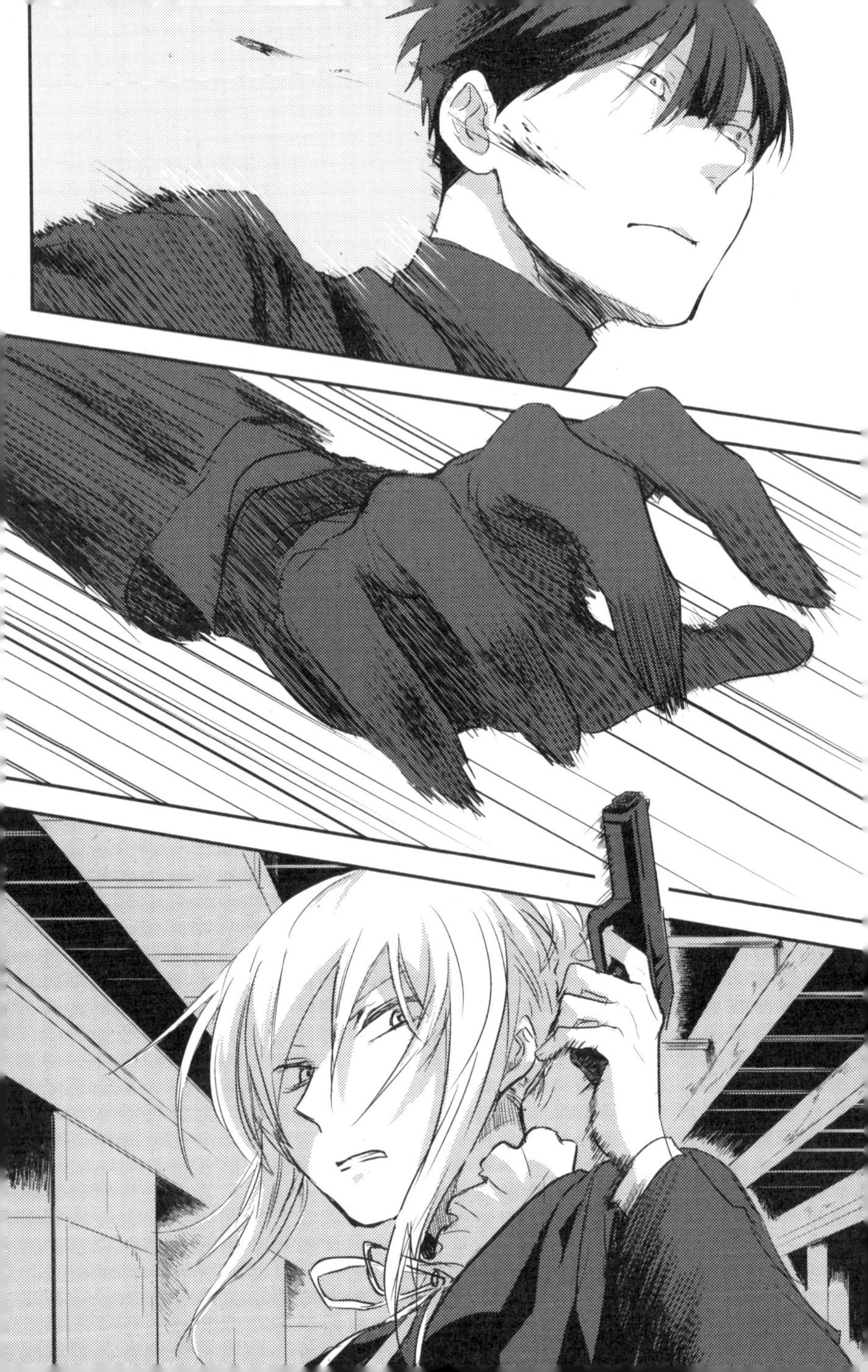

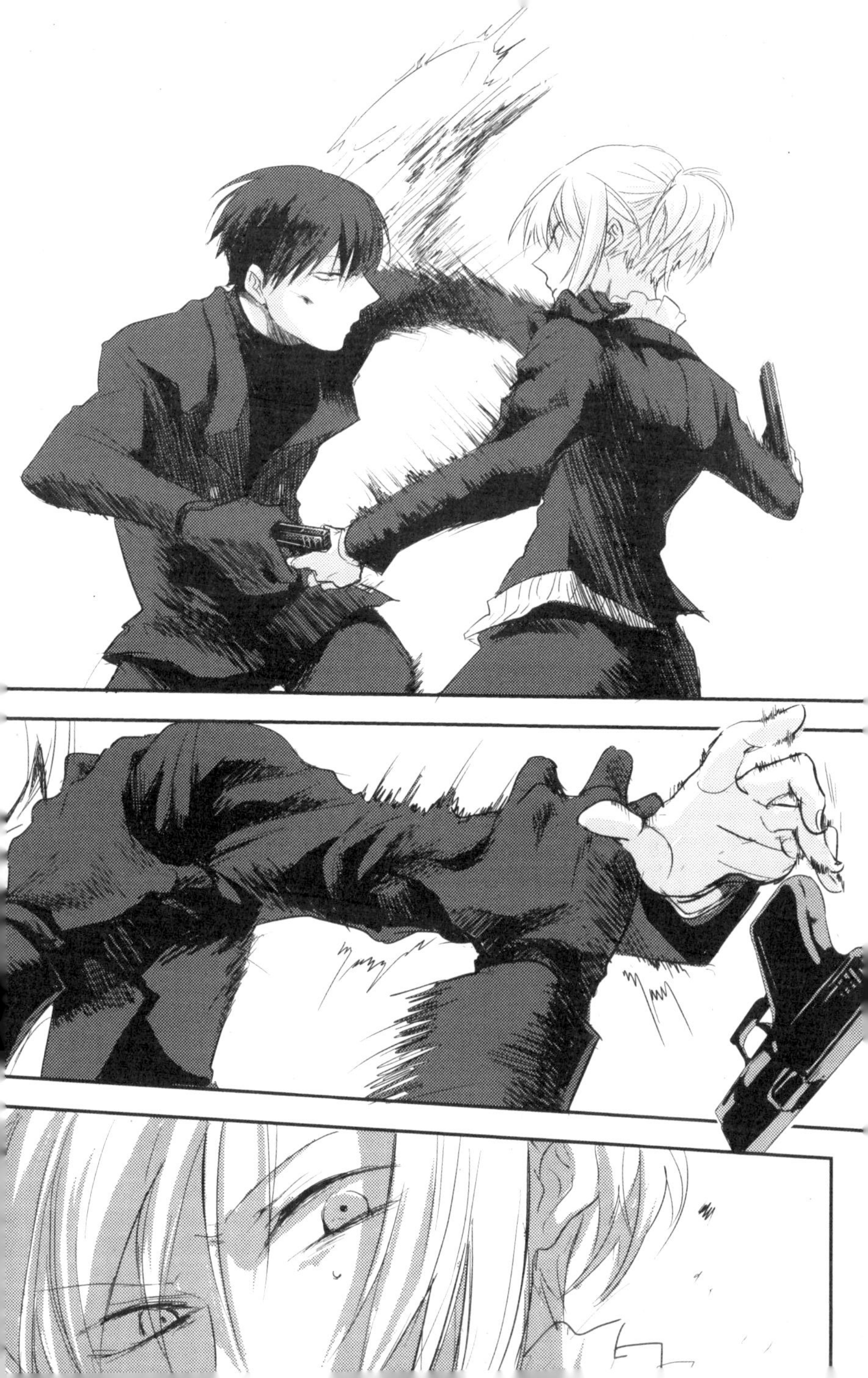

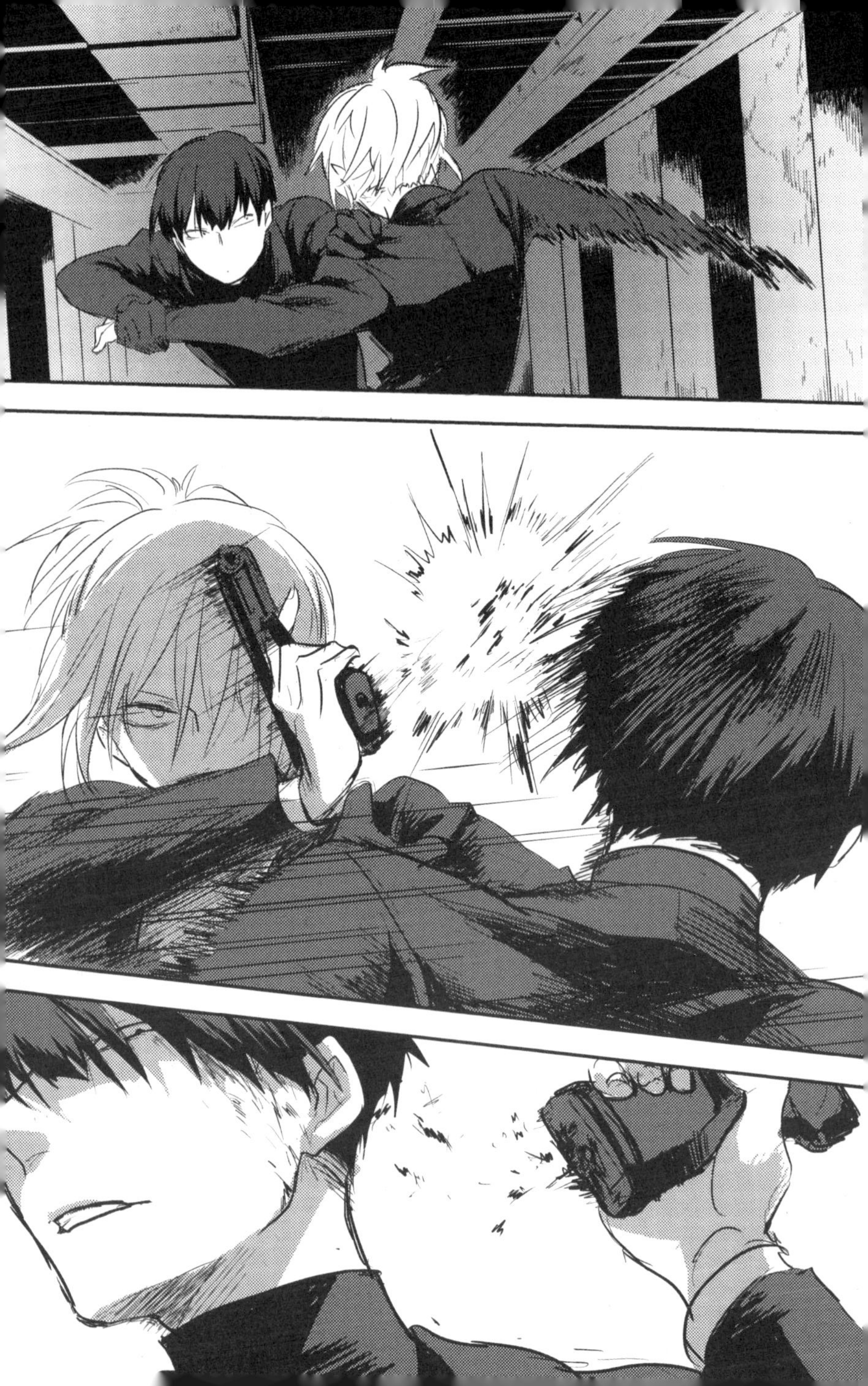

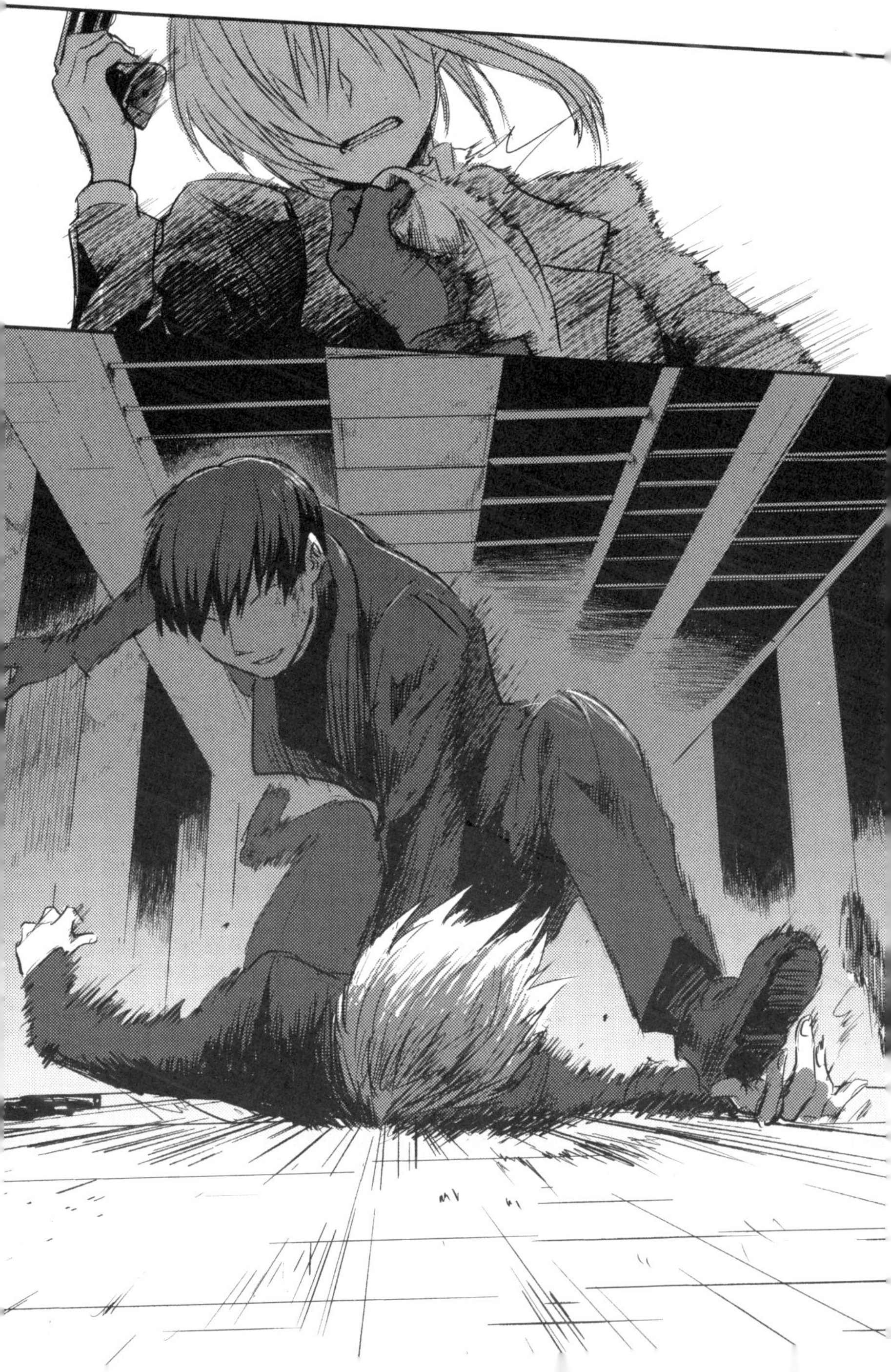

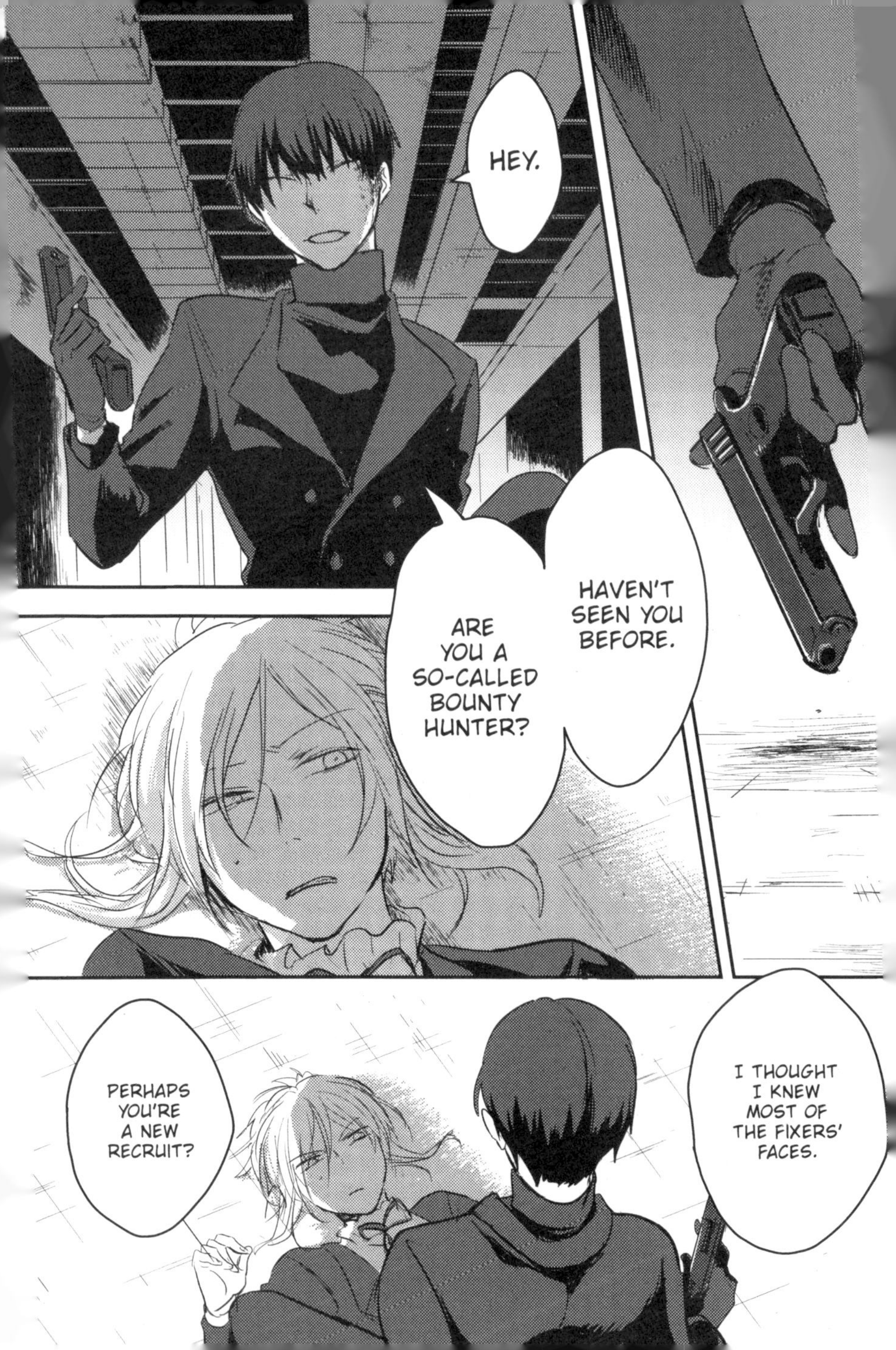
HEY.
HAVEN'T SEEN YOU BEFORE.
ARE YOU A SO-CALLED BOUNTY HUNTER?
I THOUGHT I KNEW MOST OF THE FIXERS' FACES.
PERHAPS YOU'RE A NEW RECRUIT?

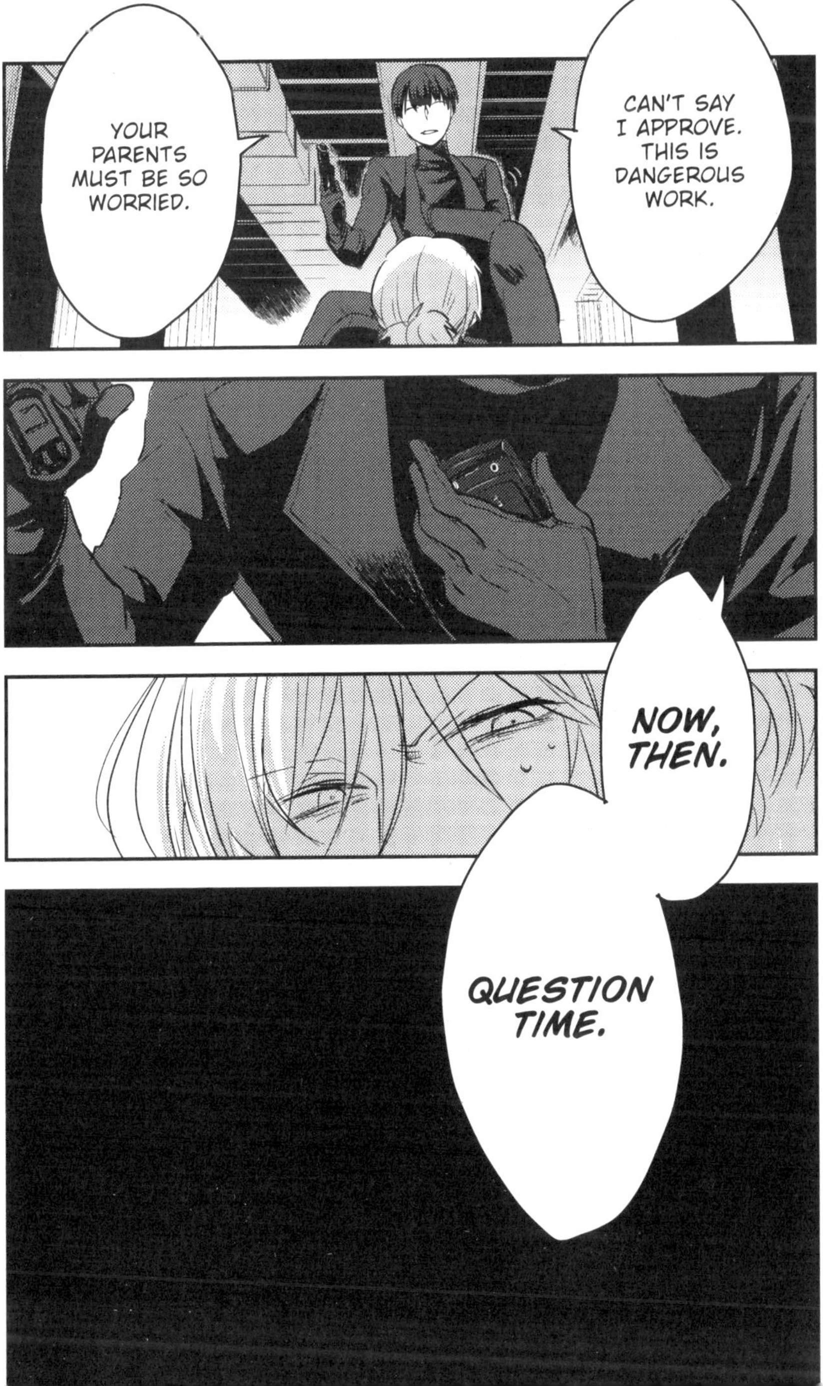
CAN'T SAY I APPROVE. THIS IS DANGEROUS WORK.
YOUR PARENTS MUST BE SO WORRIED.
NOW, THEN.
QUESTION TIME.

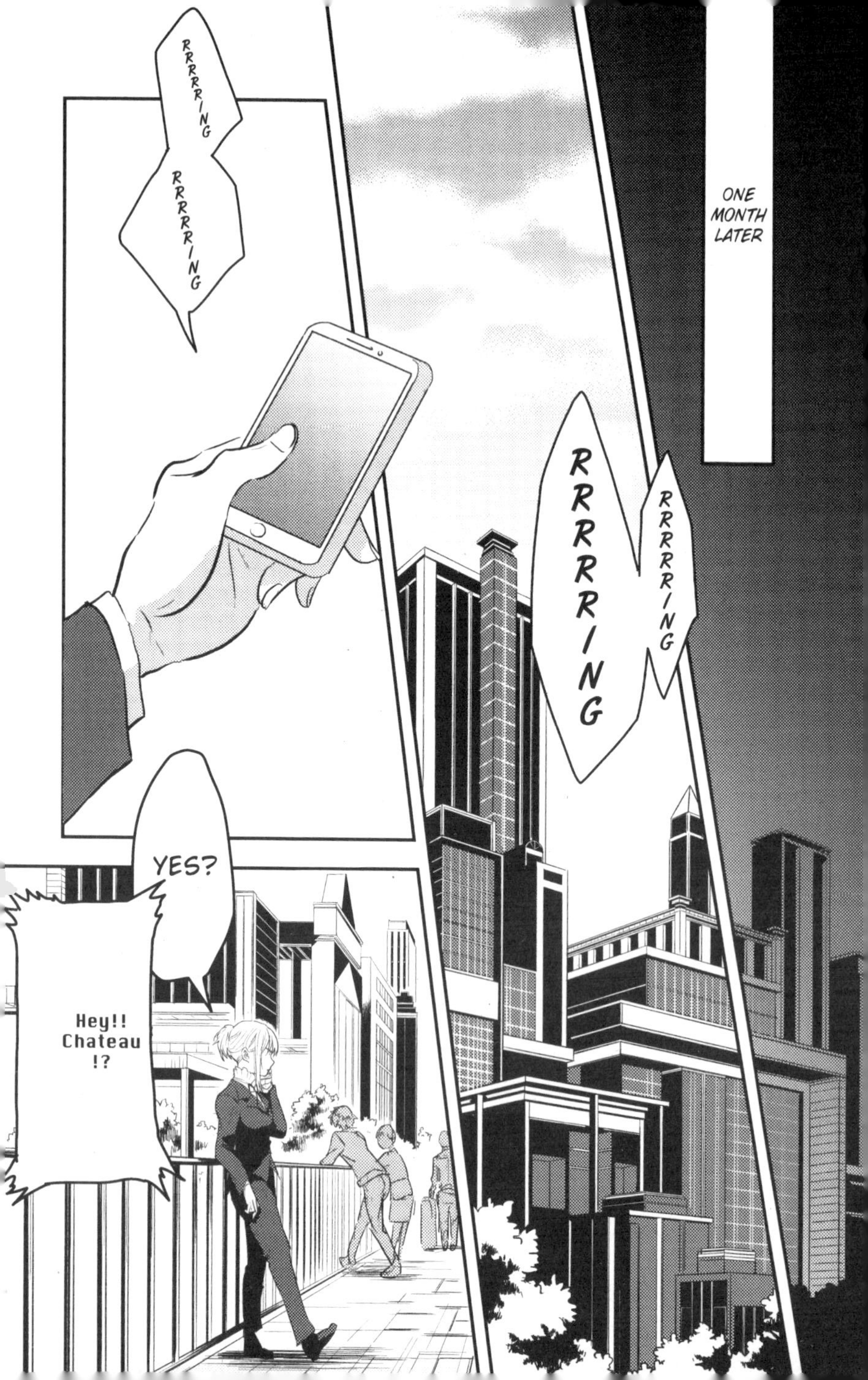
ONE MONTH LATER
RRRRRING
RRRRRING
RRRRRING
RRRRRING
YES?
Hey!! Chateau !?

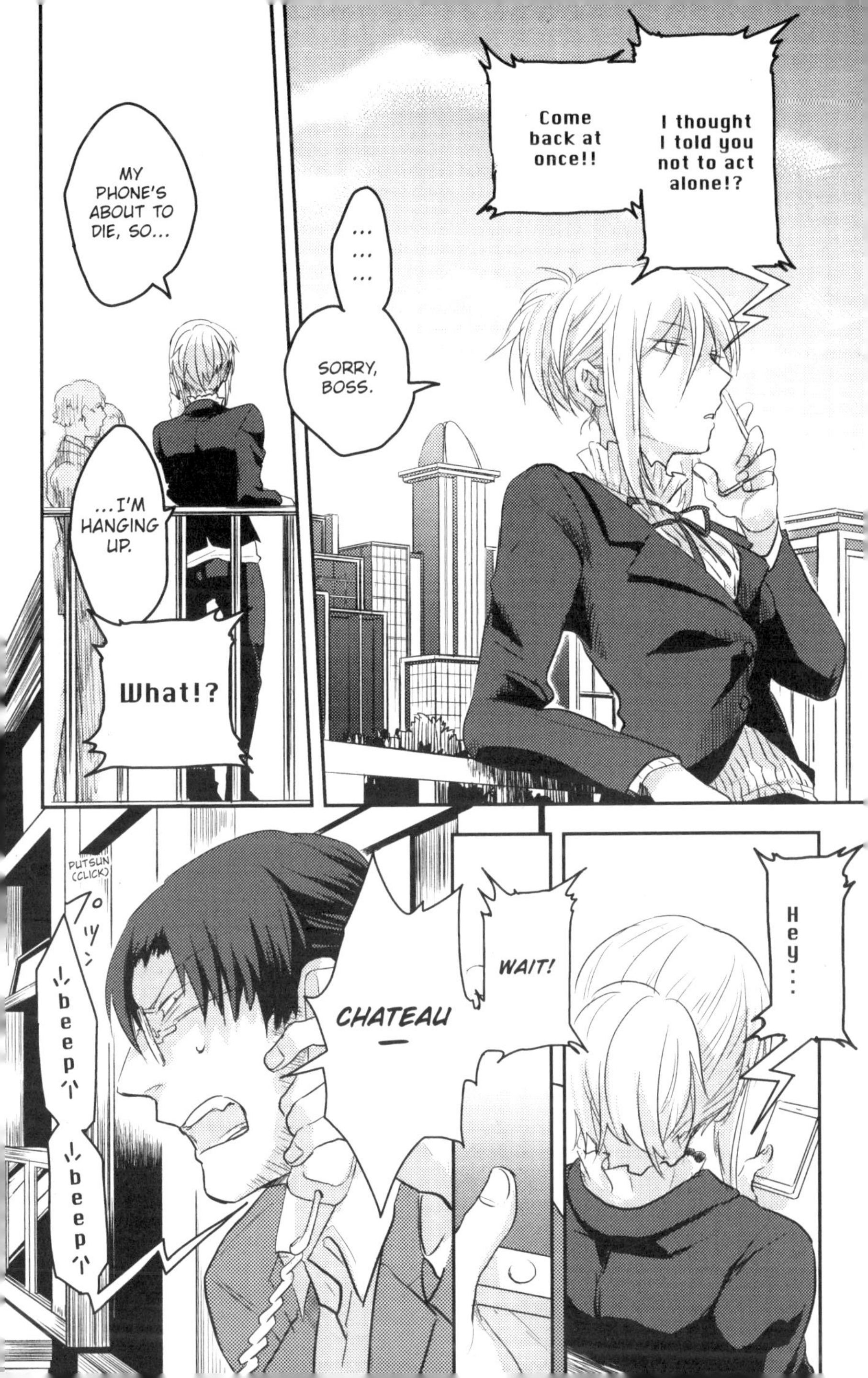

I thought I told you not to act alone!?
Come back at once!!
... ...
SORRY, BOSS.
MY PHONE'S ABOUT TO DIE, SO...
...I'M HANGING UP.
What!?
Hey...
WAIT!
CHATEAU—
PUTSUN (CLICK)
beep
beep

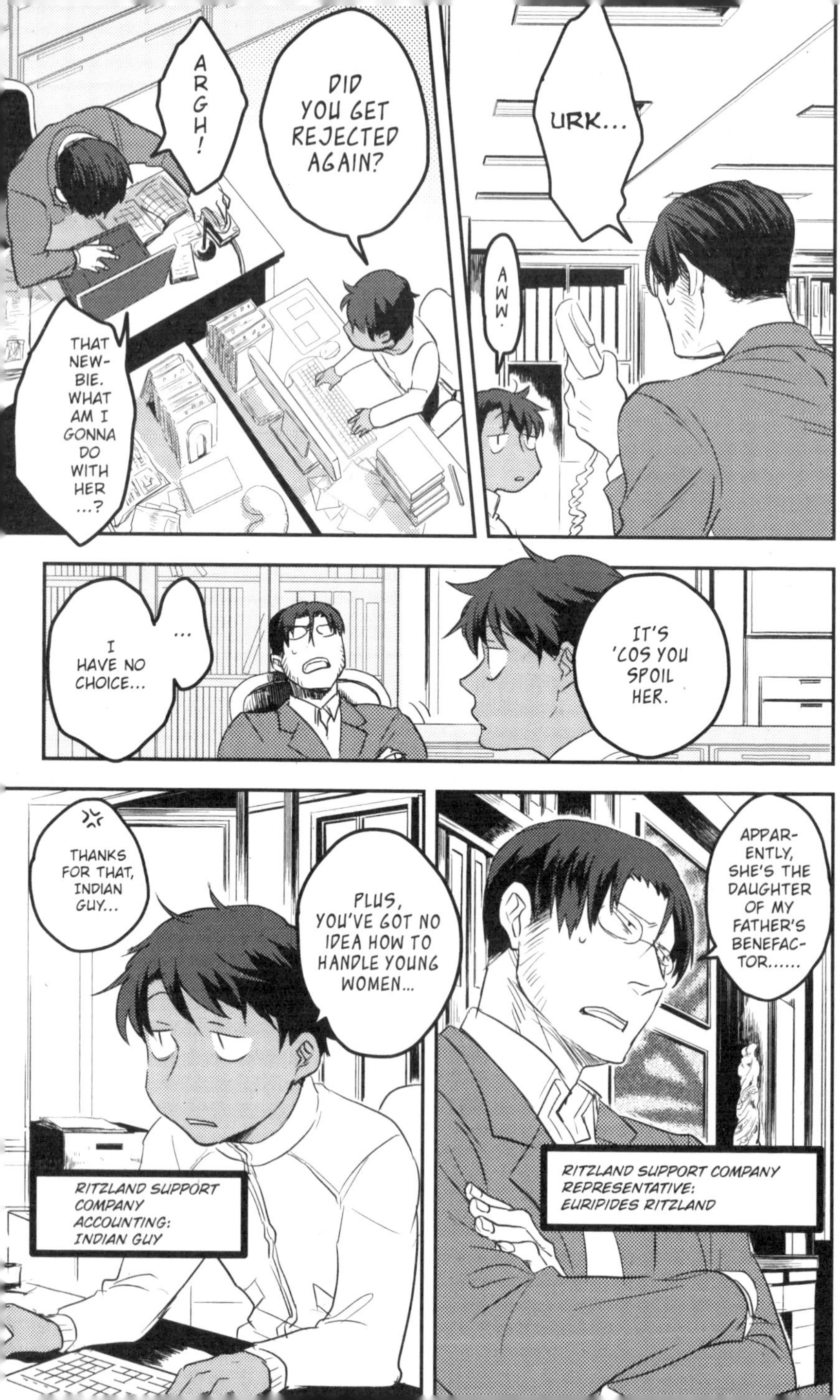
URK...
AWW.
DID YOU GET REJECTED AGAIN?
ARGH!
THAT NEWBIE. WHAT AM I GONNA DO WITH HER ...?
IT'S 'COS YOU SPOIL HER.
...
I HAVE NO CHOICE...
APPARENTLY, SHE'S THE DAUGHTER OF MY FATHER'S BENEFACTOR......
RITZLAND SUPPORT COMPANY REPRESENTATIVE: EURIPIDES RITZLAND
PLUS, YOU'VE GOT NO IDEA HOW TO HANDLE YOUNG WOMEN...
THANKS FOR THAT, INDIAN GUY...
RITZLAND SUPPORT COMPANY ACCOUNTING: INDIAN GUY

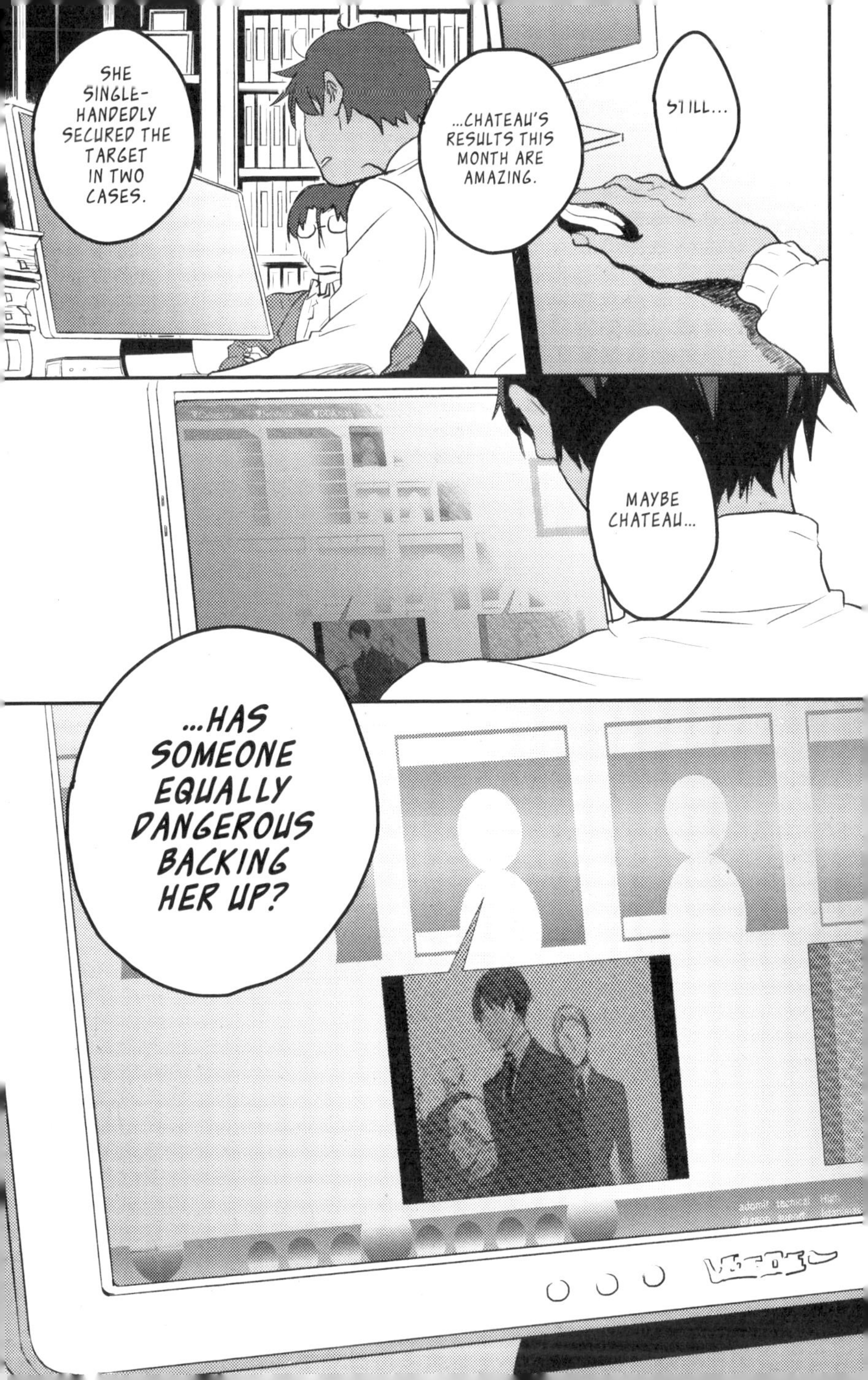
STILL...
...CHATEAU'S RESULTS THIS MONTH ARE AMAZING.
SHE SINGLE-HANDEDLY SECURED THE TARGET IN TWO CASES.
MAYBE CHATEAU...
...HAS SOMEONE EQUALLY DANGEROUS BACKING HER UP?

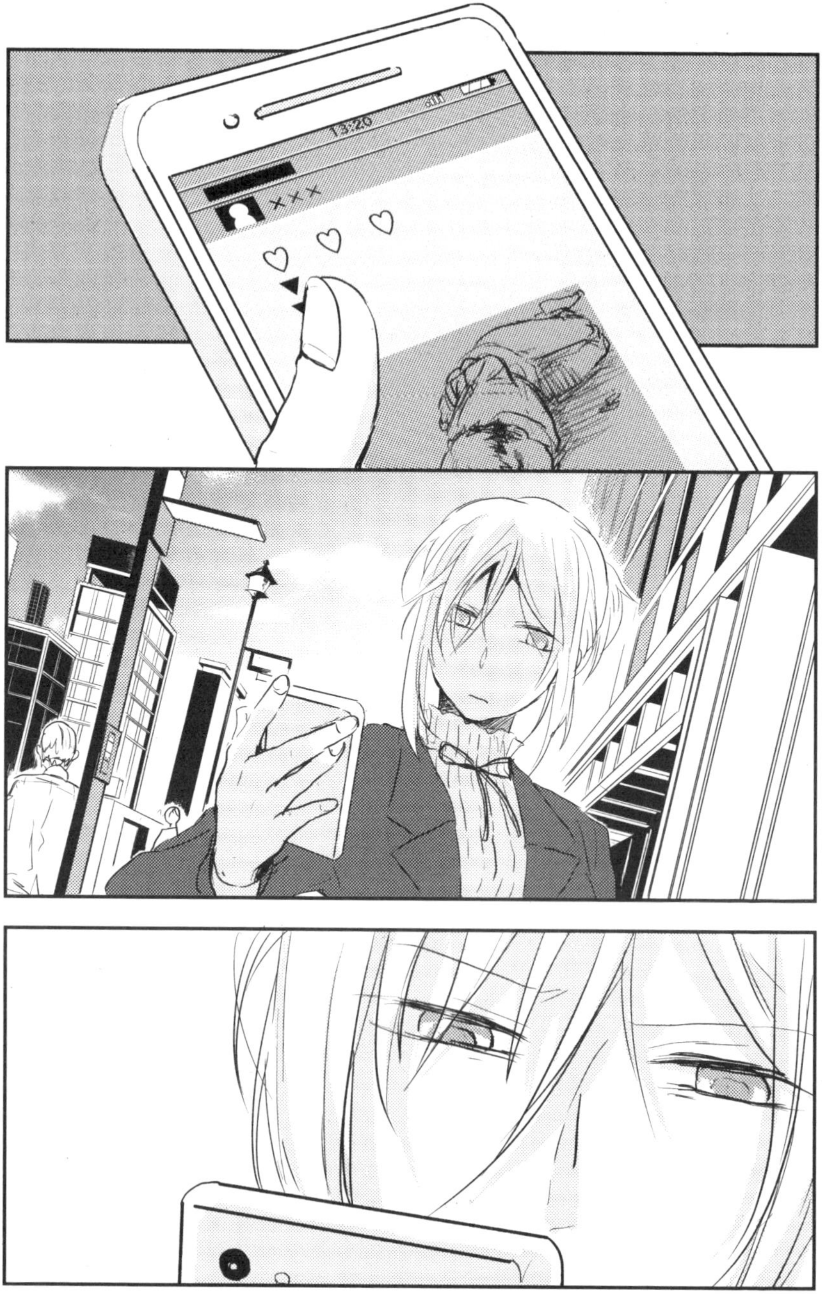
13:20
×××

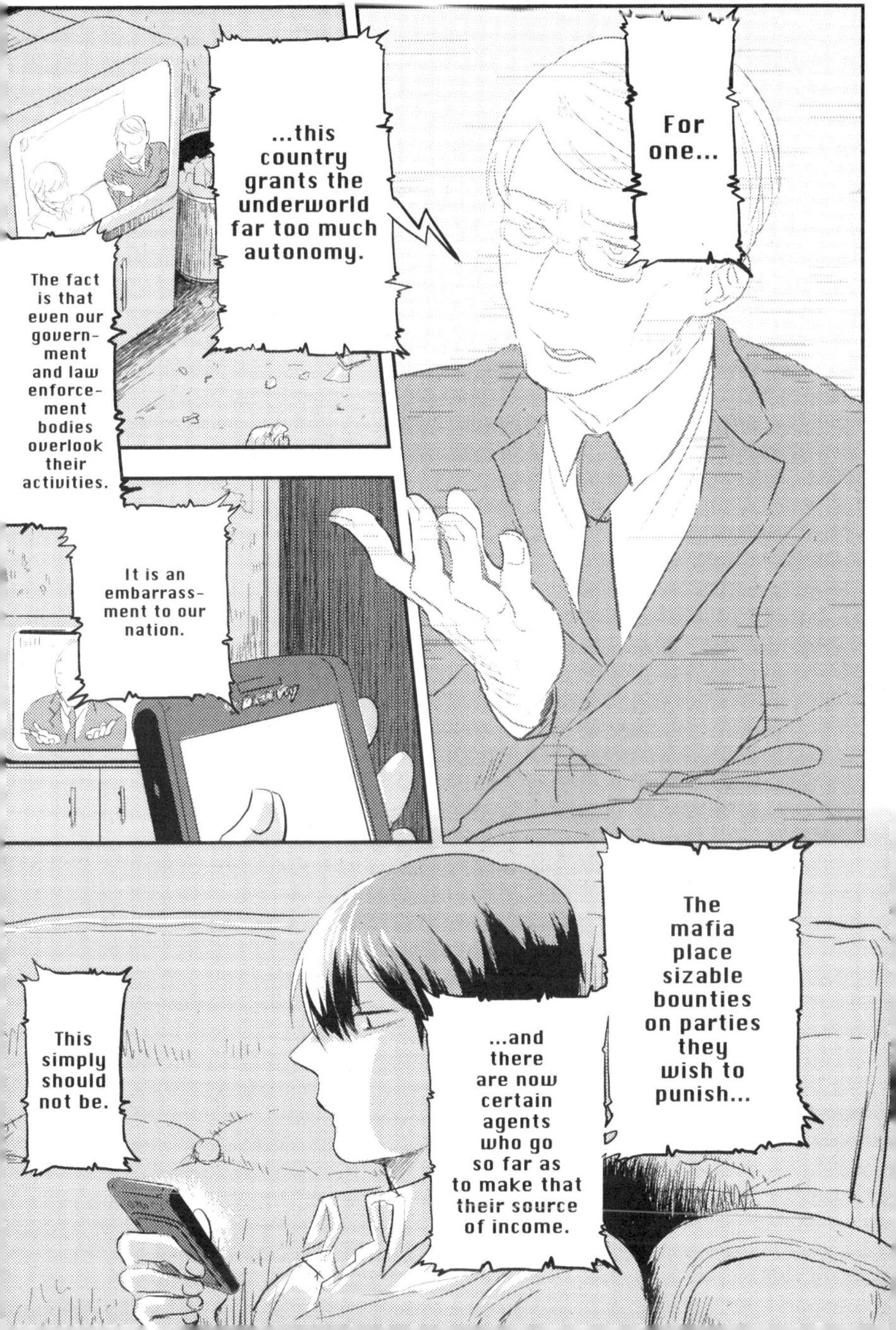
For one...
...this country grants the underworld far too much autonomy.
The fact is that even our government and law enforcement bodies overlook their activities.
It is an embarrassment to our nation.
The mafia place sizable bounties on parties they wish to punish...
...and there are now certain agents who go so far as to make that their source of income.
This simply should not be.

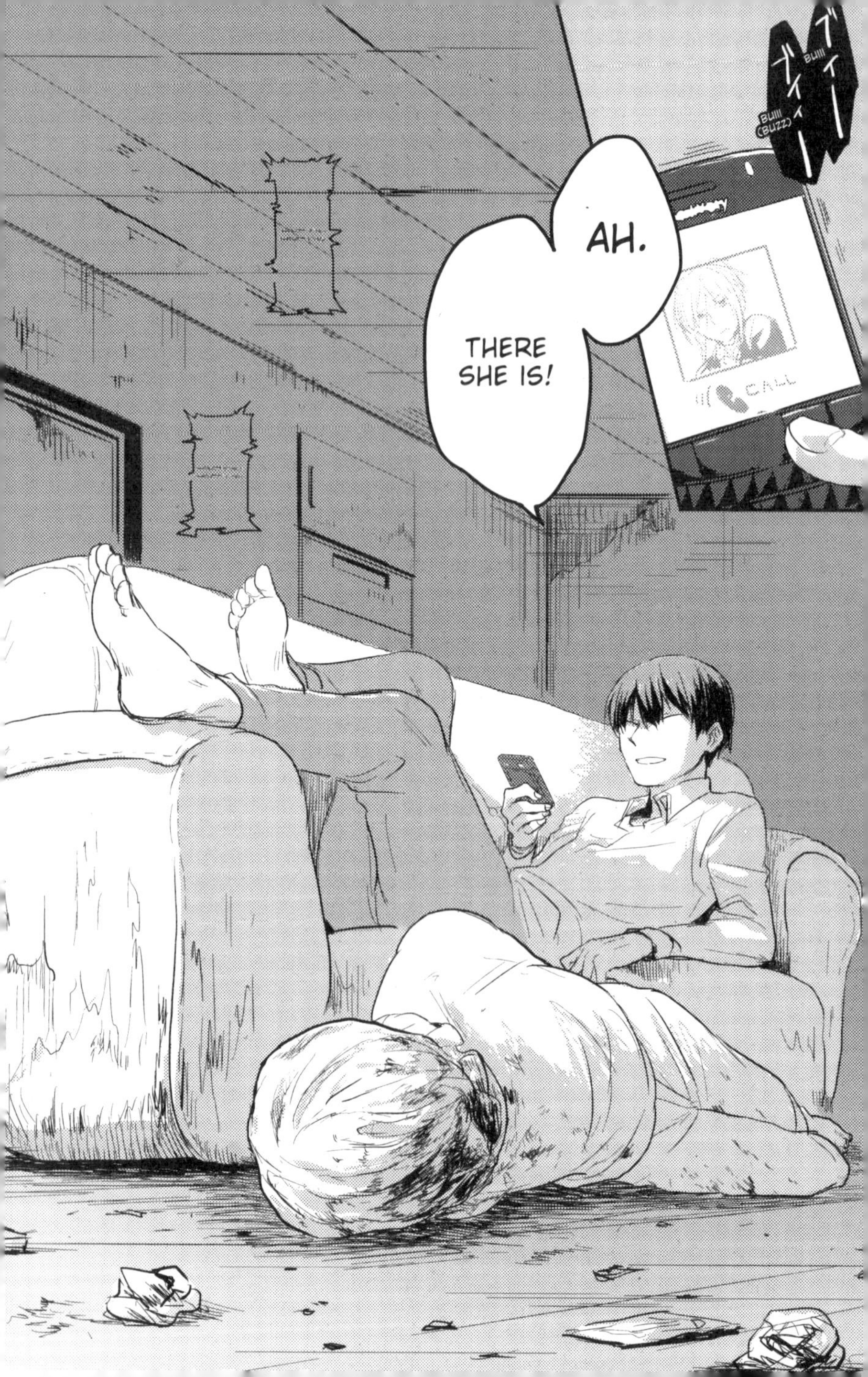
ブイー
BUIII
ブイィー
BUIII (BUZZ)
CALL
AH.
THERE SHE IS!

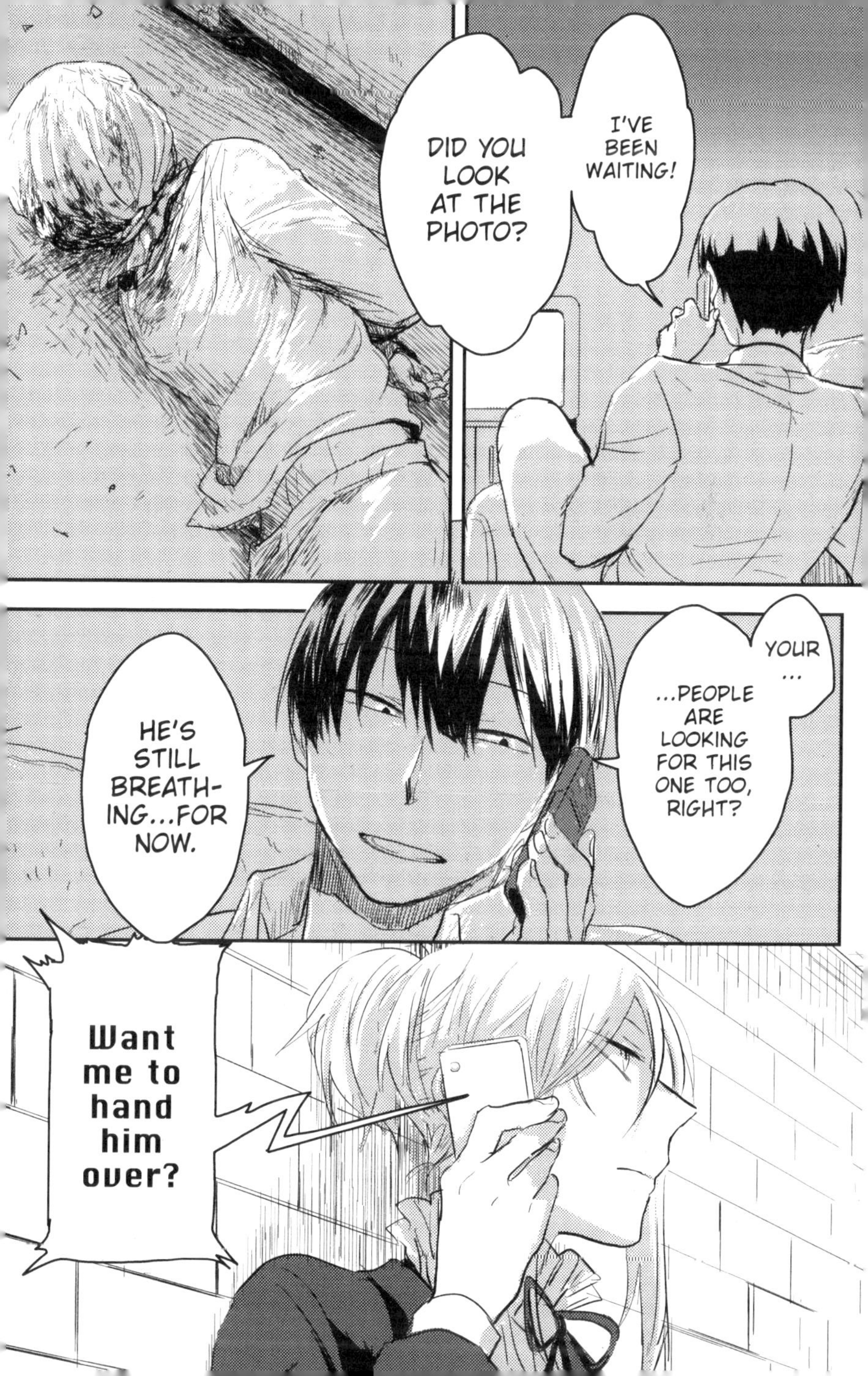
I'VE BEEN WAITING!
DID YOU LOOK AT THE PHOTO?
YOUR...
...PEOPLE ARE LOOKING FOR THIS ONE TOO, RIGHT?
HE'S STILL BREATHING...FOR NOW.
Want me to hand him over?

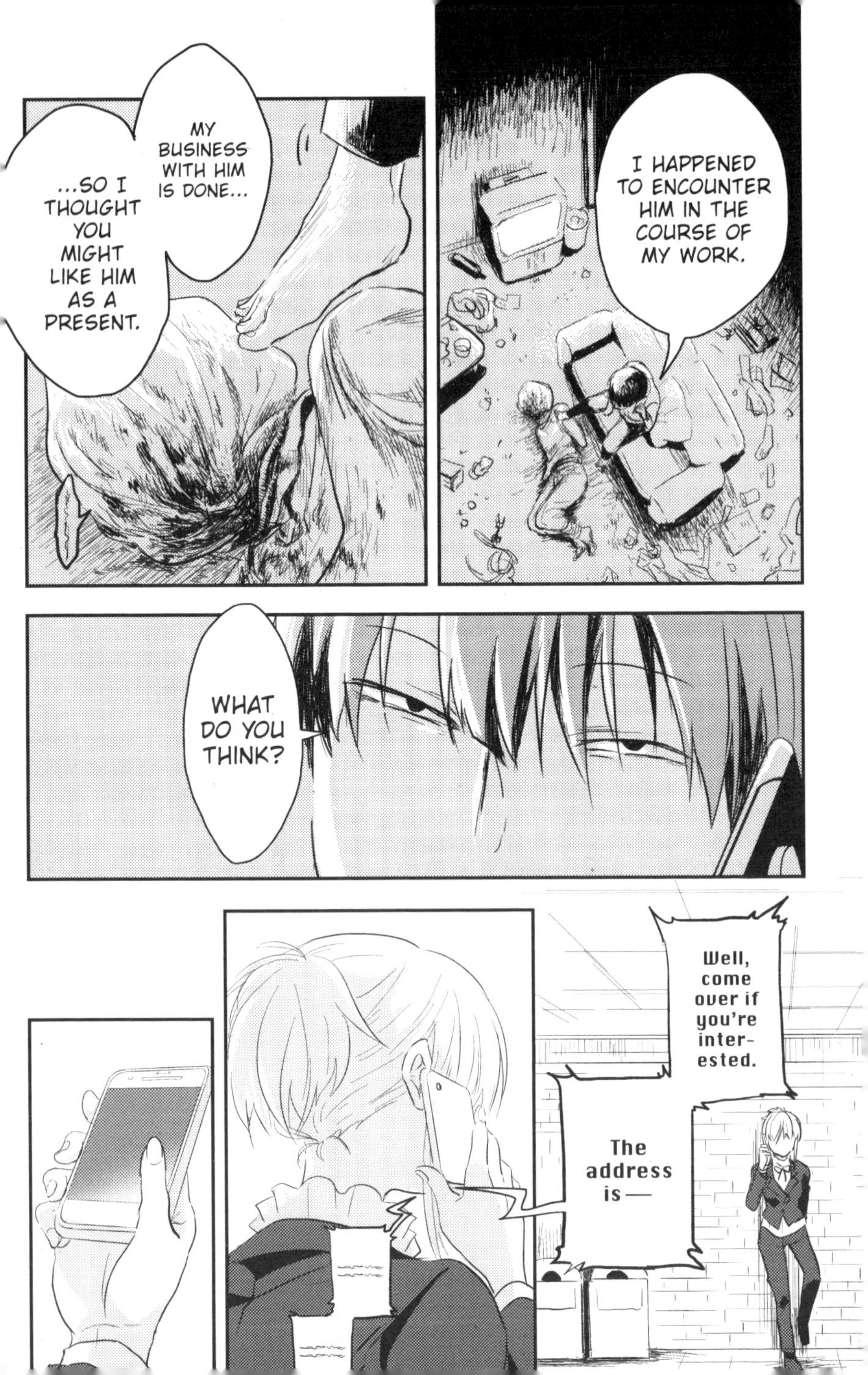
I HAPPENED TO ENCOUNTER HIM IN THE COURSE OF MY WORK.
MY BUSINESS WITH HIM IS DONE...
...SO I THOUGHT YOU MIGHT LIKE HIM AS A PRESENT.
WHAT DO YOU THINK?
Well, come over if you're inter-ested.
The address is—

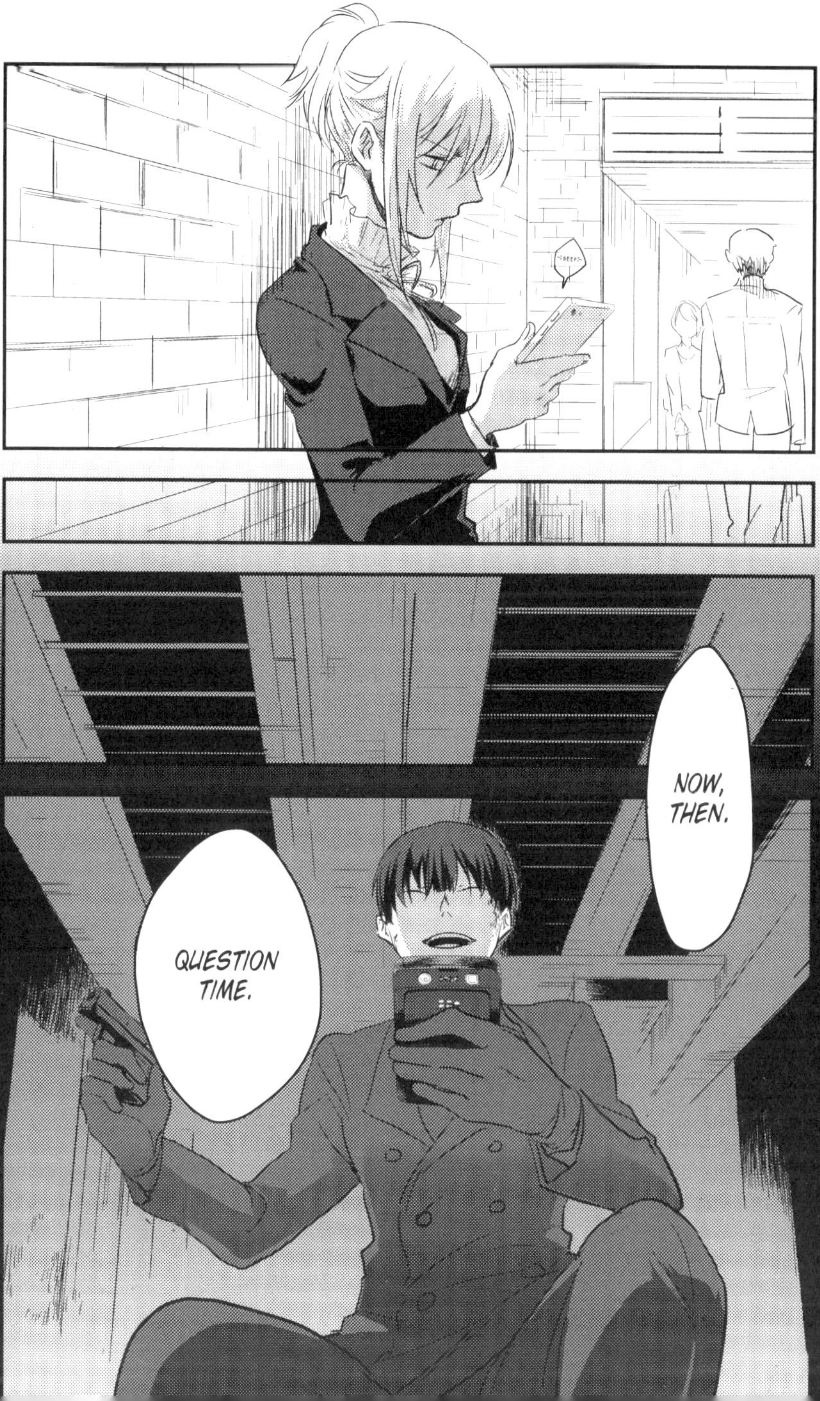
<BEEP>
NOW, THEN.
QUESTION TIME.

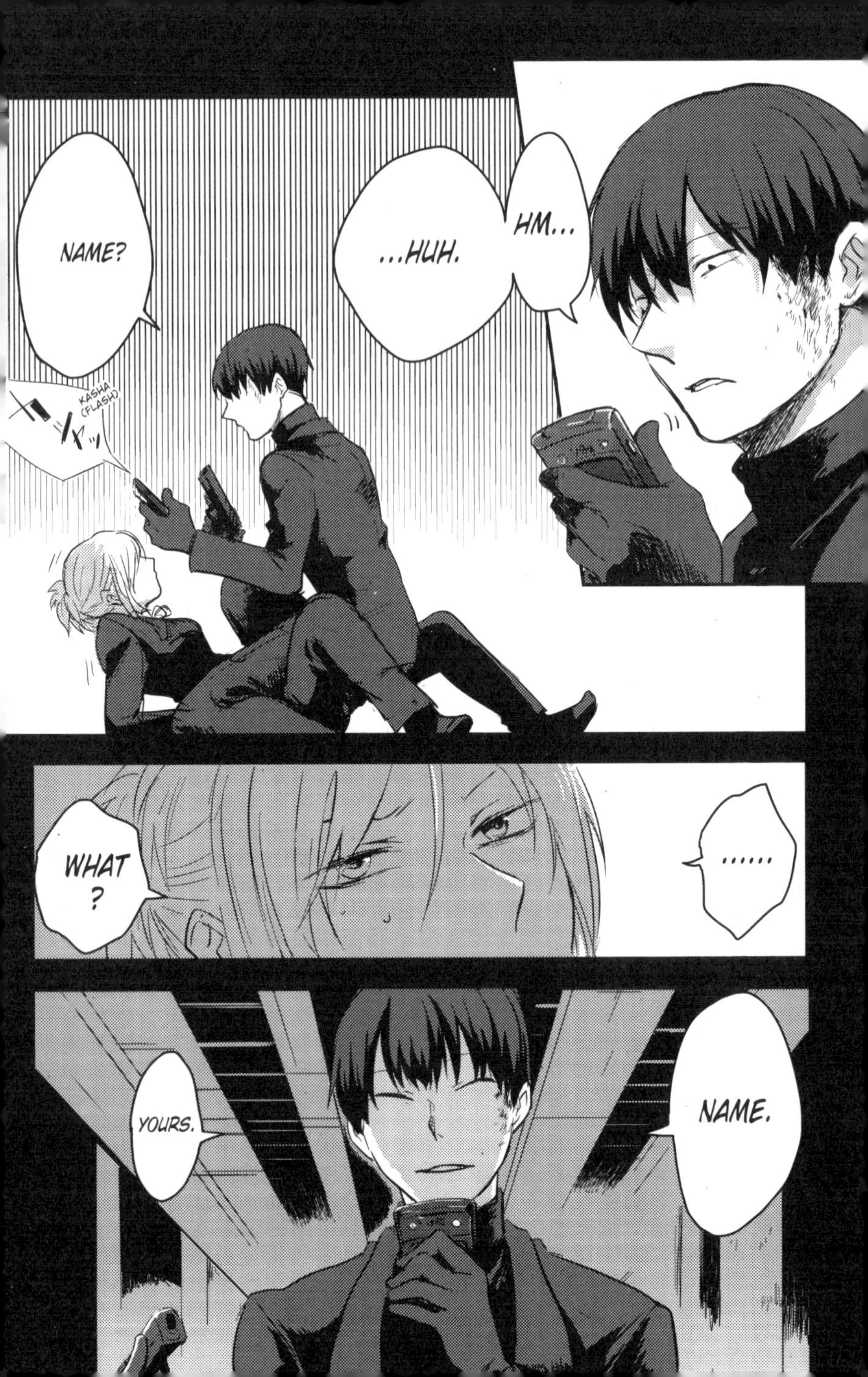
HM...
...HUH.
NAME?
KASHA (FLASH)
......
WHAT ?
NAME.
YOURS.

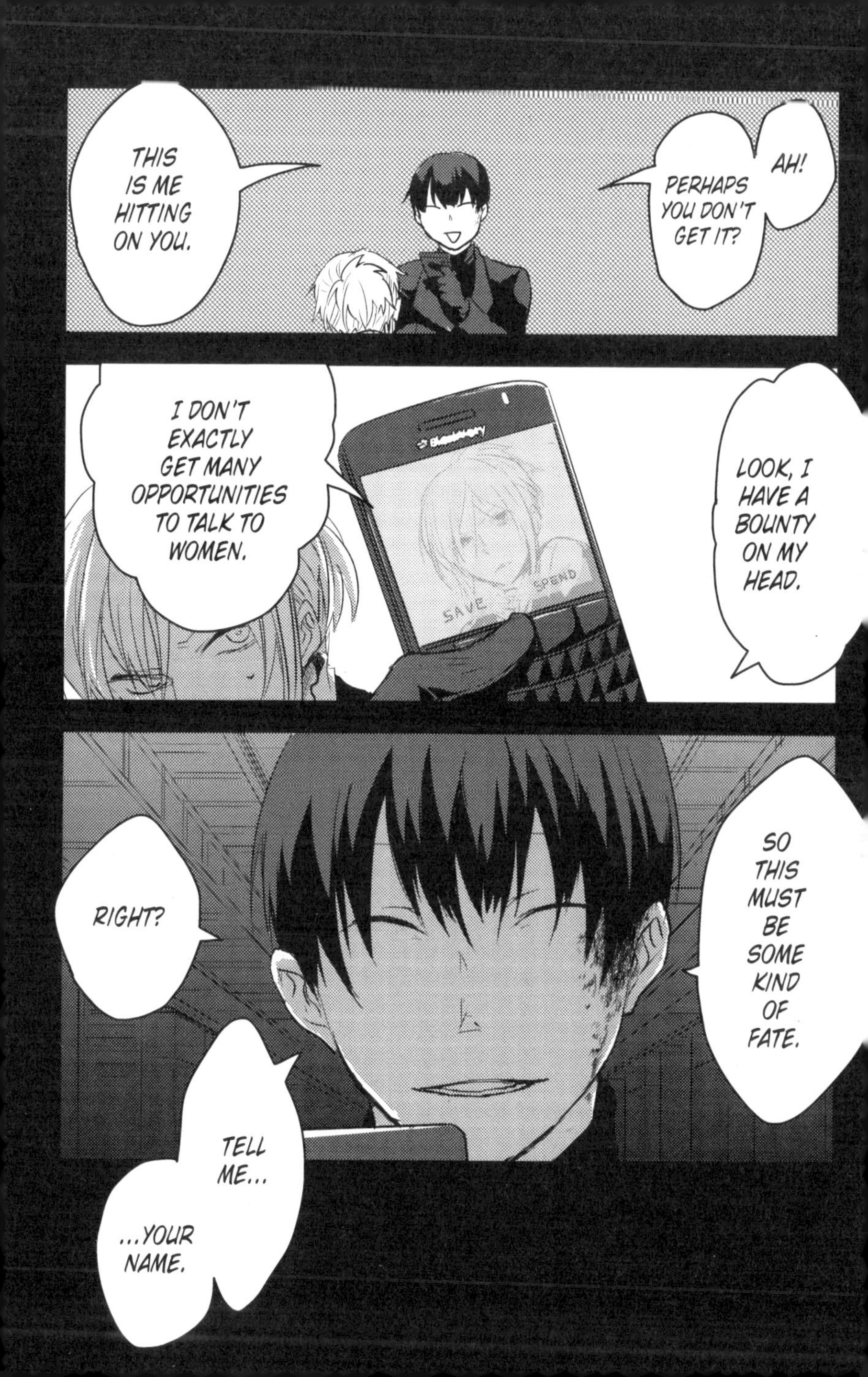
AH!
PERHAPS YOU DON'T GET IT?
THIS IS ME HITTING ON YOU.
LOOK, I HAVE A BOUNTY ON MY HEAD.
I DON'T EXACTLY GET MANY OPPORTUNITIES TO TALK TO WOMEN.
SO THIS MUST BE SOME KIND OF FATE.
RIGHT?
TELL ME...
...YOUR NAME.

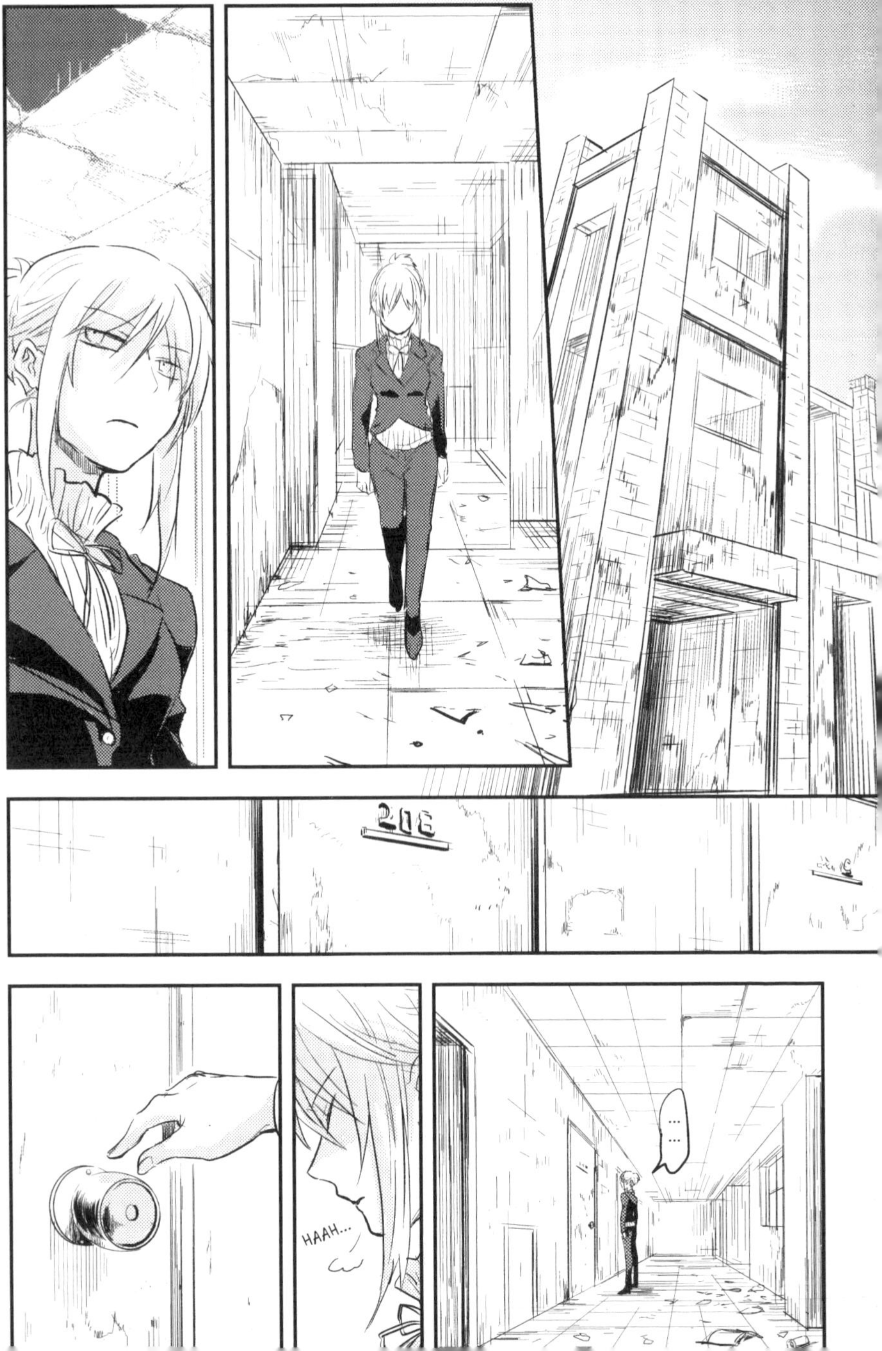
206
...
...
HAAH...

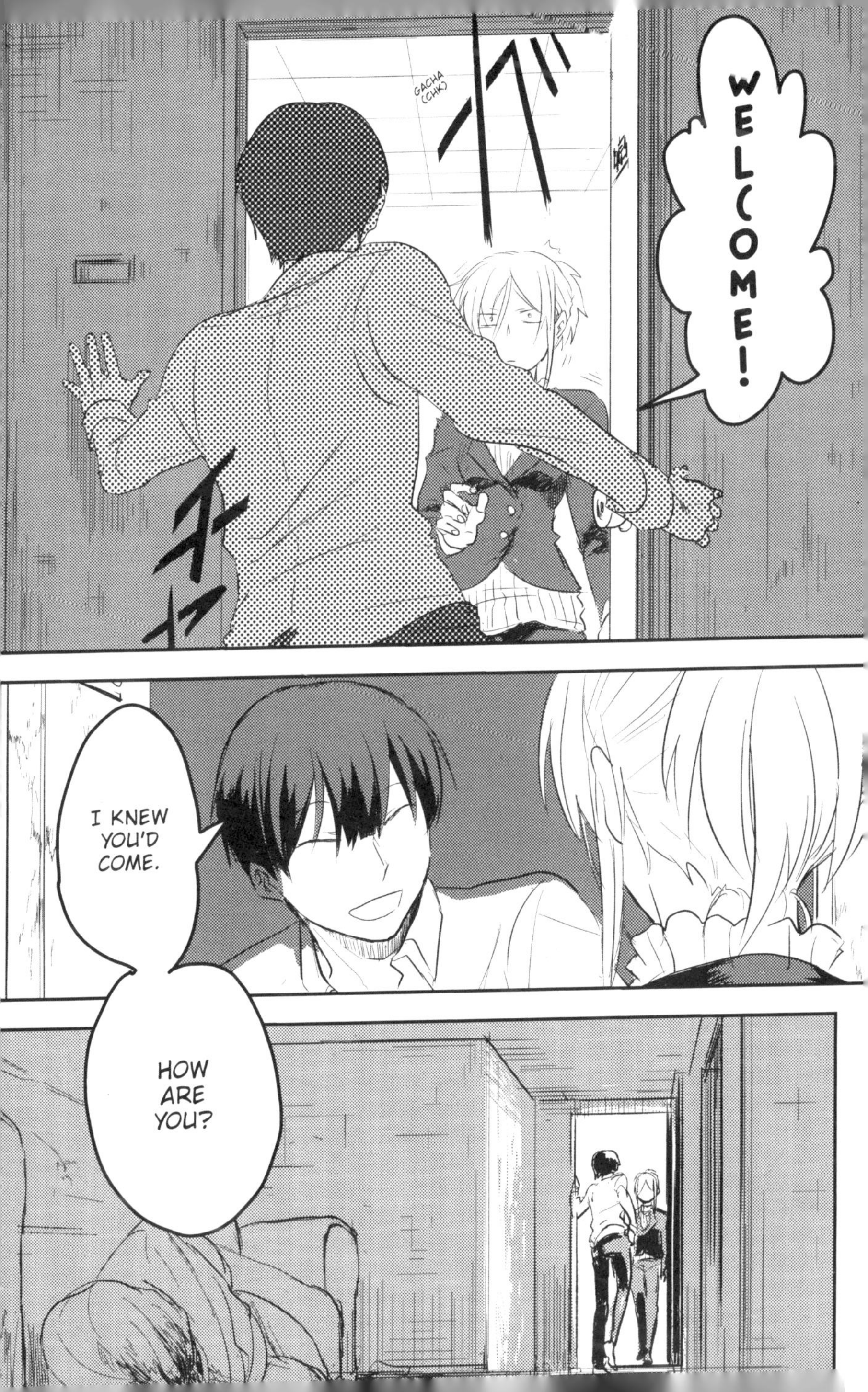
WELLCOME!
GACHA (CHK)
I KNEW YOU'D COME.
HOW ARE YOU?

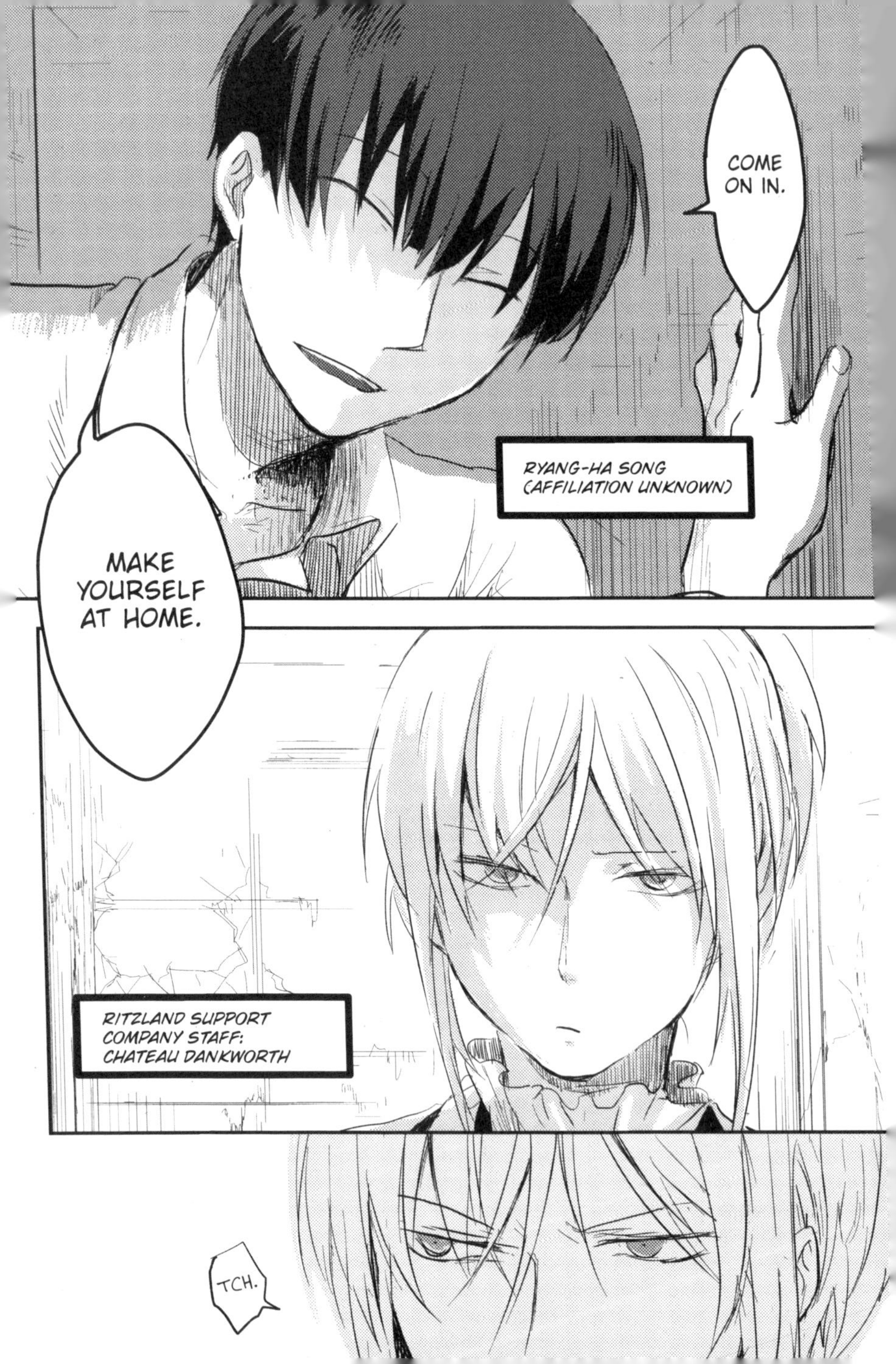
COME ON IN.
RYANG-HA SONG (AFFILIATION UNKNOWN)
MAKE YOURSELF AT HOME.
RITZLAND SUPPORT COMPANY STAFF: CHATEAU DANKWORTH
TCH.

whats your name? 1/2

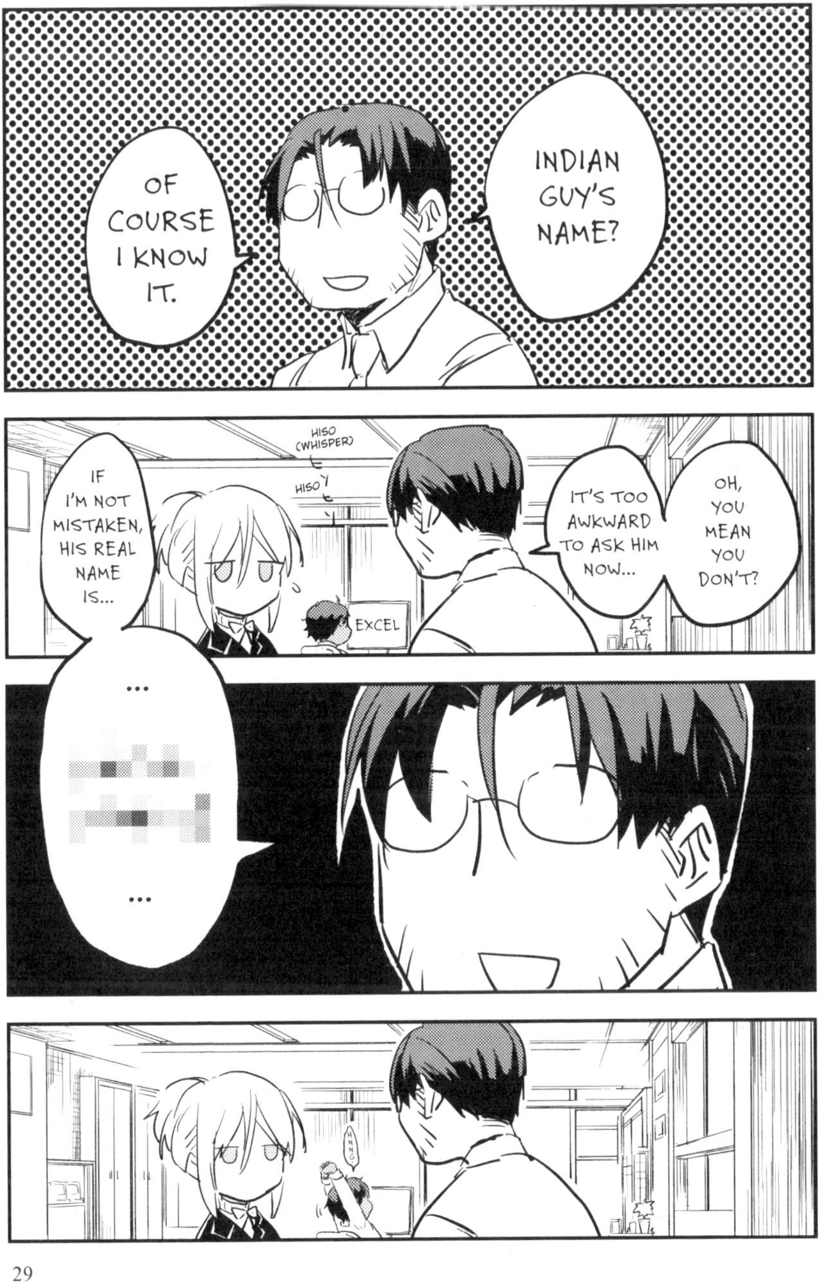
INDIAN GUY'S NAME?
OF COURSE I KNOW IT.
OH, YOU MEAN YOU DON'T?
IT'S TOO AWKWARD TO ASK HIM NOW...
HISO (WHISPER)
HISO
IF I'M NOT MISTAKEN, HIS REAL NAME IS...
EXCEL
...
...
HNNG.

whats your name? 2/2

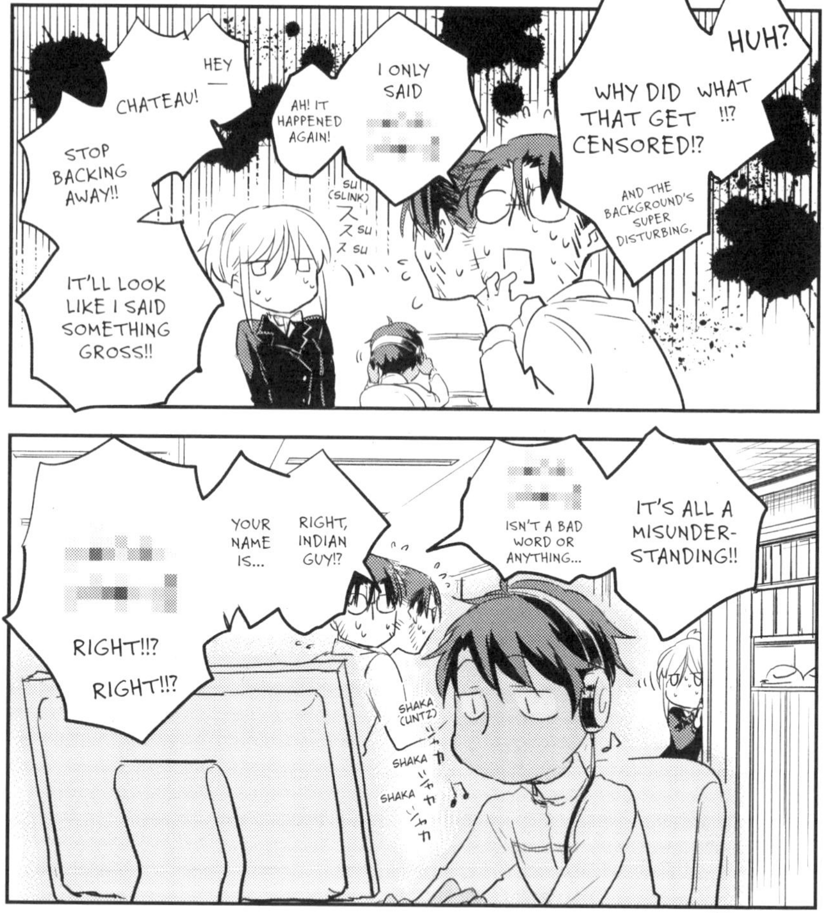
HUH?
WHAT!!?
WHY DID THAT GET CENSORED!?
AND THE BACKGROUND'S SUPER DISTURBING.
I ONLY SAID
AH! IT HAPPENED AGAIN!
HEY— CHATEAU!
STOP BACKING AWAY!!
SU (SLINK) SU SU
IT'LL LOOK LIKE I SAID SOMETHING GROSS!!
IT'S ALL A MISUNDERSTANDING!!
ISN'T A BAD WORD OR ANYTHING...
RIGHT, INDIAN GUY!?
YOUR NAME IS...
RIGHT!!? RIGHT!!?
SHAKA (UNTZ)
SHAKA
SHAKA

INDIAN GUY: REAL NAME:

NATIONALITY: UNKNOWN

AGE: UNKNOWN (ADULT)

PAST EXPERIENCE: UNKNOWN

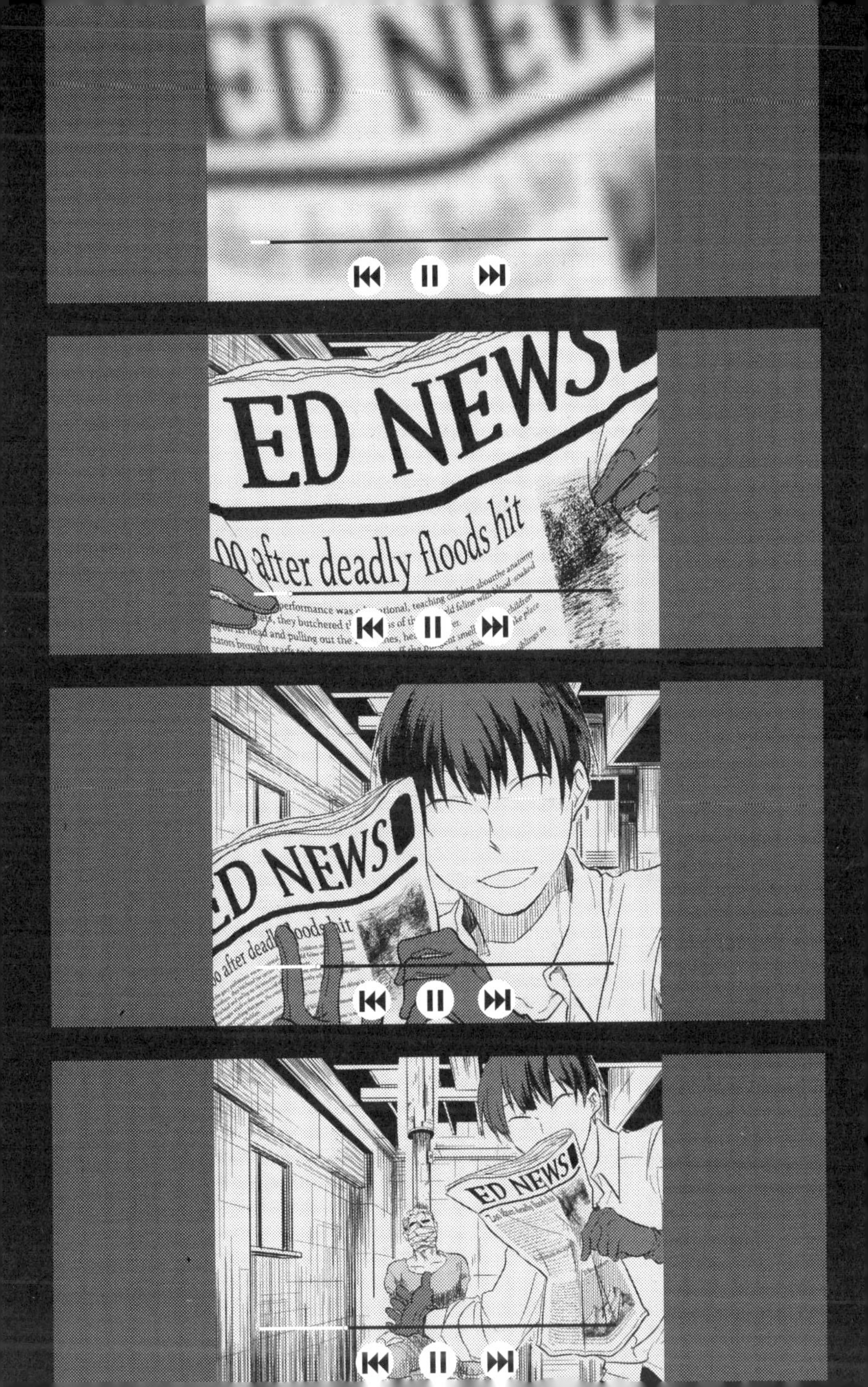
ED NEWS
00 after deadly floods hit

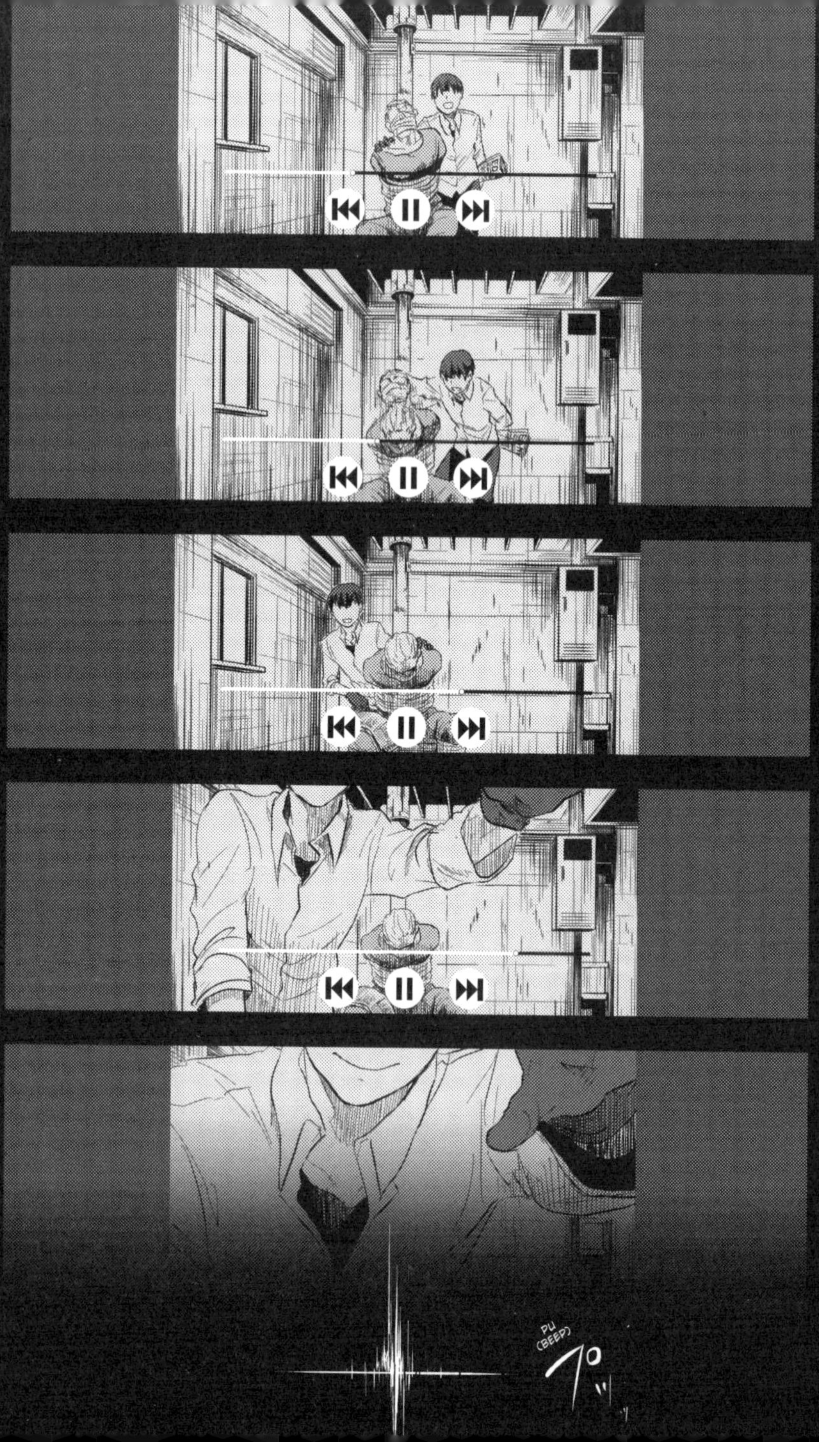
プッ
PU
(BEEP)

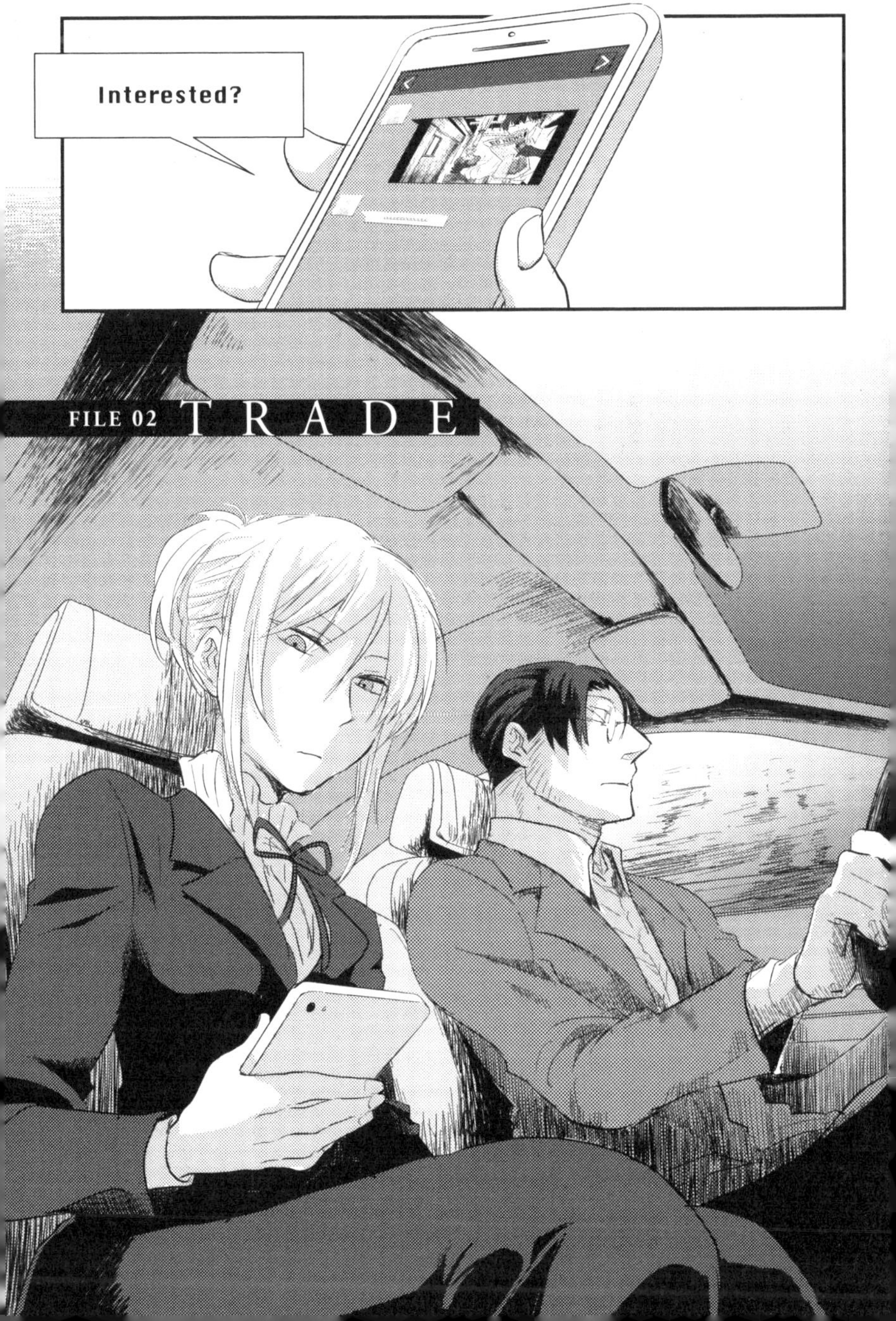
Interested?
FILE 02 TRADE

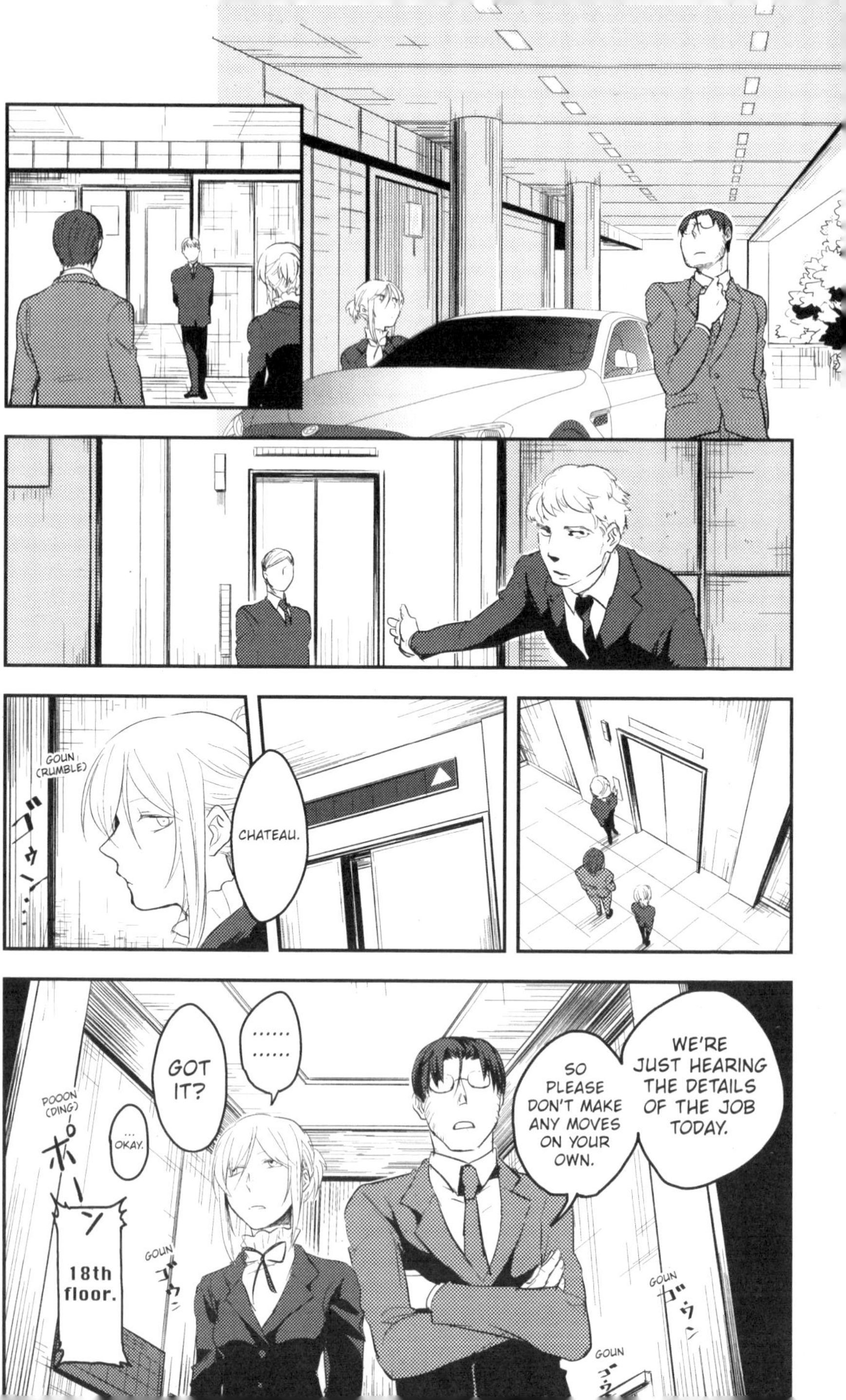
CHATEAU.
GOUN (RUMBLE)
WE'RE JUST HEARING THE DETAILS OF THE JOB TODAY.
SO PLEASE DON'T MAKE ANY MOVES ON YOUR OWN.
......
......
GOT IT?
...OKAY.
GOUN
GOUN
GOUN
POOON (DING)
18th floor.

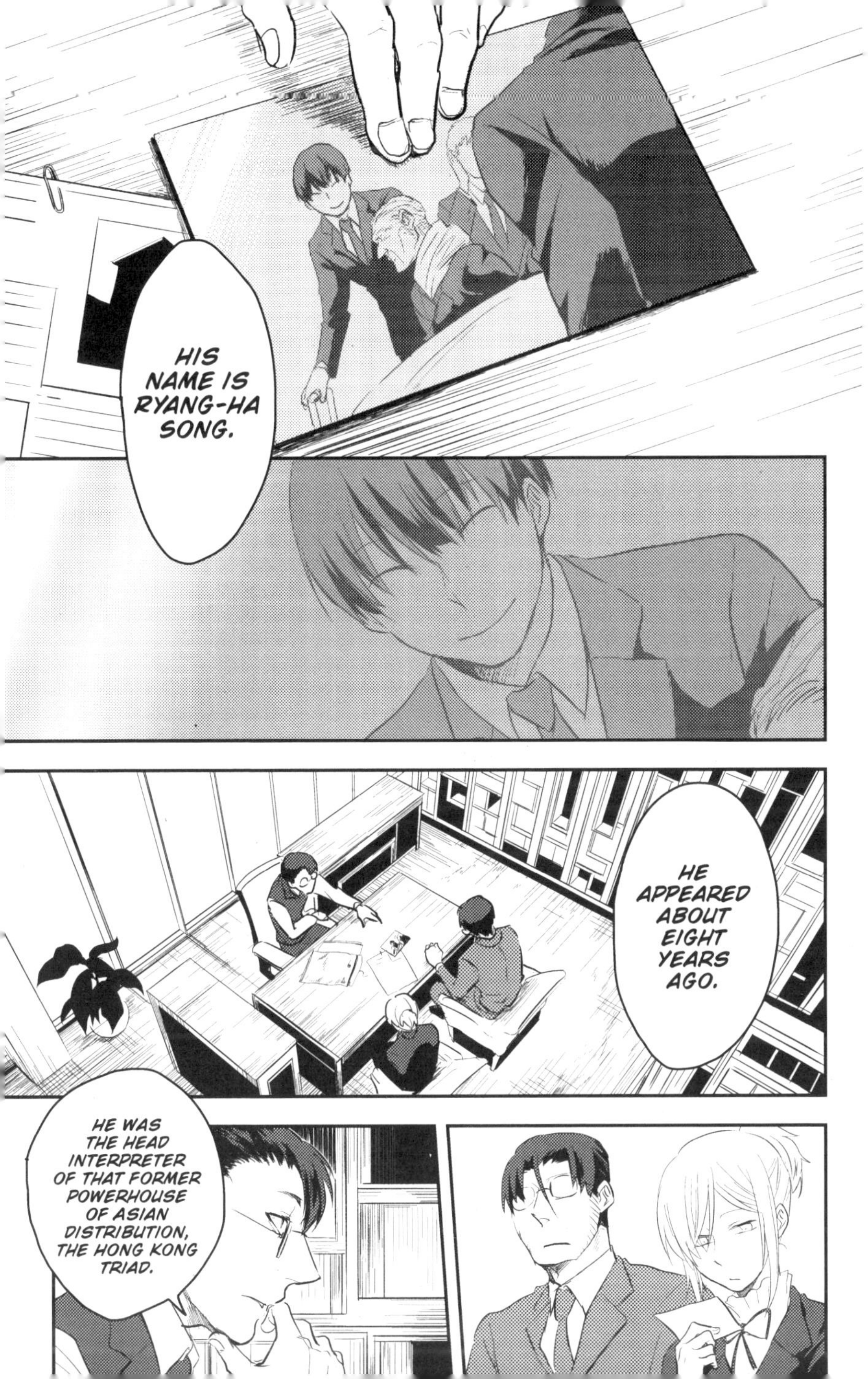
HIS NAME IS RYANG-HA SONG.
HE APPEARED ABOUT EIGHT YEARS AGO.
HE WAS THE HEAD INTERPRETER OF THAT FORMER POWERHOUSE OF ASIAN DISTRIBUTION, THE HONG KONG TRIAD.

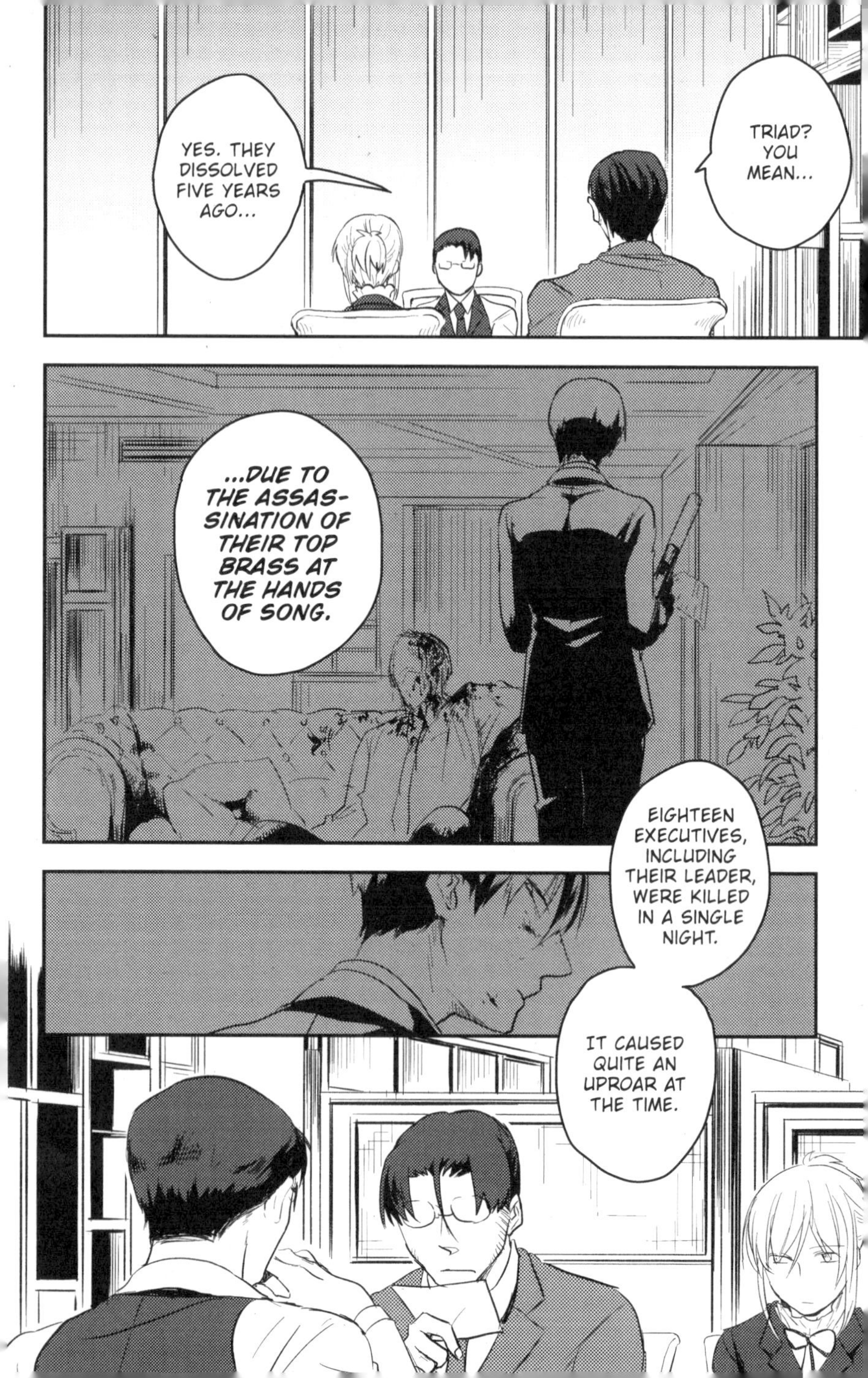
TRIAD? YOU MEAN...
YES. THEY DISSOLVED FIVE YEARS AGO...
...DUE TO THE ASSAS-SINATION OF THEIR TOP BRASS AT THE HANDS OF SONG.
EIGHTEEN EXECUTIVES, INCLUDING THEIR LEADER, WERE KILLED IN A SINGLE NIGHT.
IT CAUSED QUITE AN UPROAR AT THE TIME.

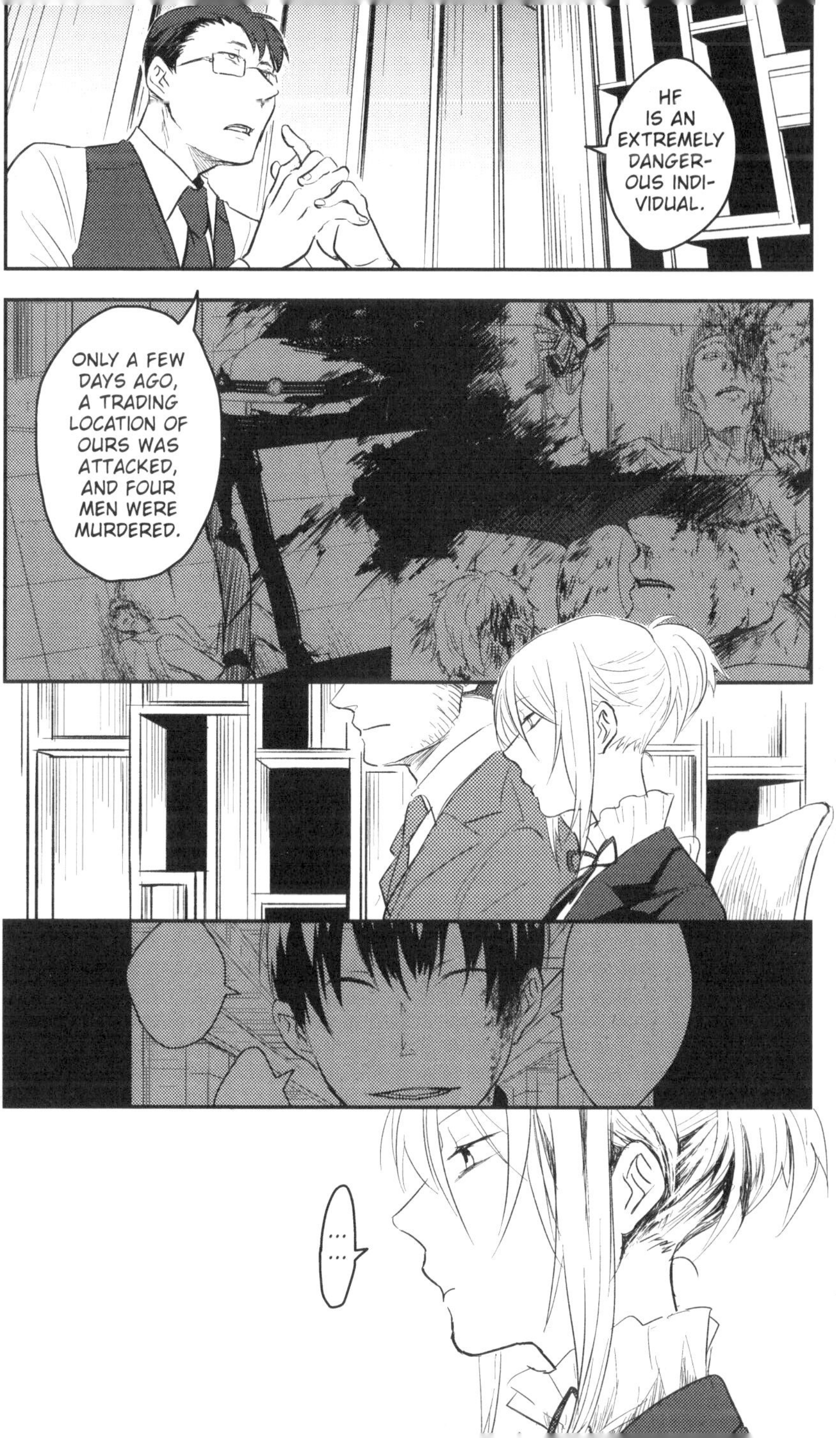
HF IS AN EXTREMELY DANGER-OUS INDI-VIDUAL.
ONLY A FEW DAYS AGO, A TRADING LOCATION OF OURS WAS ATTACKED, AND FOUR MEN WERE MURDERED.
......

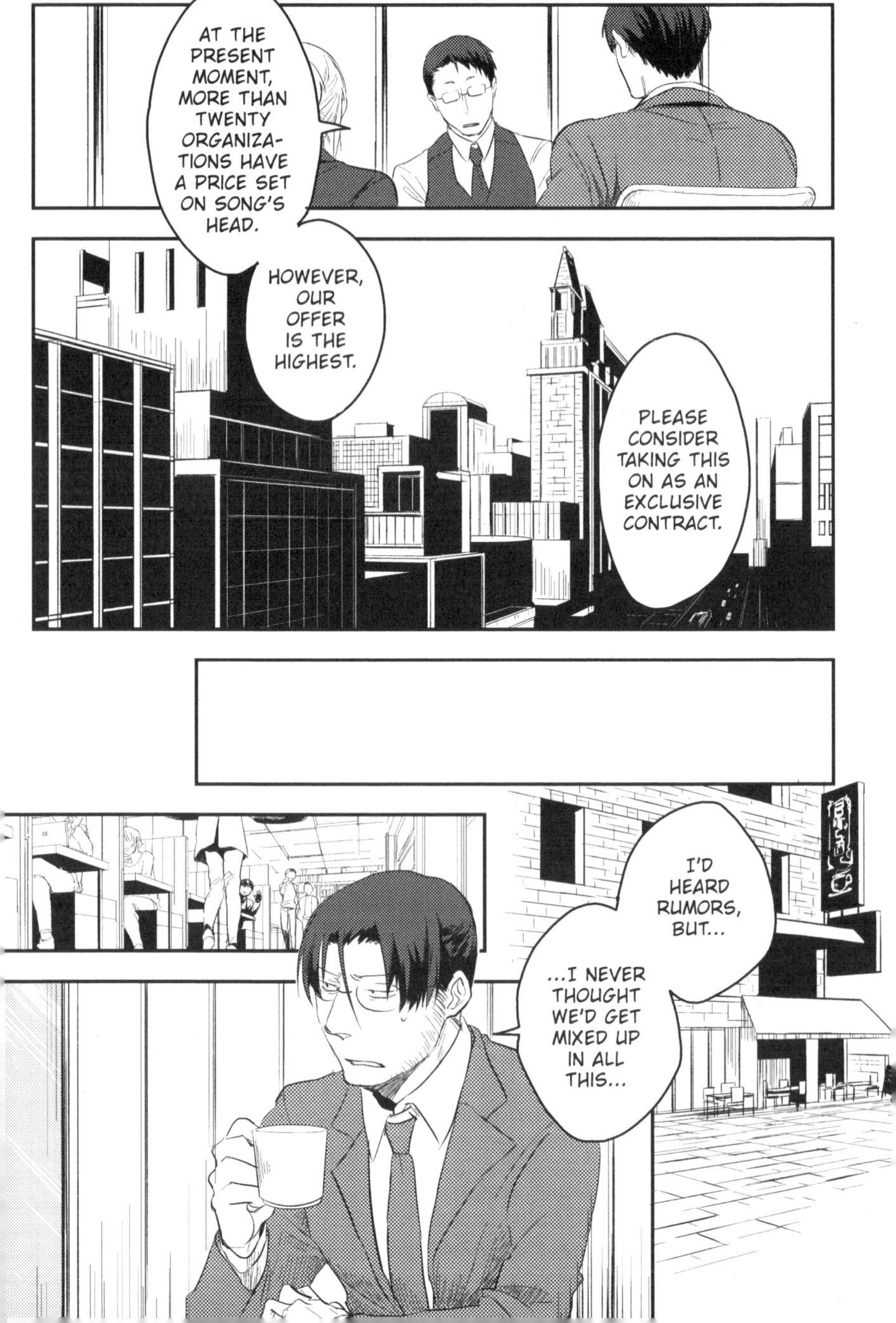
AT THE PRESENT MOMENT, MORE THAN TWENTY ORGANIZA-TIONS HAVE A PRICE SET ON SONG'S HEAD.
HOWEVER, OUR OFFER IS THE HIGHEST.
PLEASE CONSIDER TAKING THIS ON AS AN EXCLUSIVE CONTRACT.
I'D HEARD RUMORS, BUT...
...I NEVER THOUGHT WE'D GET MIXED UP IN ALL THIS...

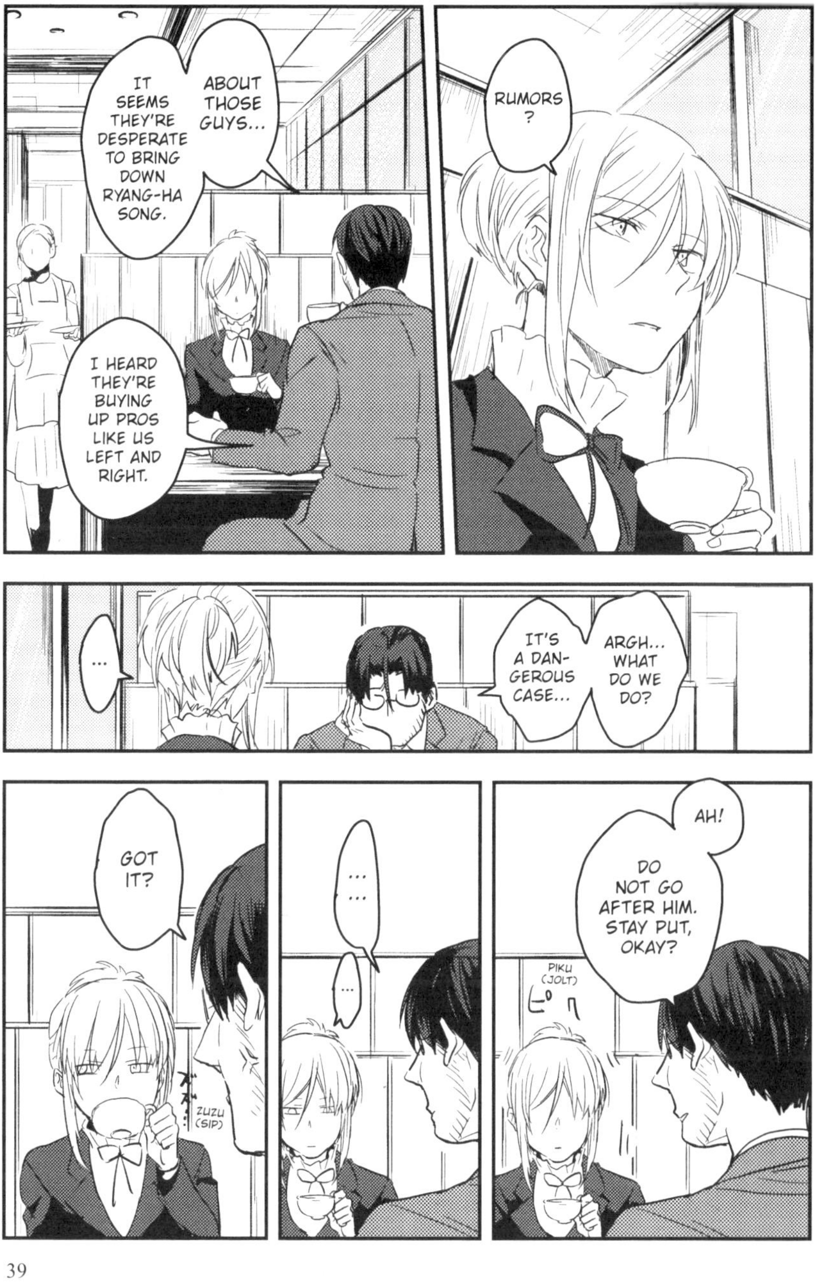
RUMORS?
ABOUT THOSE GUYS...
IT SEEMS THEY'RE DESPERATE TO BRING DOWN RYANG-HA SONG.
I HEARD THEY'RE BUYING UP PROS LIKE US LEFT AND RIGHT.
ARGH... WHAT DO WE DO?
IT'S A DANGEROUS CASE...
...
AH!
DO NOT GO AFTER HIM. STAY PUT, OKAY?
PIKU (JOLT)
... ...
...
GOT IT?
ZUZU (SIP)

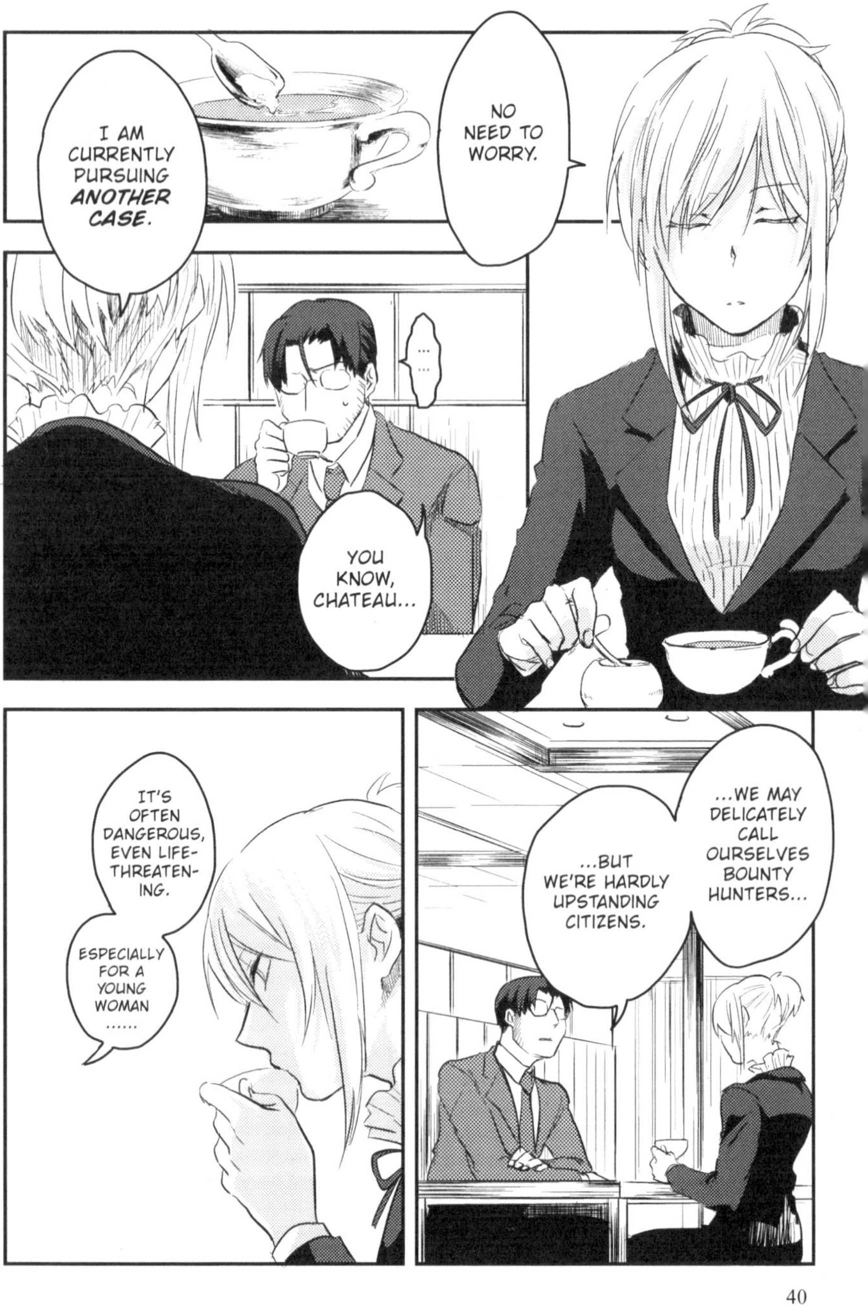
NO NEED TO WORRY.
I AM CURRENTLY PURSUING **ANOTHER CASE**.
......
YOU KNOW, CHATEAU...
...WE MAY DELICATELY CALL OURSELVES BOUNTY HUNTERS...
...BUT WE'RE HARDLY UPSTANDING CITIZENS.
IT'S OFTEN DANGEROUS, EVEN LIFE-THREATENING.
ESPECIALLY FOR A YOUNG WOMAN ......

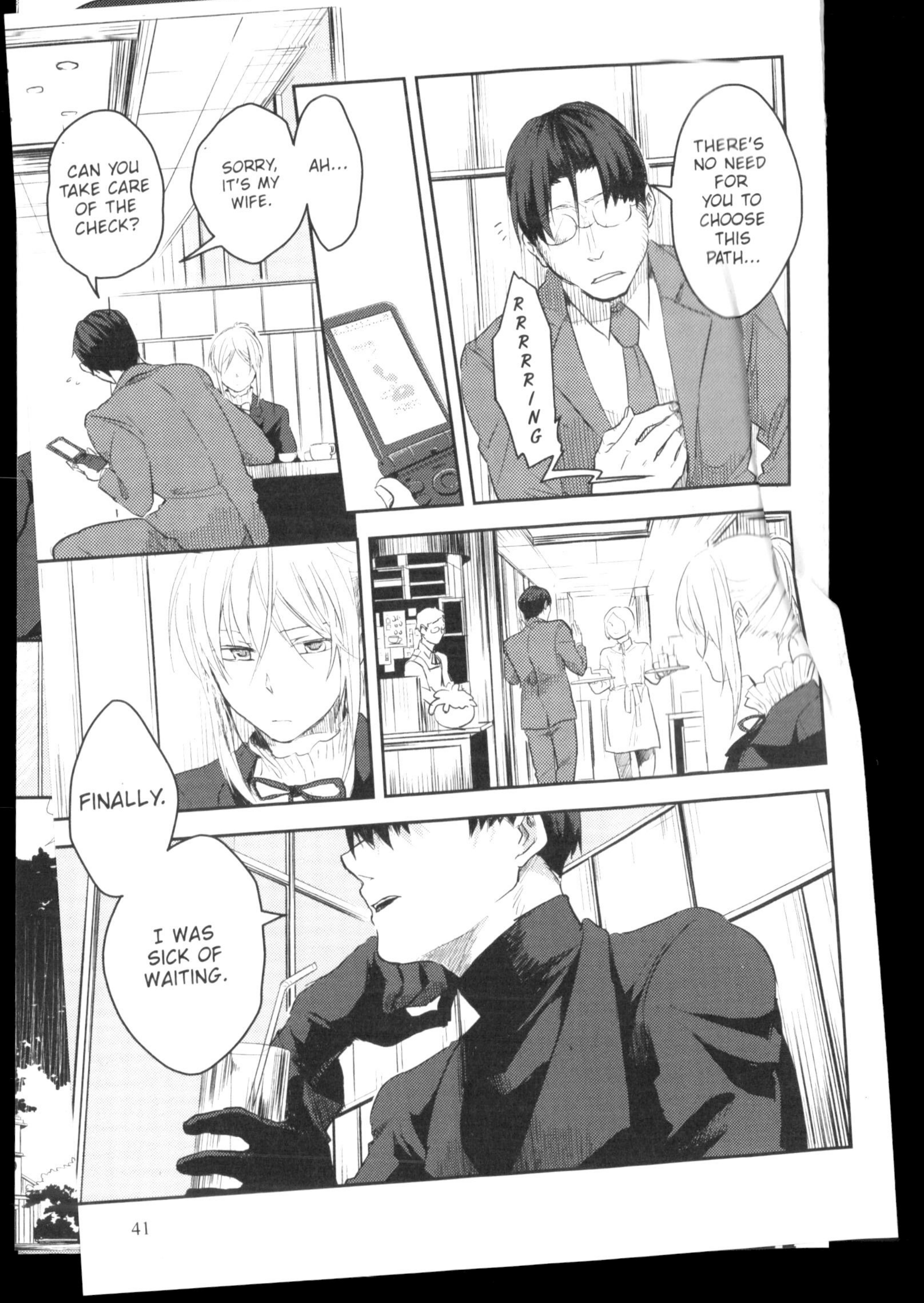
THERE'S NO NEED FOR YOU TO CHOOSE THIS PATH...
RRRRING
AH...
SORRY, IT'S MY WIFE.
CAN YOU TAKE CARE OF THE CHECK?
FINALLY.
I WAS SICK OF WAITING.

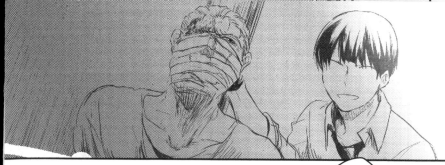

THIS IS THE PERSON I AM CURRENTLY CHASING.

WHAT ARE YOUR TERMS?

HMM.

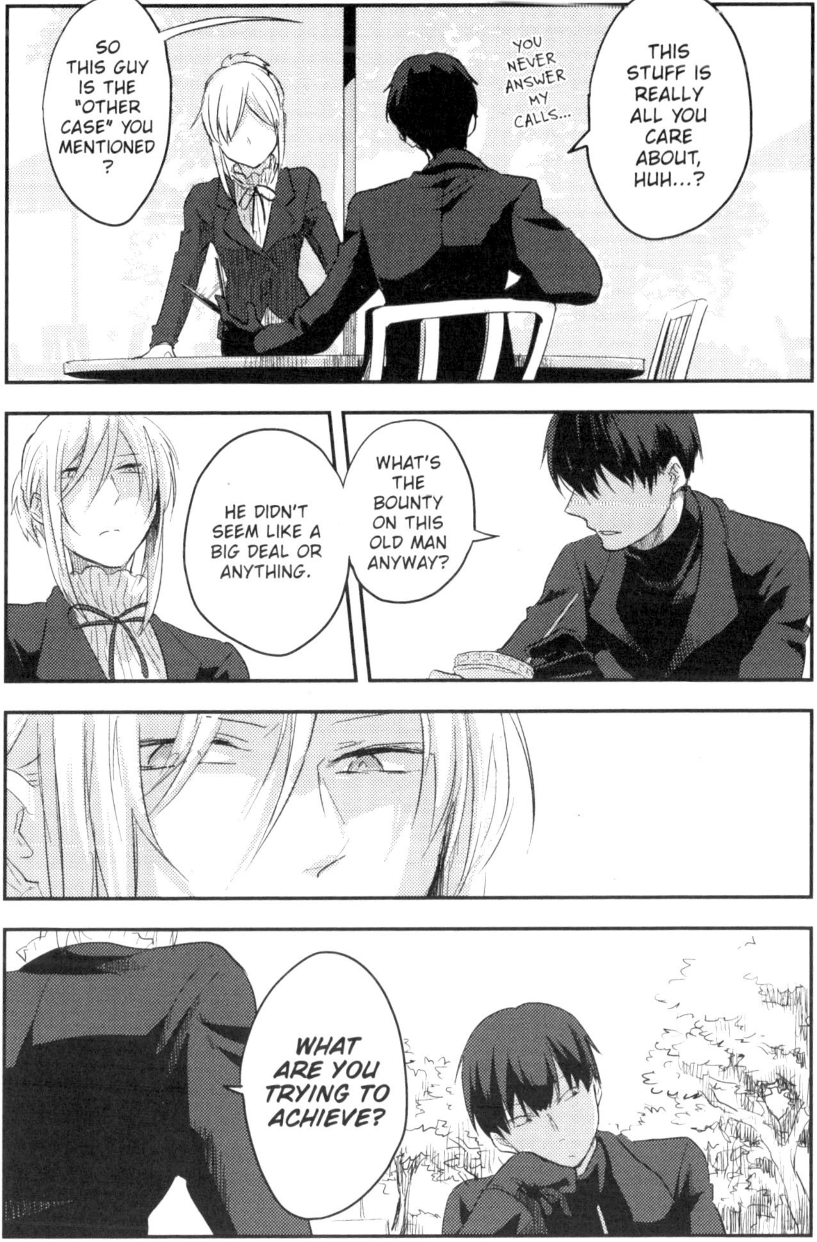
THIS STUFF IS REALLY ALL YOU CARE ABOUT, HUH...?
YOU NEVER ANSWER MY CALLS...
SO THIS GUY IS THE "OTHER CASE" YOU MENTIONED ?
WHAT'S THE BOUNTY ON THIS OLD MAN ANYWAY?
HE DIDN'T SEEM LIKE A BIG DEAL OR ANYTHING.
WHAT ARE YOU TRYING TO ACHIEVE?

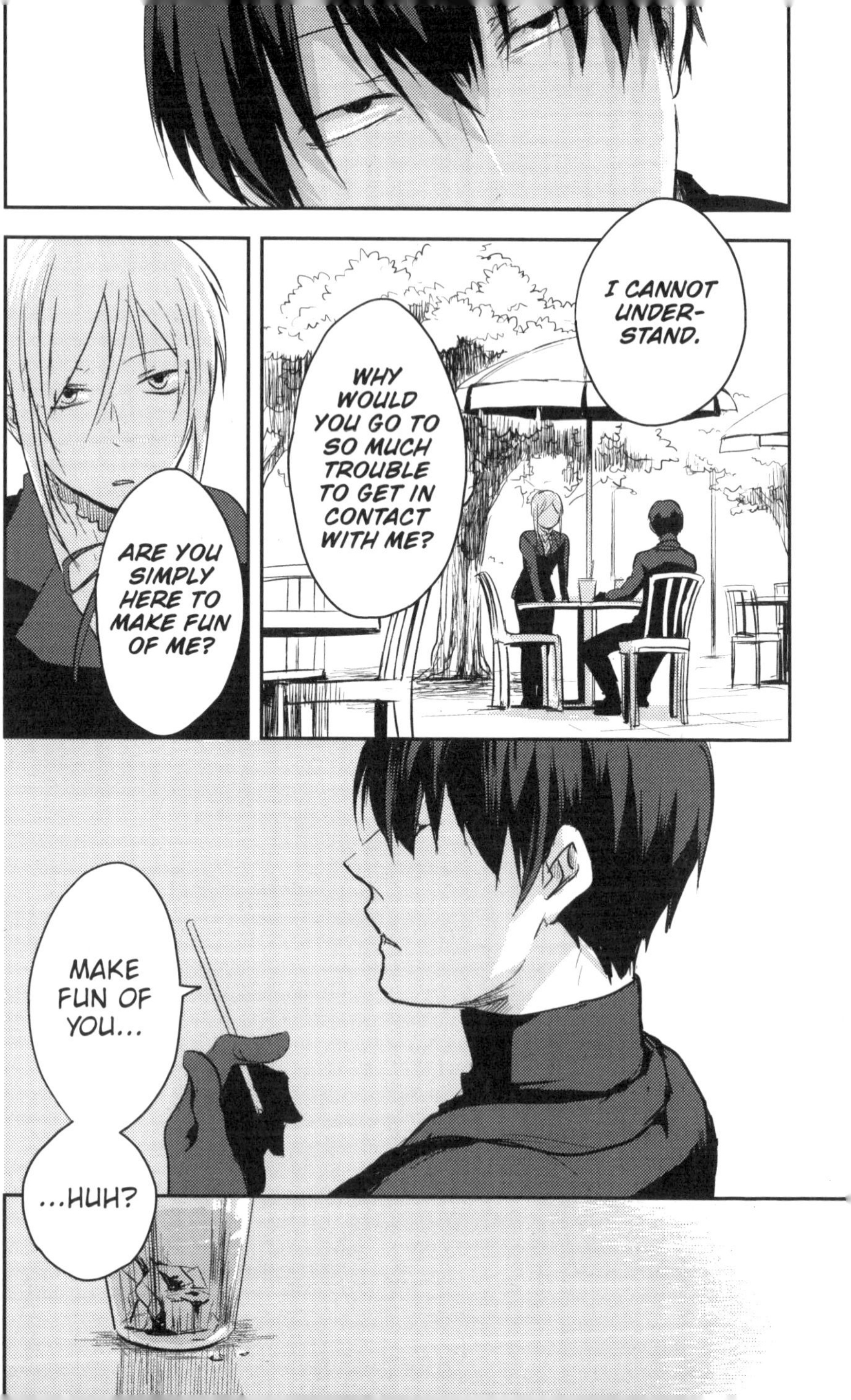
I CANNOT UNDER-STAND.
WHY WOULD YOU GO TO SO MUCH TROUBLE TO GET IN CONTACT WITH ME?
ARE YOU SIMPLY HERE TO MAKE FUN OF ME?
MAKE FUN OF YOU...
...HUH?

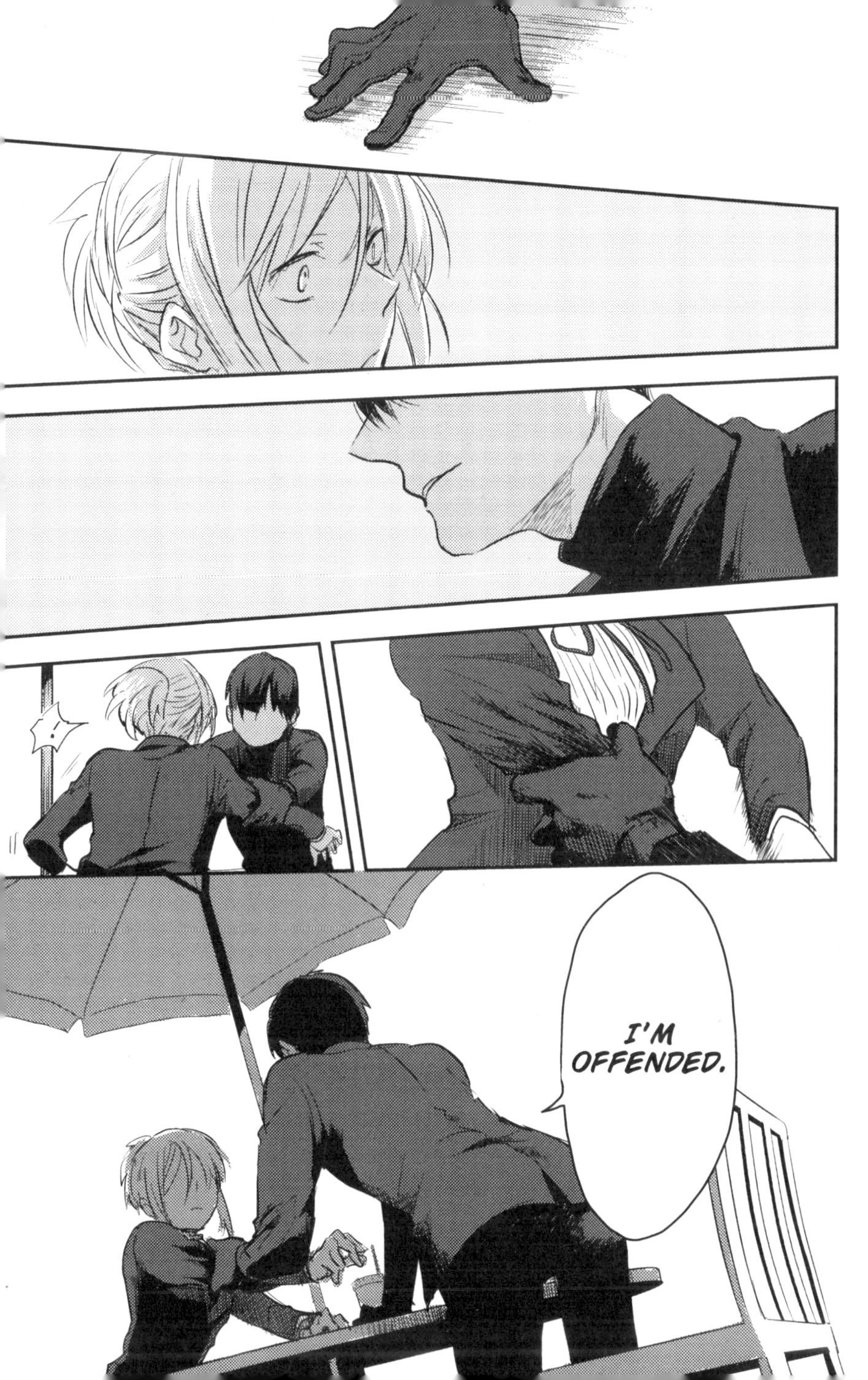
!
I'M OFFENDED.

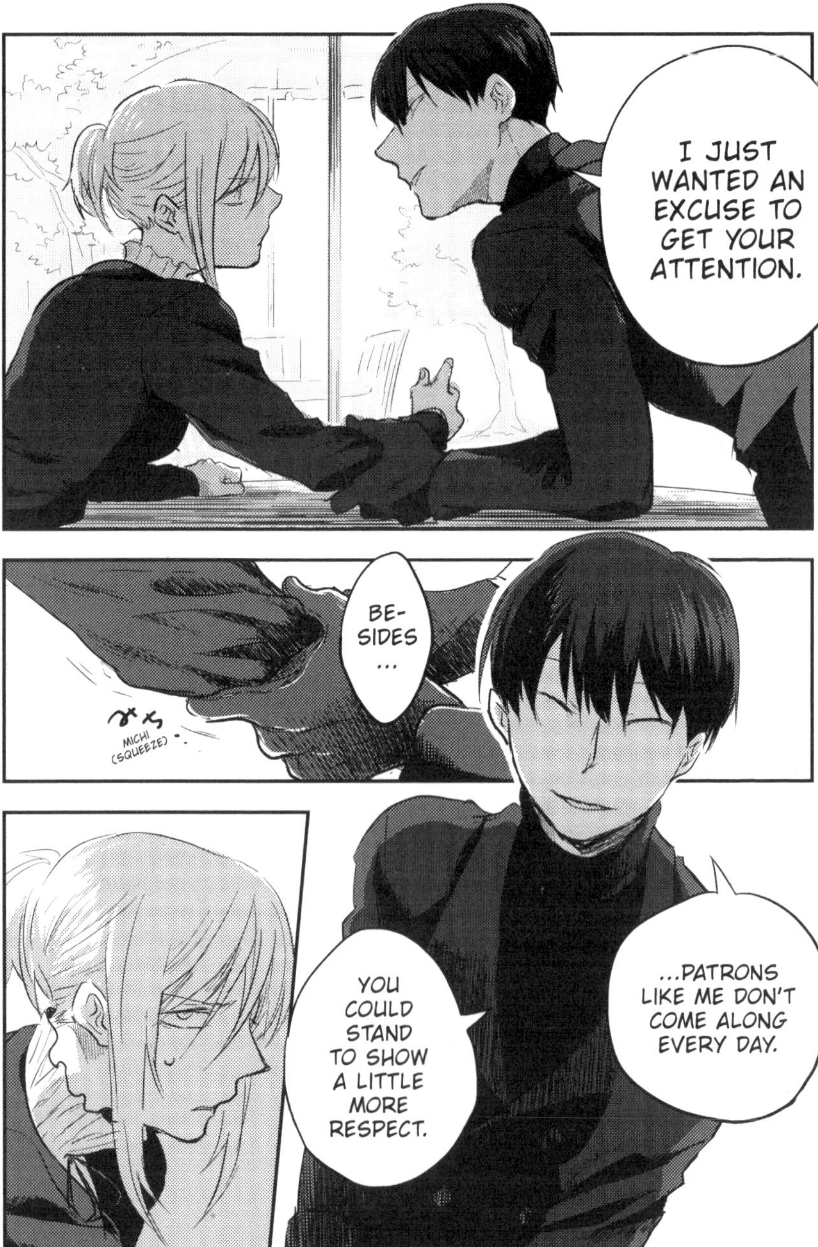
I JUST WANTED AN EXCUSE TO GET YOUR ATTENTION.
BE-SIDES...
みち
MICHI (SQUEEZE)
...PATRONS LIKE ME DON'T COME ALONG EVERY DAY.
YOU COULD STAND TO SHOW A LITTLE MORE RESPECT.

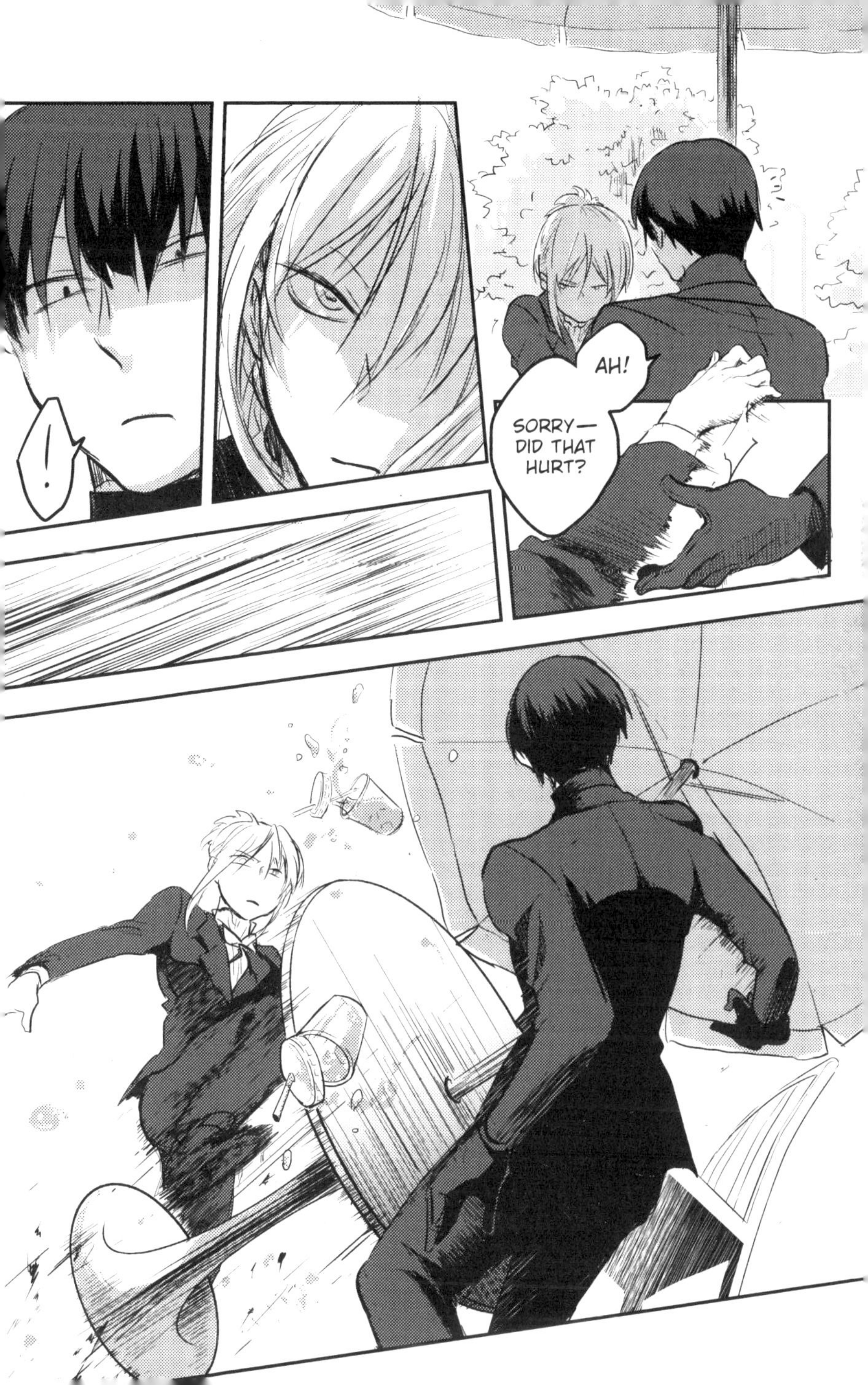
AH!
SORRY—DID THAT HURT?
!

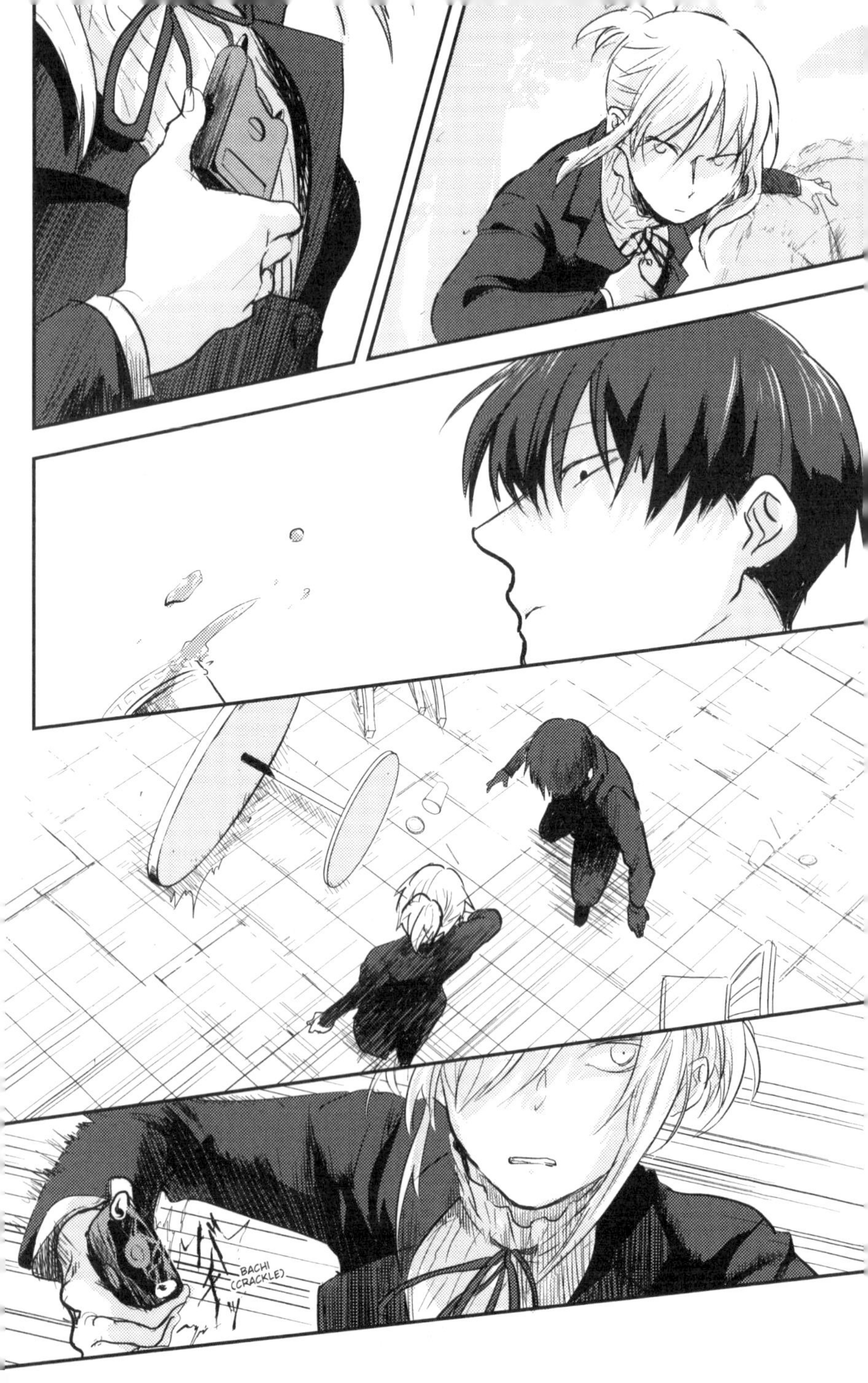
BACHI
(CRACKLE)

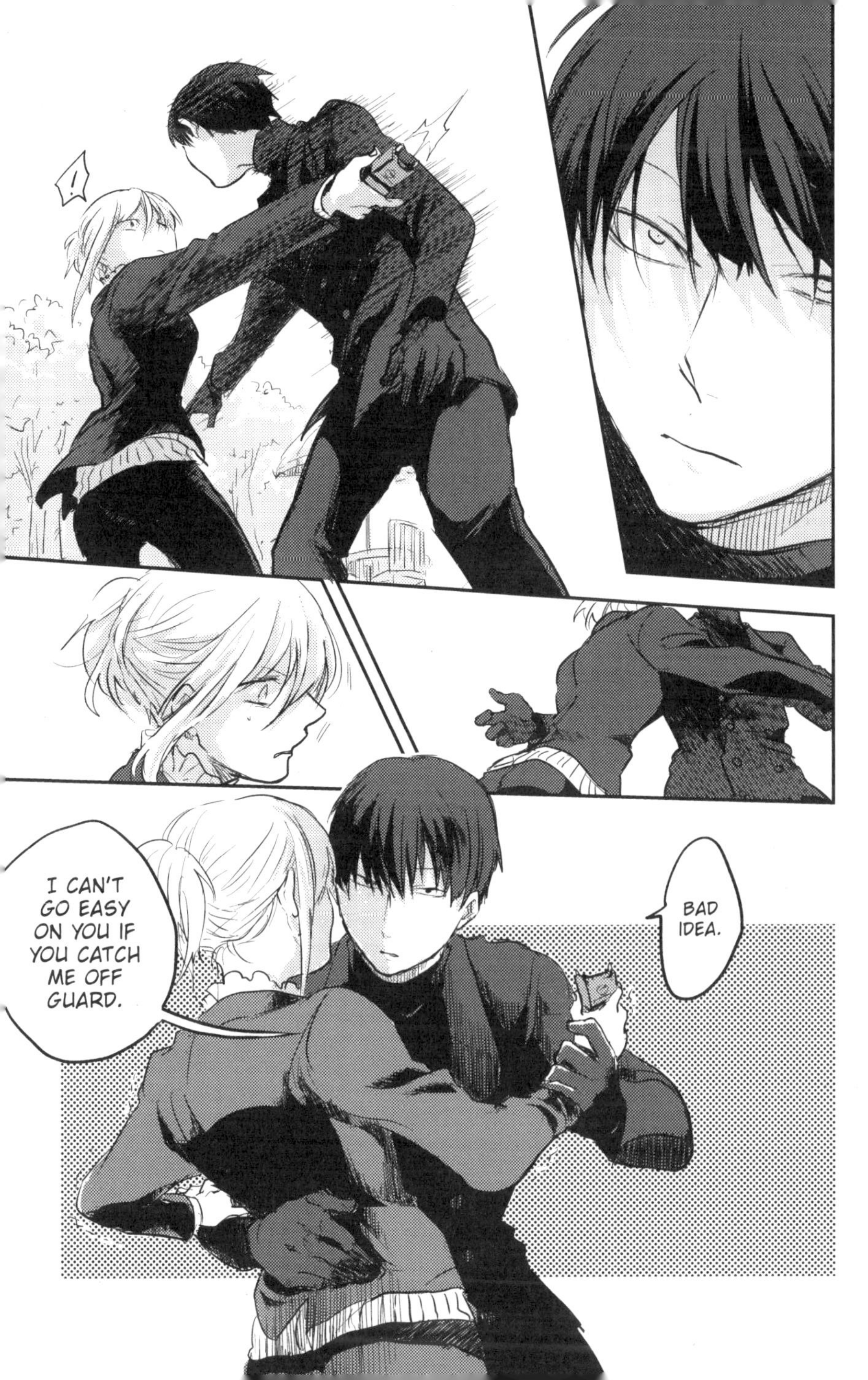
!
BAD IDEA.
I CAN'T GO EASY ON YOU IF YOU CATCH ME OFF GUARD.

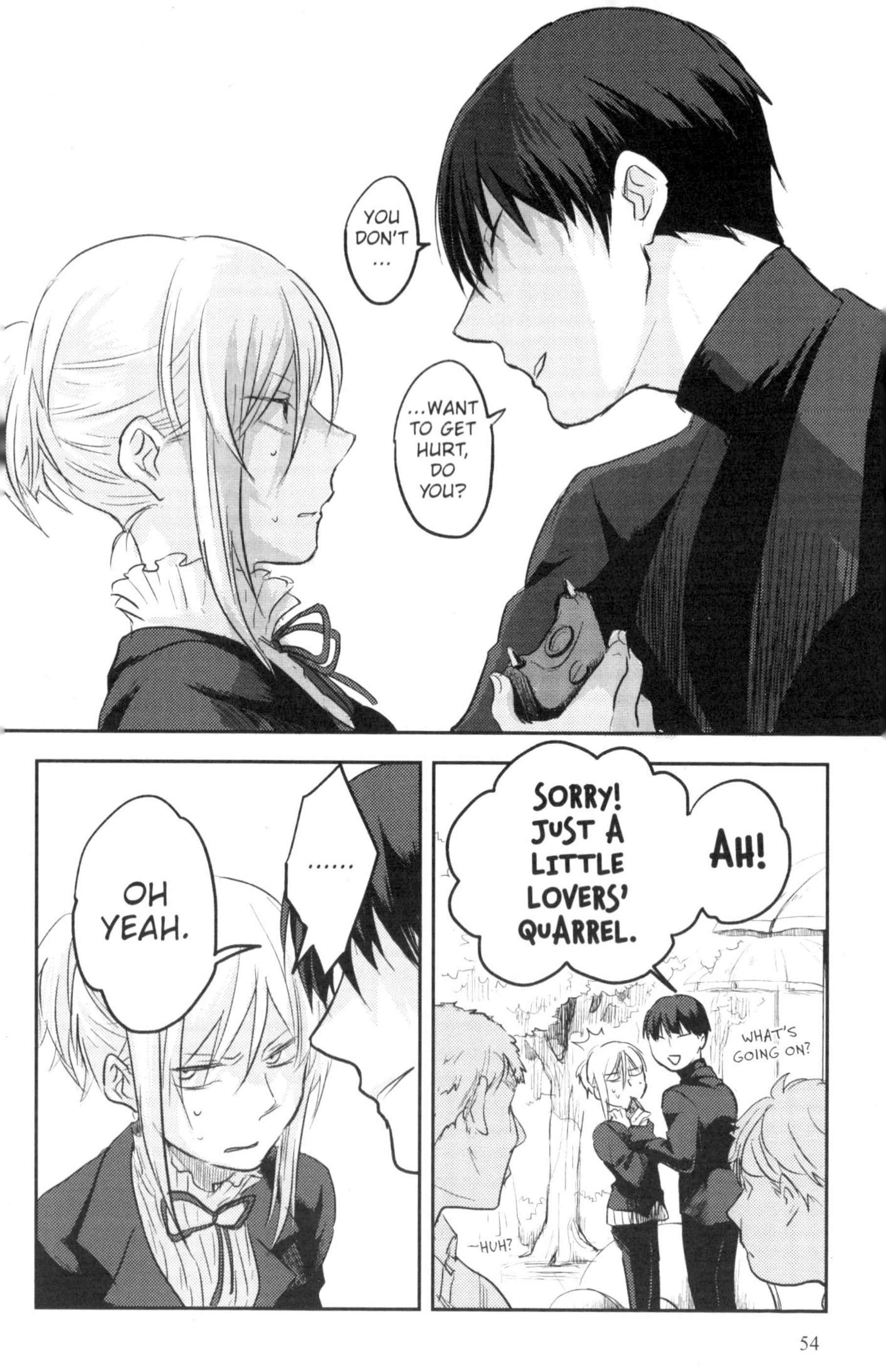
YOU DON'T ...
...WANT TO GET HURT, DO YOU?
AH!
SORRY! JUST A LITTLE LOVERS' QUARREL.
WHAT'S GOING ON?
—HUH?
......
OH YEAH.

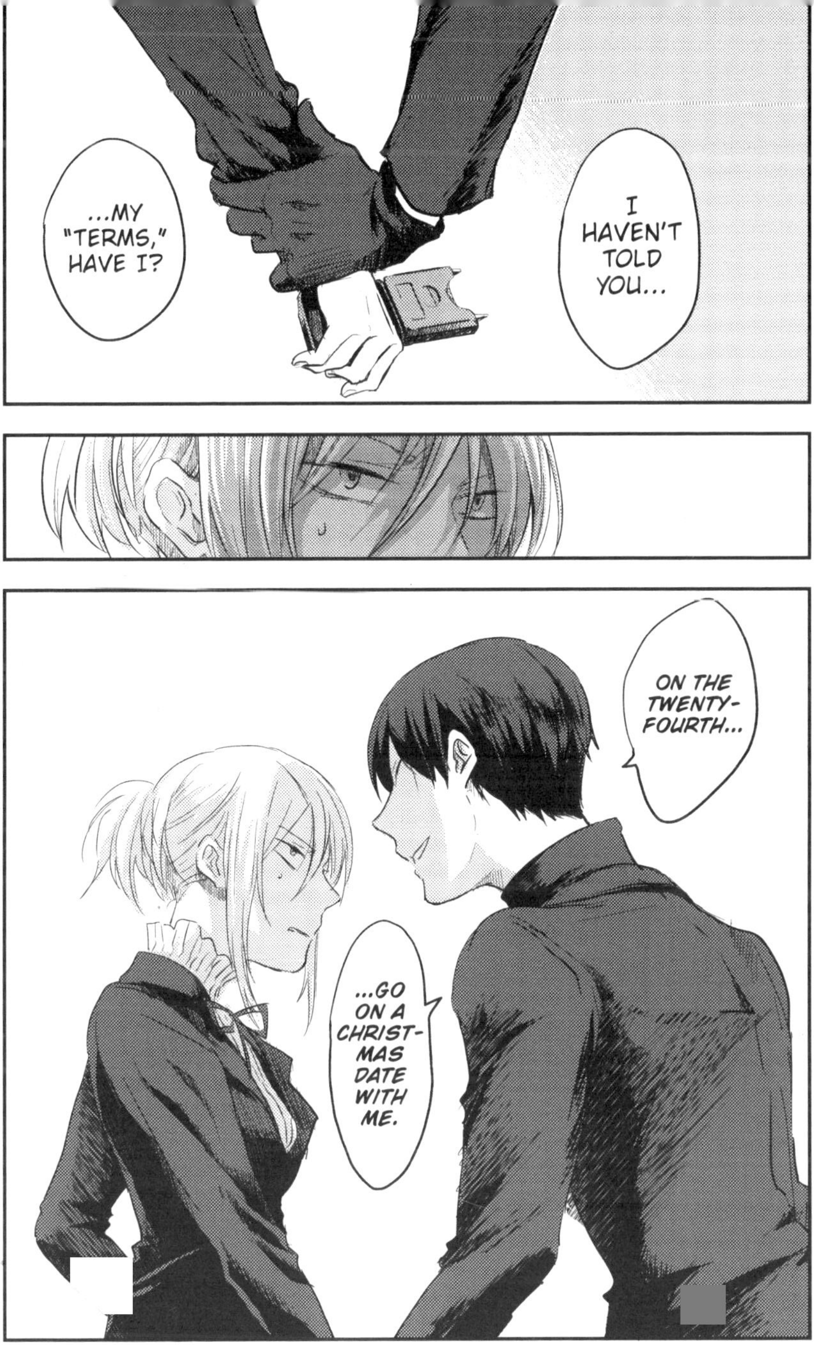
I HAVEN'T TOLD YOU...
...MY "TERMS," HAVE I?
ON THE TWENTY-FOURTH...
...GO ON A CHRIST-MAS DATE WITH ME.

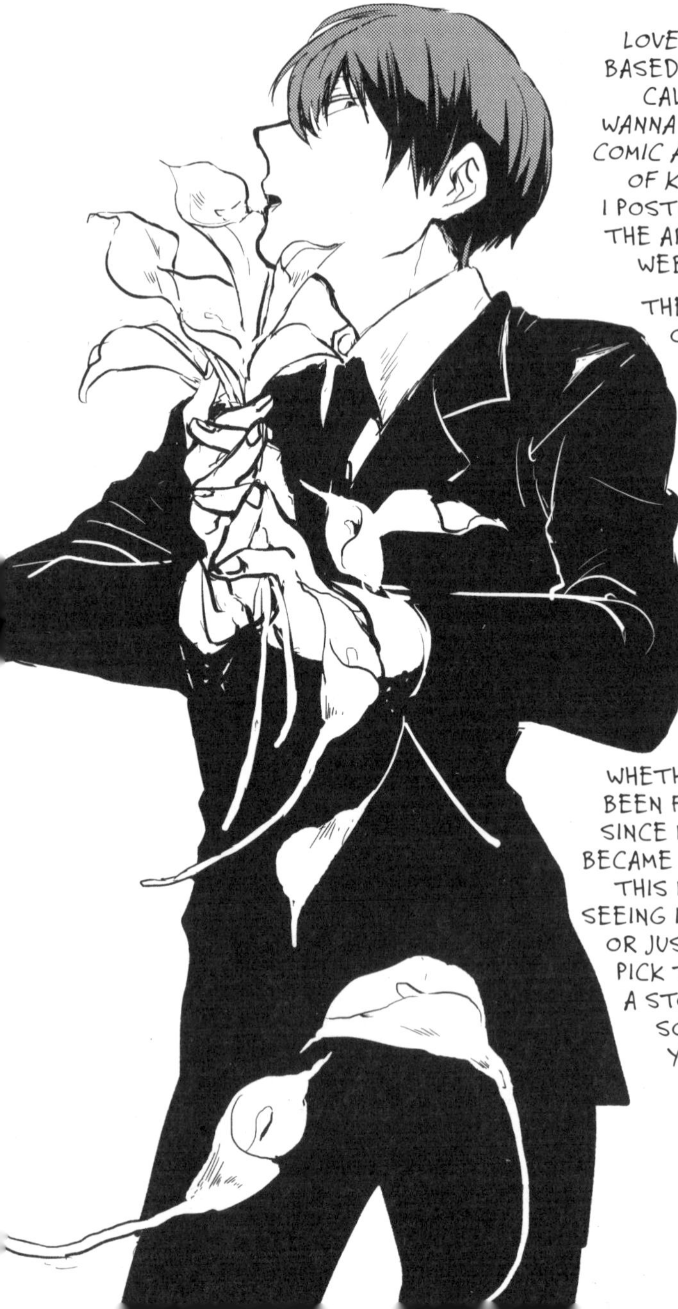

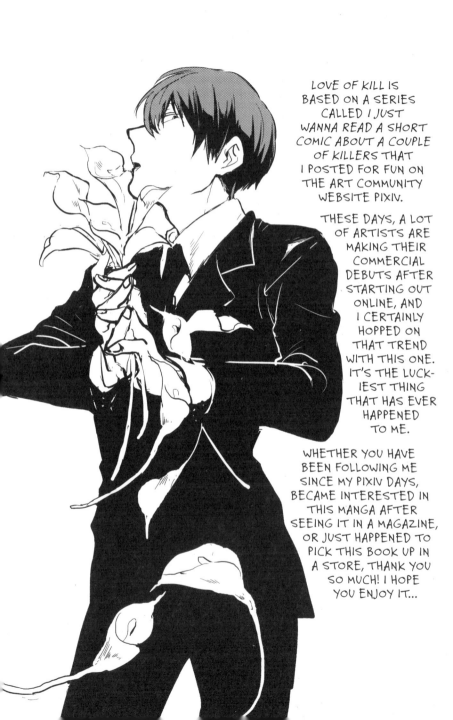

LOVE OF KILL IS BASED ON A SERIES CALLED I JUST WANNA READ A SHORT COMIC ABOUT A COUPLE OF KILLERS THAT I POSTED FOR FUN ON THE ART COMMUNITY WEBSITE PIXIV.

THESE DAYS, A LOT OF ARTISTS ARE MAKING THEIR COMMERCIAL DEBUTS AFTER STARTING OUT ONLINE, AND I CERTAINLY HOPPED ON THAT TREND WITH THIS ONE. IT'S THE LUCKIEST THING THAT HAS EVER HAPPENED TO ME.

WHETHER YOU HAVE BEEN FOLLOWING ME SINCE MY PIXIV DAYS, BECAME INTERESTED IN THIS MANGA AFTER SEEING IT IN A MAGAZINE, OR JUST HAPPENED TO PICK THIS BOOK UP IN A STORE, THANK YOU SO MUCH! I HOPE YOU ENJOY IT...

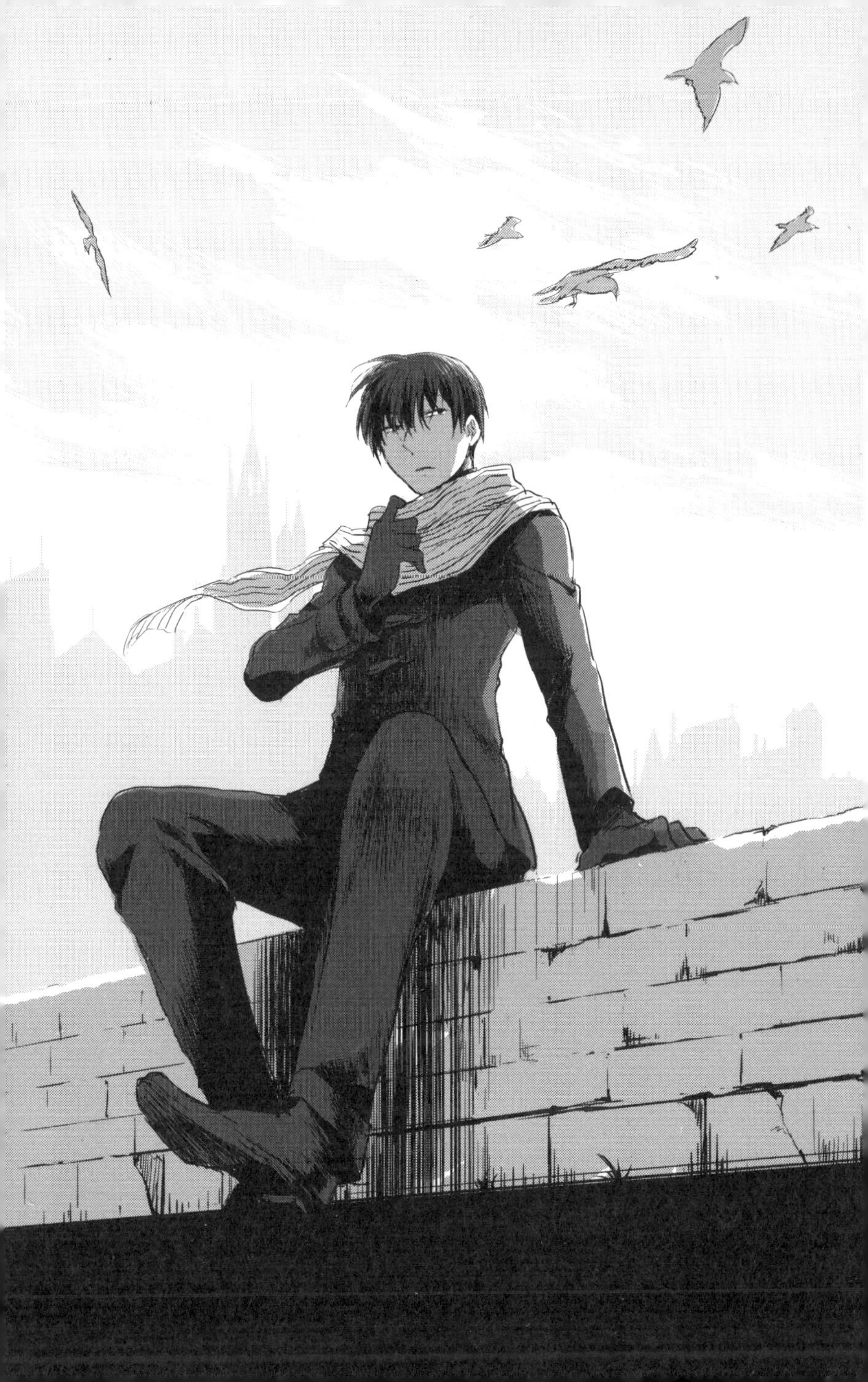

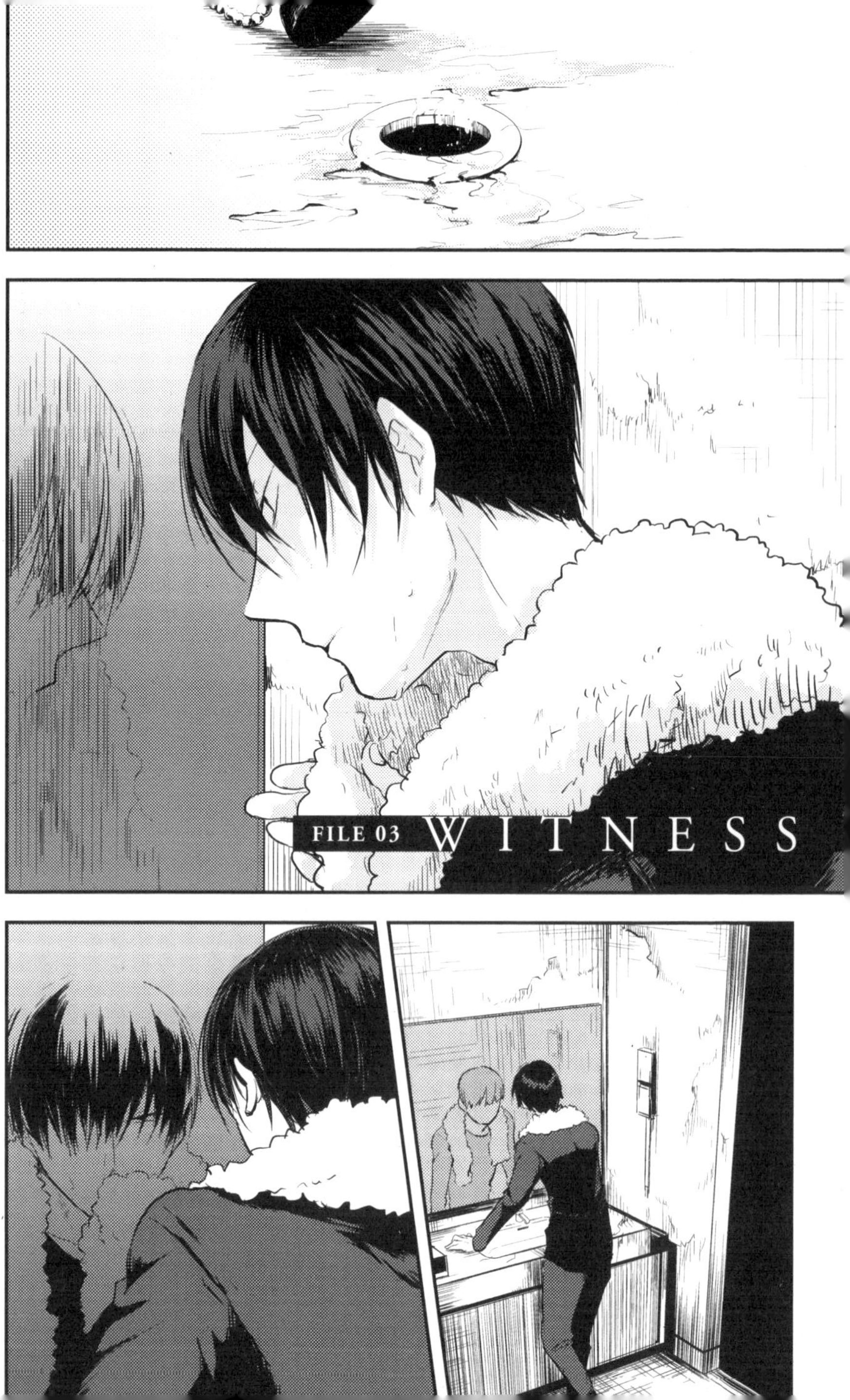
FILE 03
WITNESS

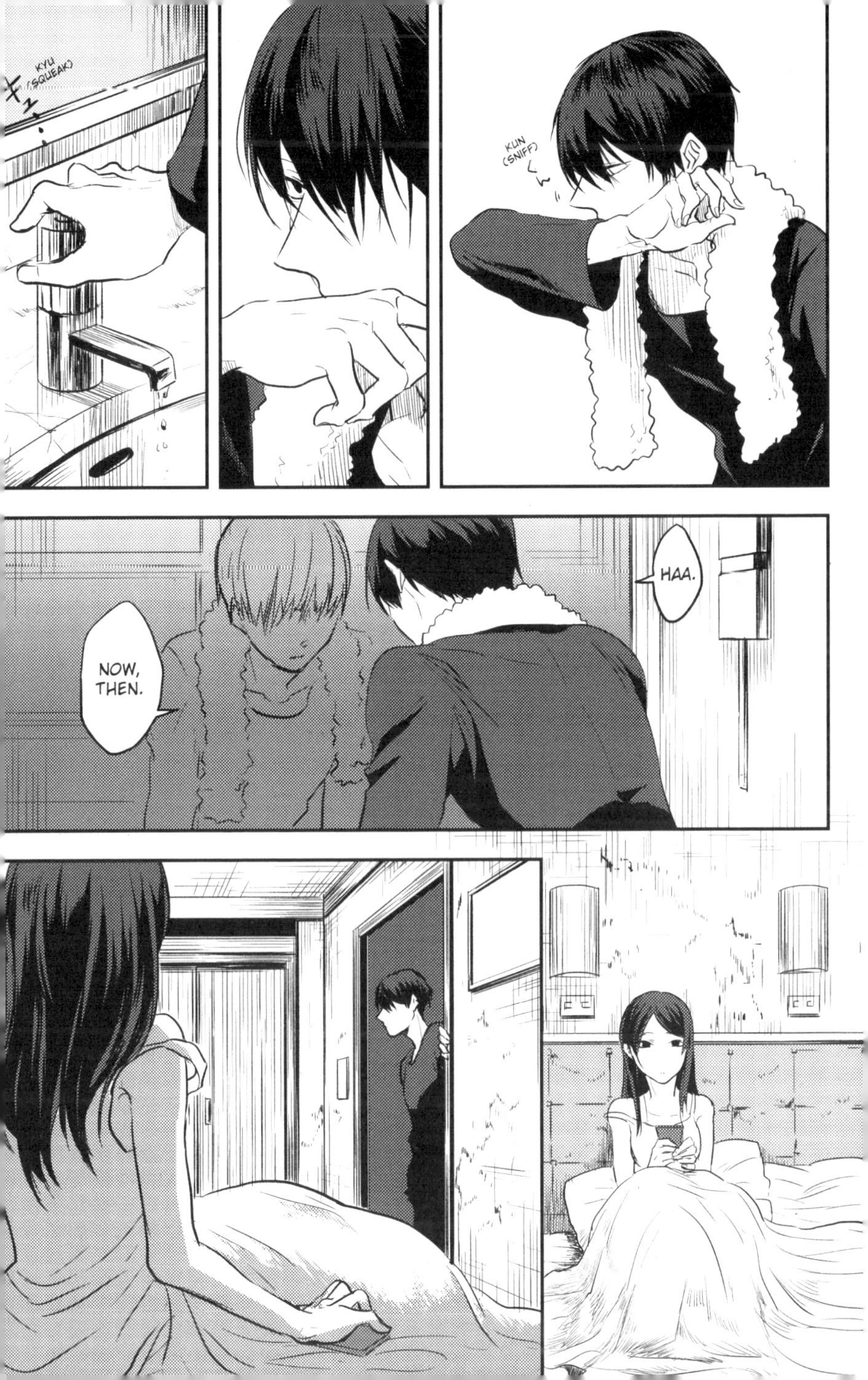
KUN (SNIFF)
くん
KYU (SQUEAK)
キュ
HAA.
NOW, THEN.

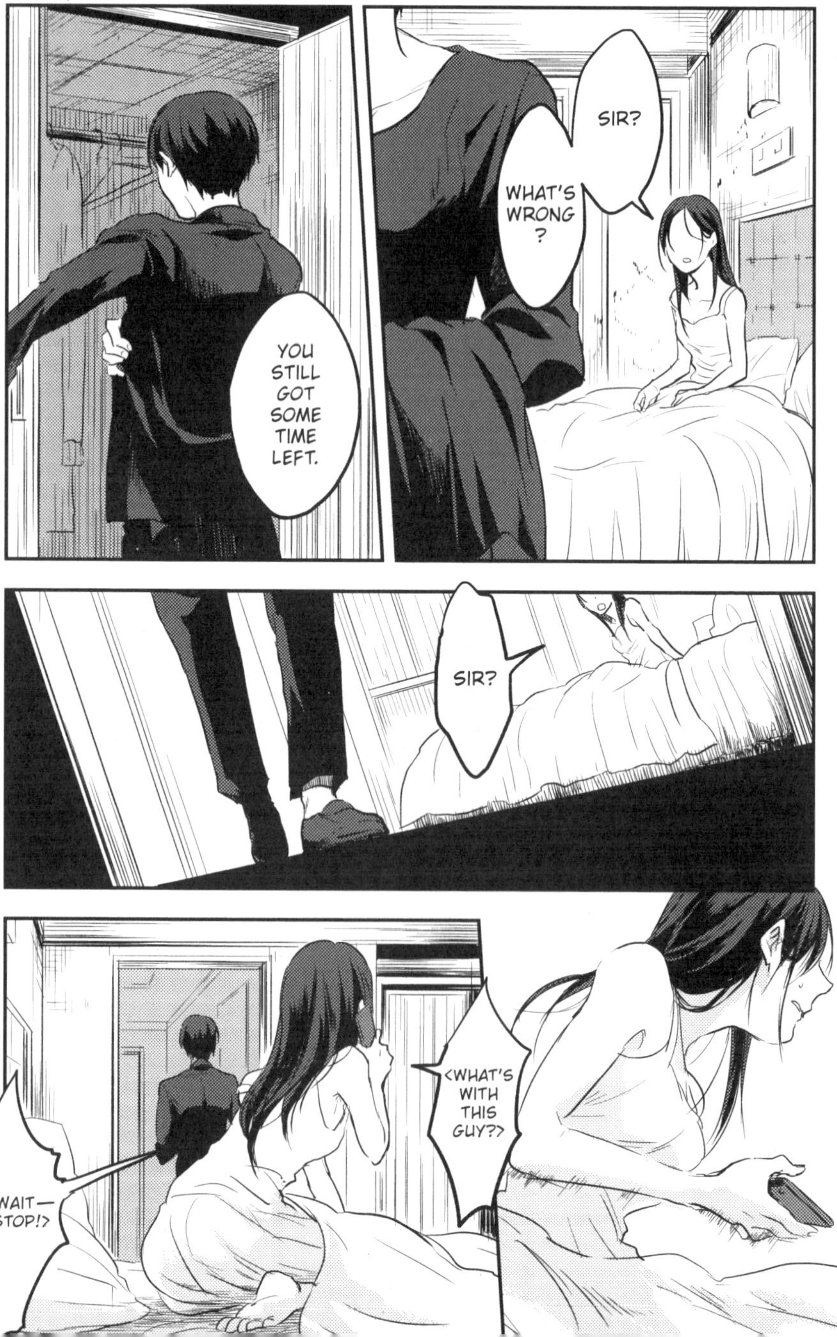
SIR?
WHAT'S WRONG?
YOU STILL GOT SOME TIME LEFT.
SIR?
<WHAT'S WITH THIS GUY?>
<WAIT— STOP!>

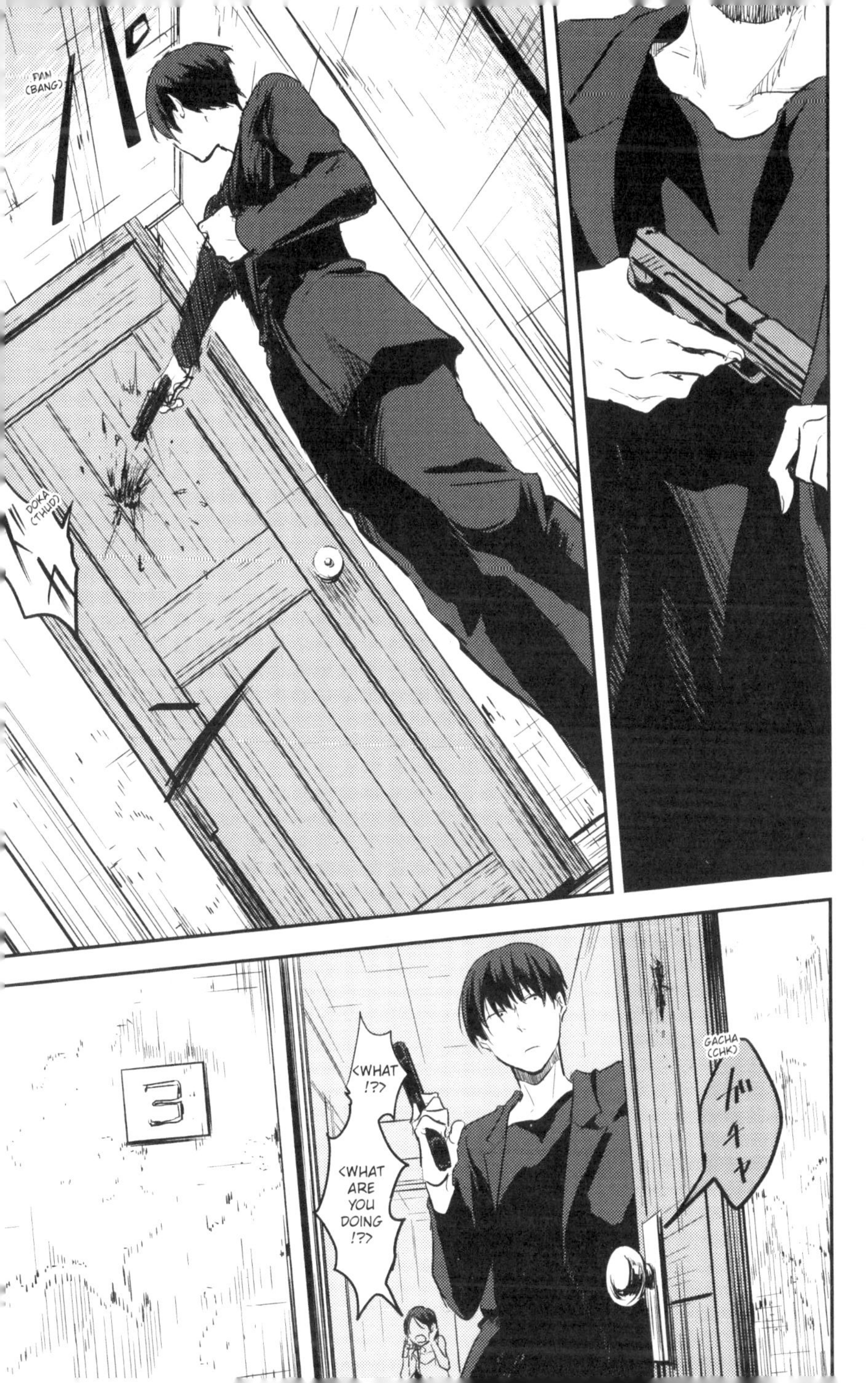

FAN (BANG)
DOKA (THUD)
GACHA (CHK)
ガチャ
<WHAT!?>
<WHAT ARE YOU DOING!?>

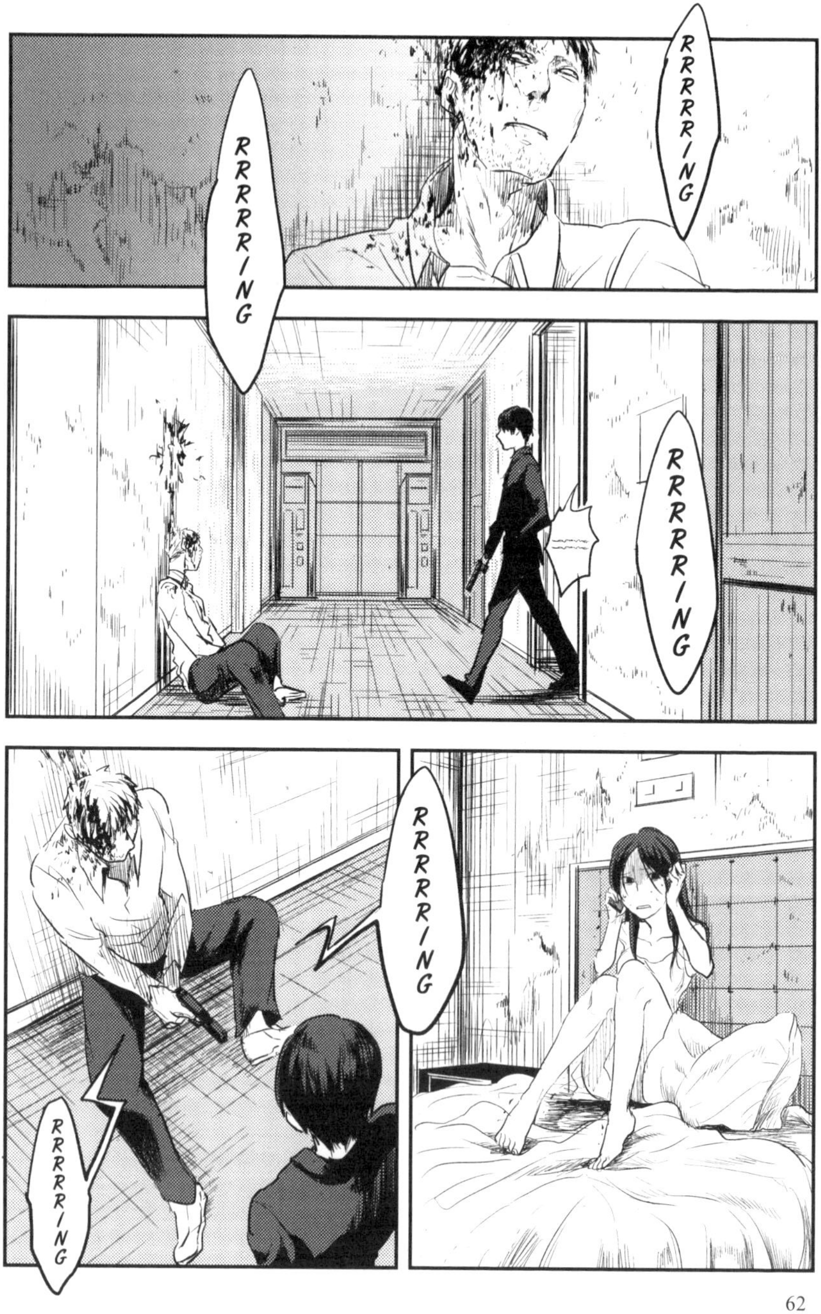
RRRRRING
RRRRRING
RRRRRING
RRRRRING
RRRRRING

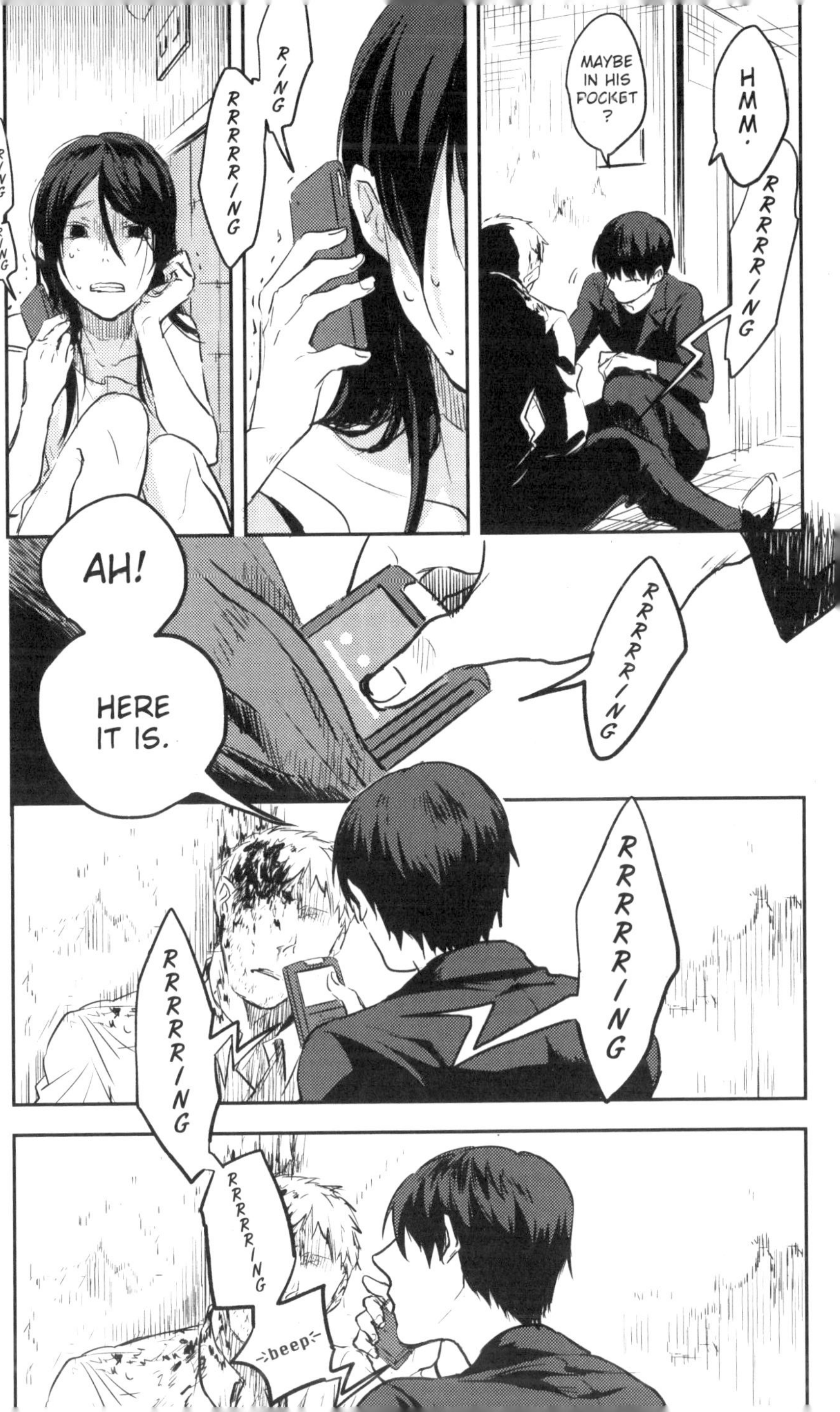
HMM.
MAYBE IN HIS POCKET ?
RRRRRING
RING
RRRRRING
RING RING
RRRRRING
AH!
HERE IT IS.
RRRRRING
RRRRRING
RRRRRING
beep

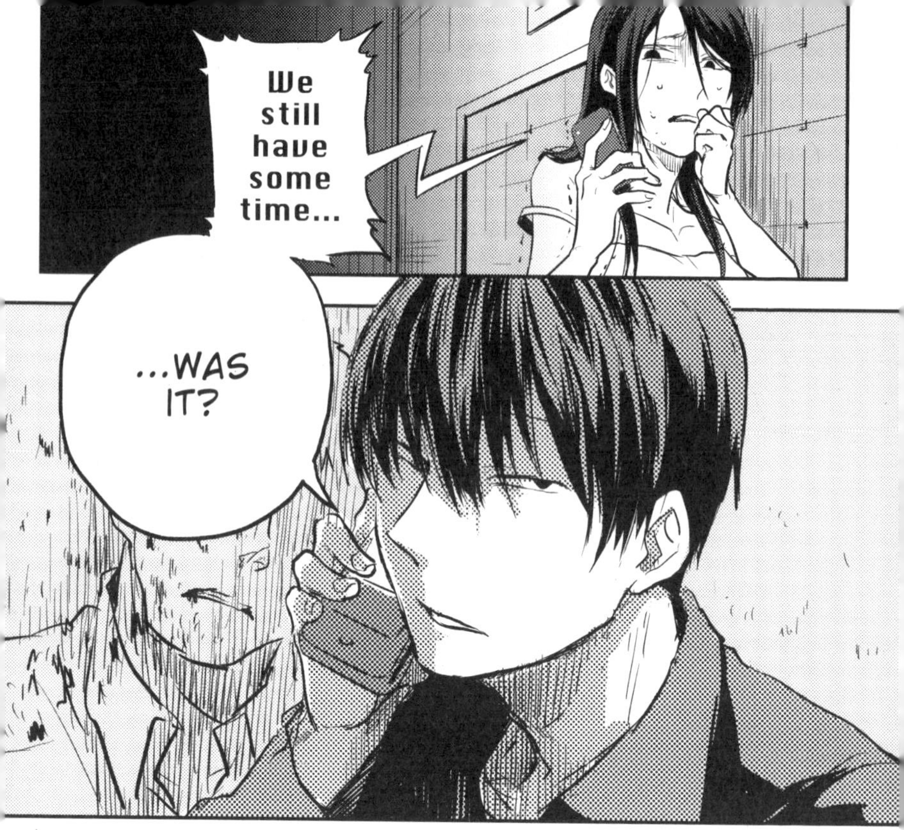
We still have some time...
...WAS IT?

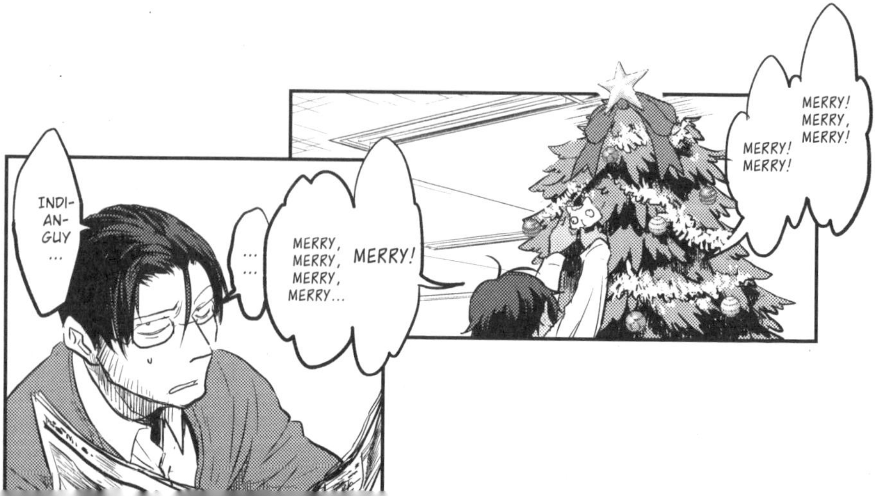
MERRY! MERRY, MERRY!
MERRY! MERRY!
MERRY!
MERRY, MERRY, MERRY, MERRY...
... ...
INDI-AN-GUY ...

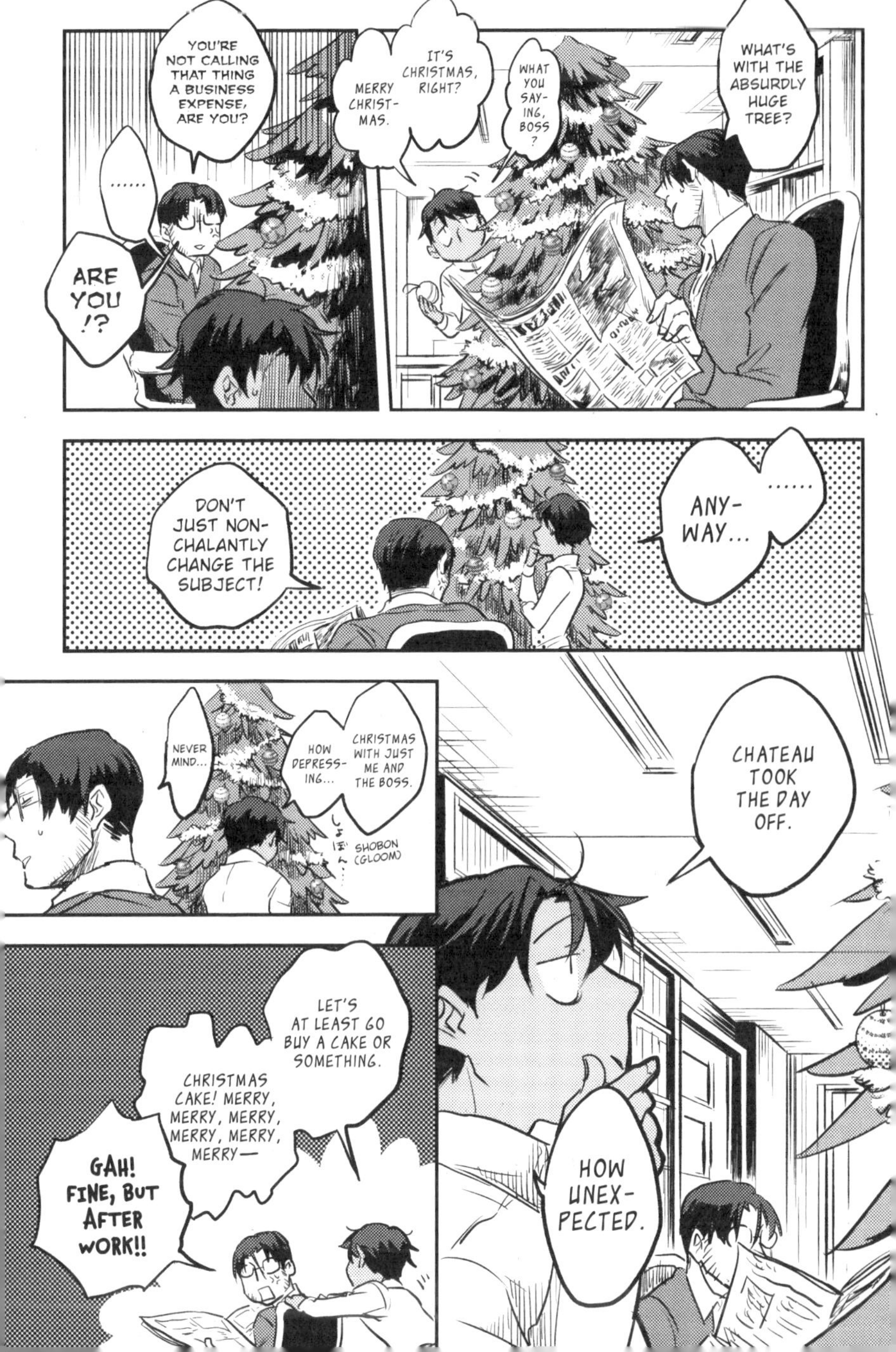
WHAT'S WITH THE ABSURDLY HUGE TREE?
WHAT YOU SAYING, BOSS?
IT'S CHRISTMAS, RIGHT?
MERRY CHRISTMAS.
YOU'RE NOT CALLING THAT THING A BUSINESS EXPENSE, ARE YOU?
......
ARE YOU!?
......
ANYWAY...
DON'T JUST NONCHALANTLY CHANGE THE SUBJECT!
CHATEAU TOOK THE DAY OFF.
HOW UNEXPECTED.
CHRISTMAS WITH JUST ME AND THE BOSS.
HOW DEPRESSING...
NEVER MIND...
しょぼん...
SHOBON (GLOOM)
LET'S AT LEAST GO BUY A CAKE OR SOMETHING.
CHRISTMAS CAKE! MERRY, MERRY, MERRY, MERRY, MERRY, MERRY—
GAH! FINE, BUT AFTER WORK!!

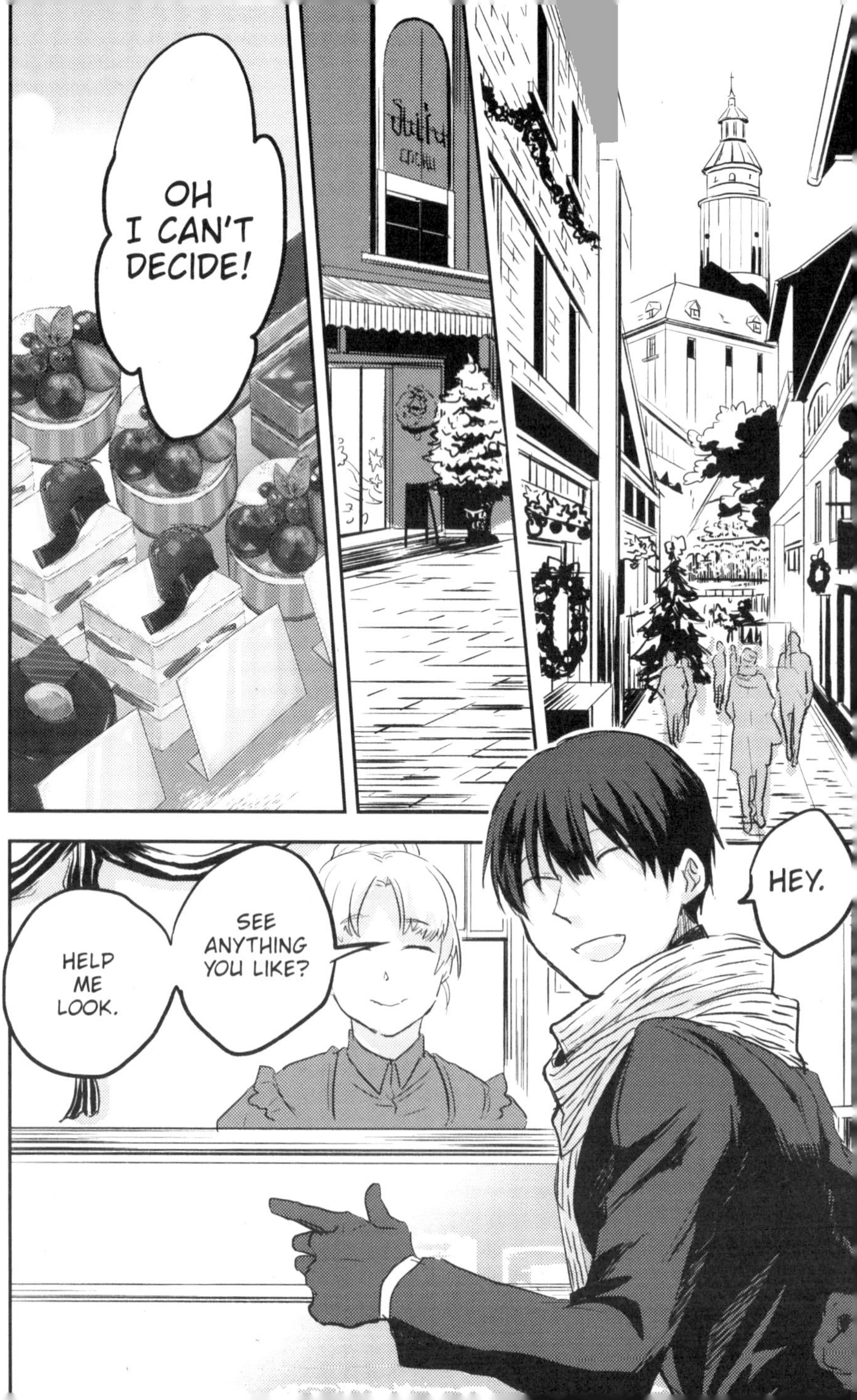
OH I CAN'T DECIDE!
HEY.
SEE ANYTHING YOU LIKE?
HELP ME LOOK.

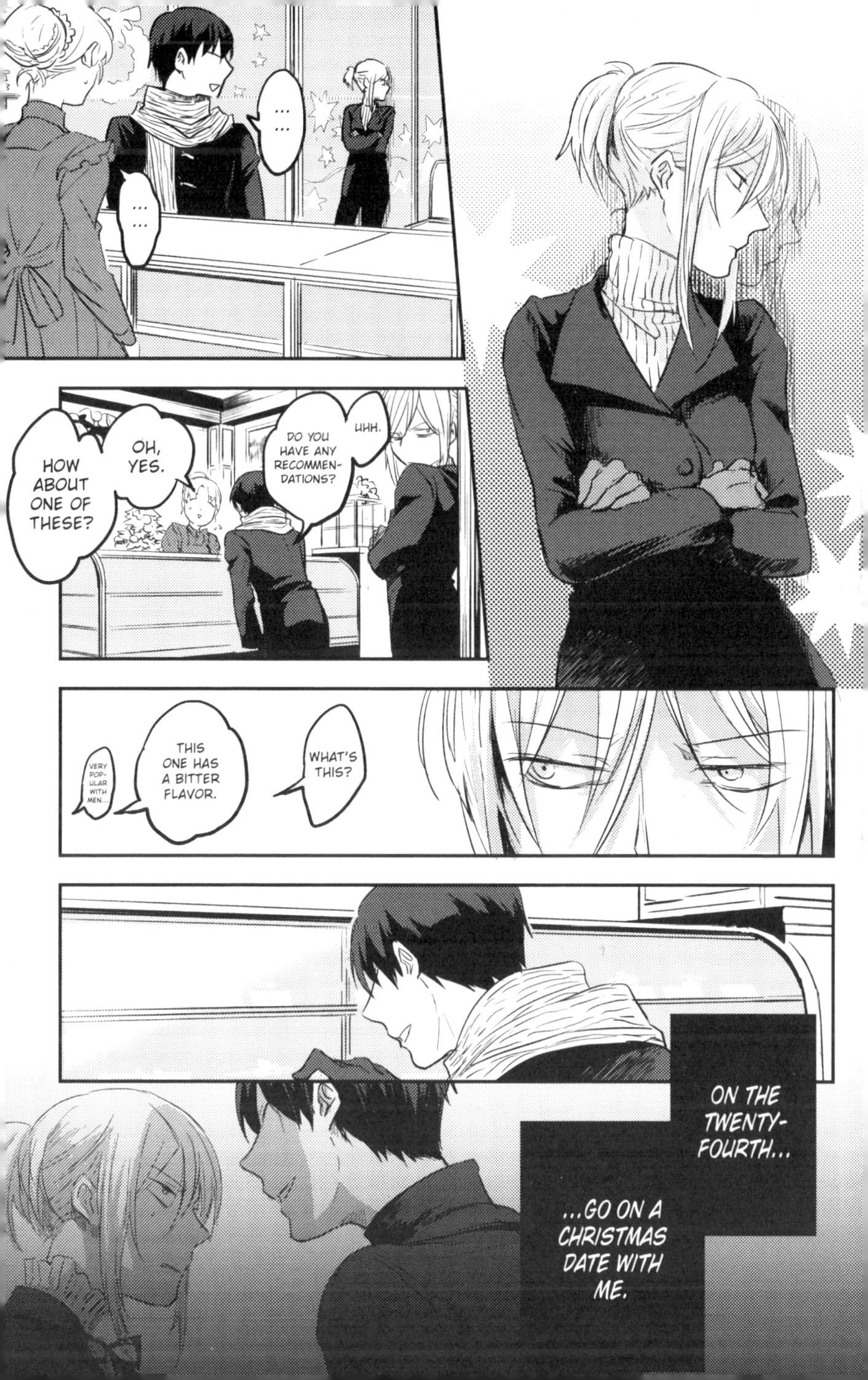
......
......
UHH.
DO YOU HAVE ANY RECOMMENDATIONS?
OH, YES.
HOW ABOUT ONE OF THESE?
WHAT'S THIS?
THIS ONE HAS A BITTER FLAVOR.
VERY POPULAR WITH MEN...
ON THE TWENTY-FOURTH...
...GO ON A CHRISTMAS DATE WITH ME.

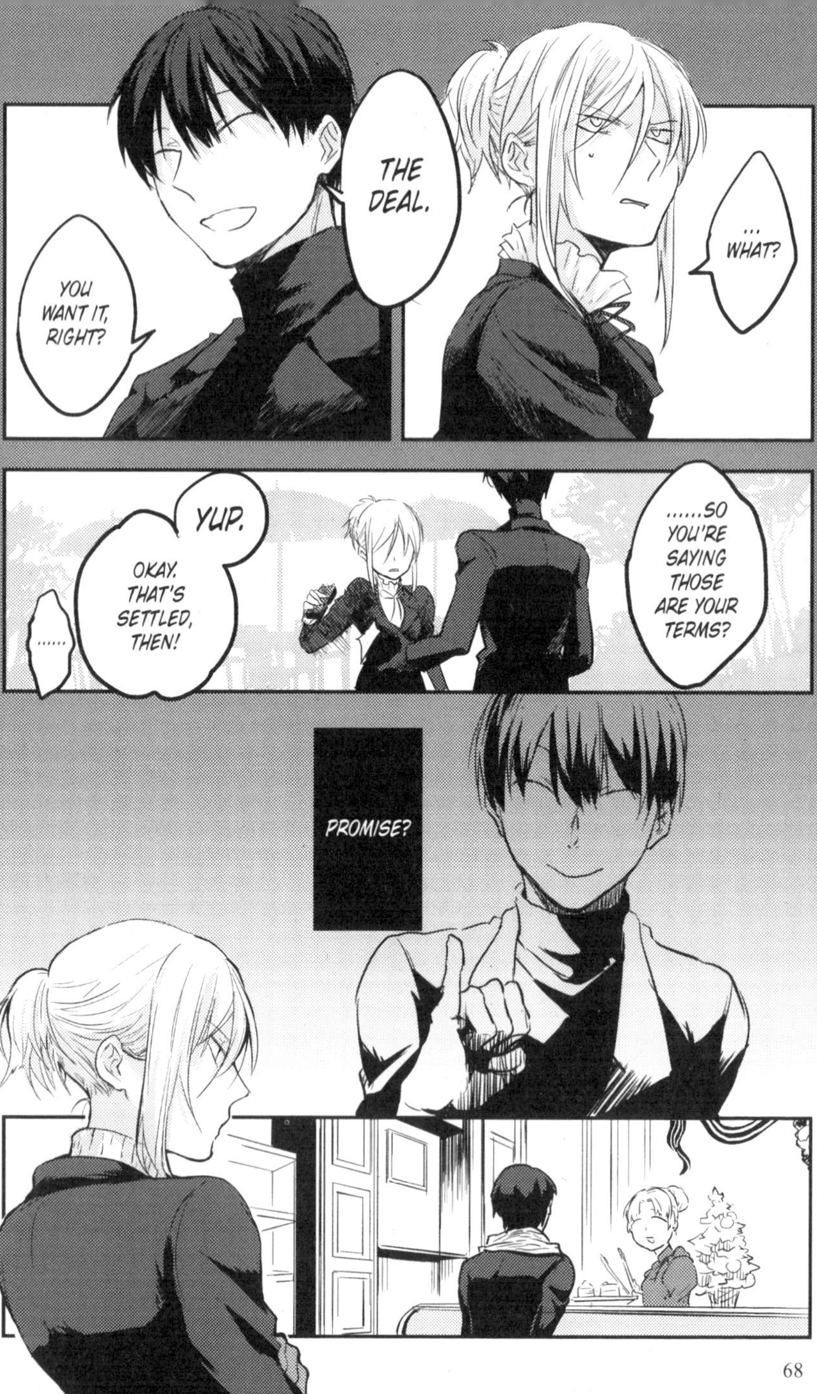
... WHAT?
THE DEAL.
YOU WANT IT, RIGHT?
......SO YOU'RE SAYING THOSE ARE YOUR TERMS?
YUP.
OKAY. THAT'S SETTLED, THEN!
......
PROMISE?

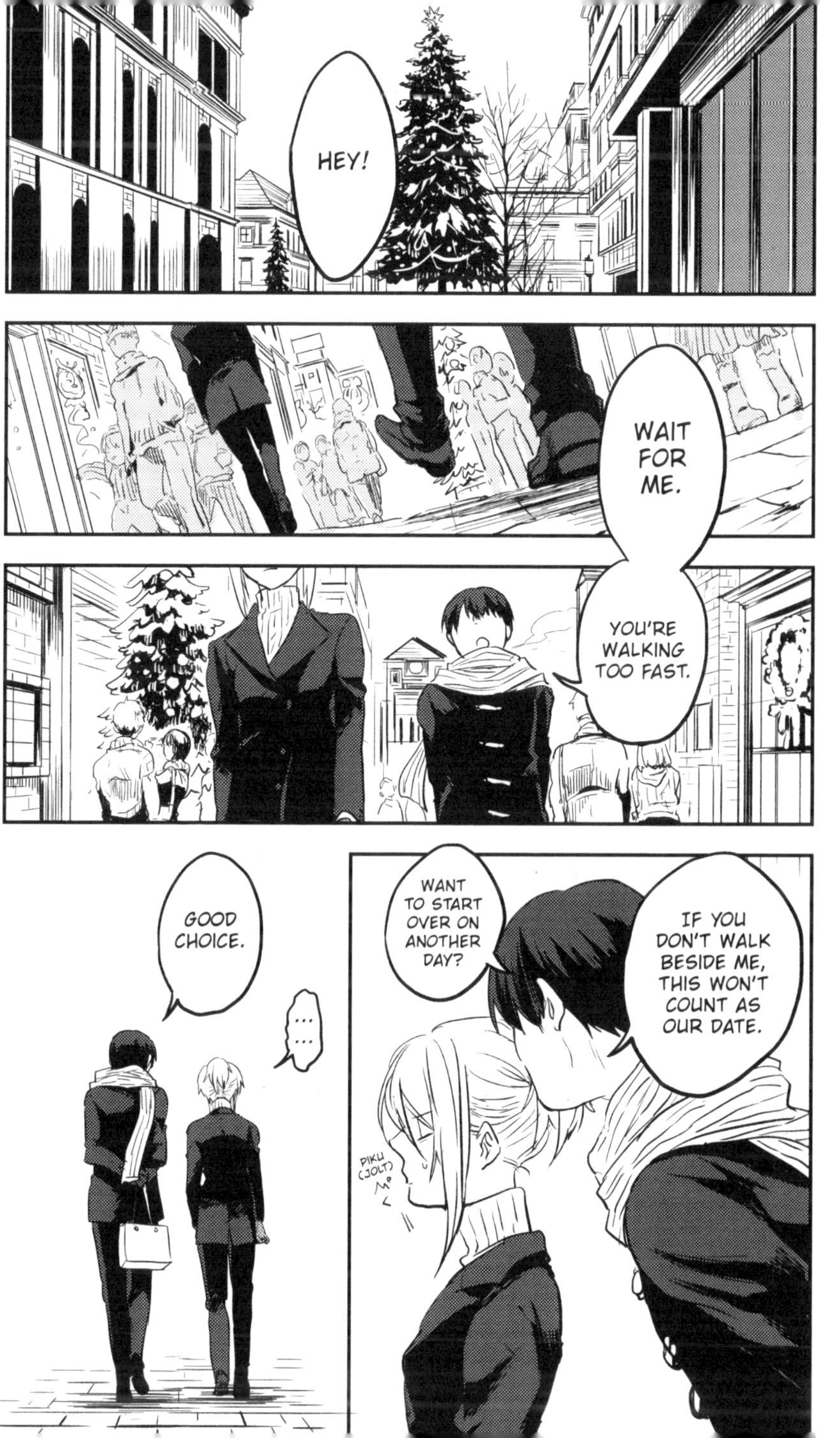

HEY!
WAIT FOR ME.
YOU'RE WALKING TOO FAST.
IF YOU DON'T WALK BESIDE ME, THIS WON'T COUNT AS OUR DATE.
WANT TO START OVER ON ANOTHER DAY?
PIKU (JOLT)
GOOD CHOICE.
... ...

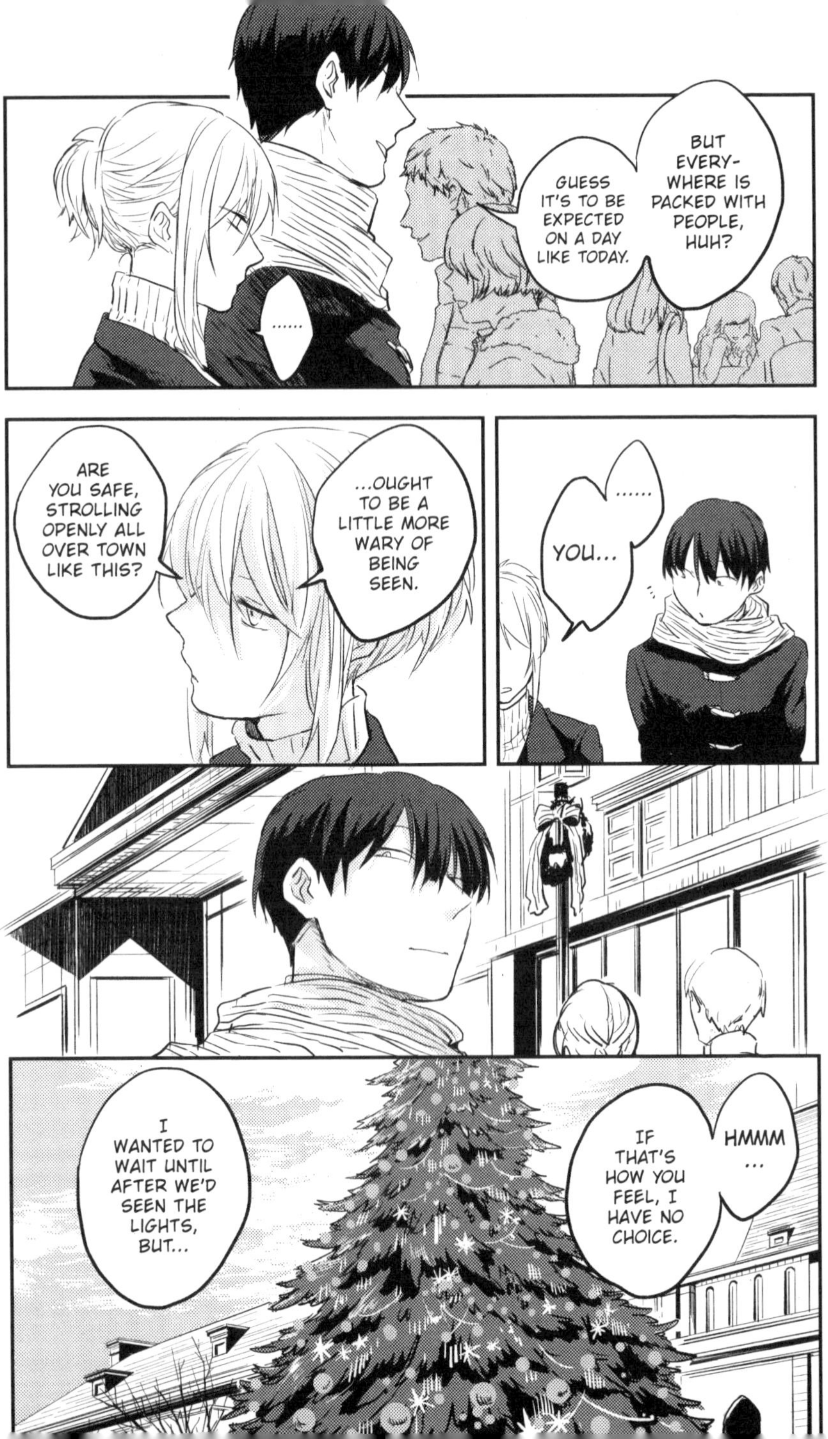
BUT EVERY-WHERE IS PACKED WITH PEOPLE, HUH?
GUESS IT'S TO BE EXPECTED ON A DAY LIKE TODAY.
......
......
YOU...
...OUGHT TO BE A LITTLE MORE WARY OF BEING SEEN.
ARE YOU SAFE, STROLLING OPENLY ALL OVER TOWN LIKE THIS?
HMMM...
IF THAT'S HOW YOU FEEL, I HAVE NO CHOICE.
I WANTED TO WAIT UNTIL AFTER WE'D SEEN THE LIGHTS, BUT...

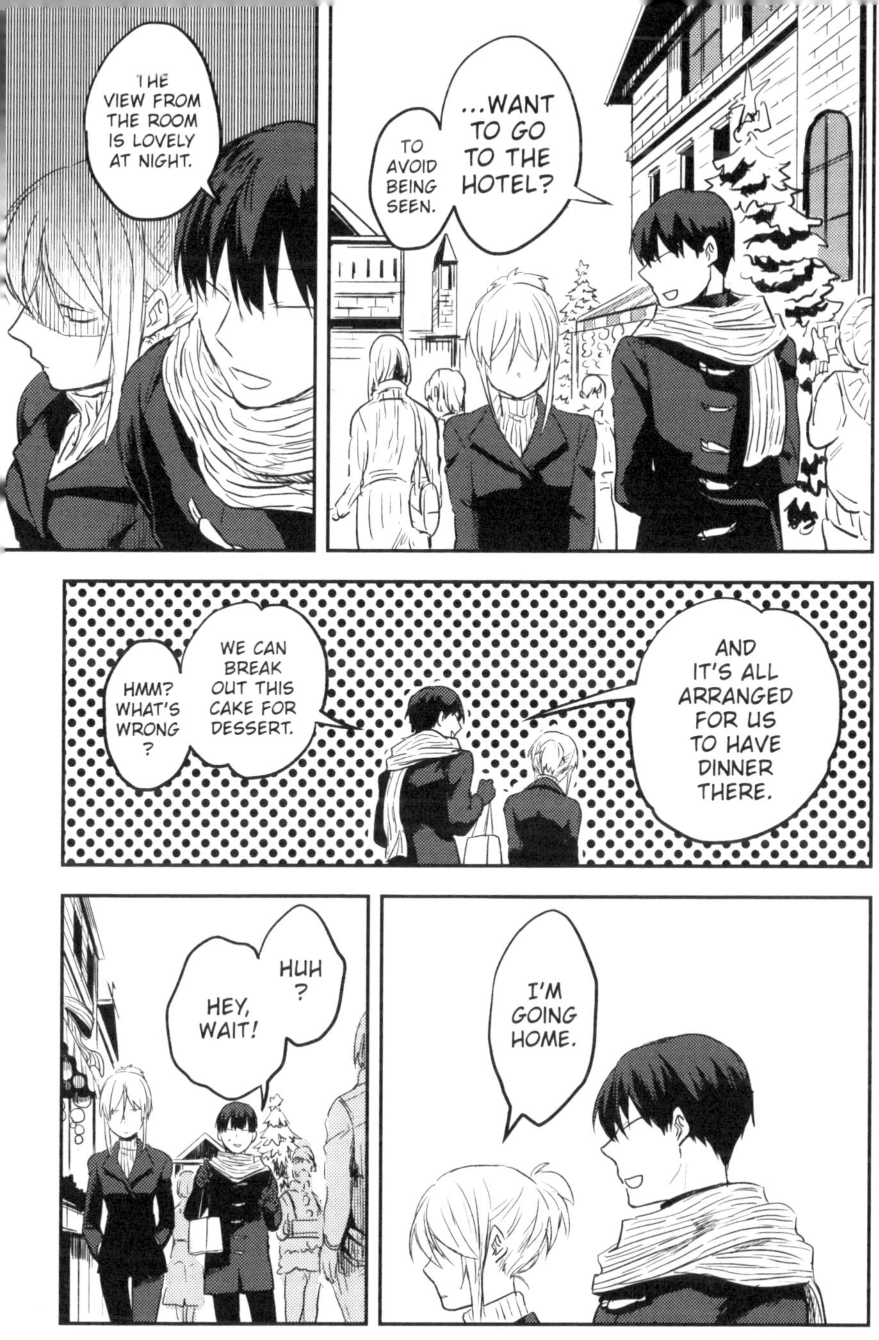
...WANT TO GO TO THE HOTEL?
TO AVOID BEING SEEN.
THE VIEW FROM THE ROOM IS LOVELY AT NIGHT.
AND IT'S ALL ARRANGED FOR US TO HAVE DINNER THERE.
WE CAN BREAK OUT THIS CAKE FOR DESSERT.
HMM? WHAT'S WRONG?
I'M GOING HOME.
HUH?
HEY, WAIT!

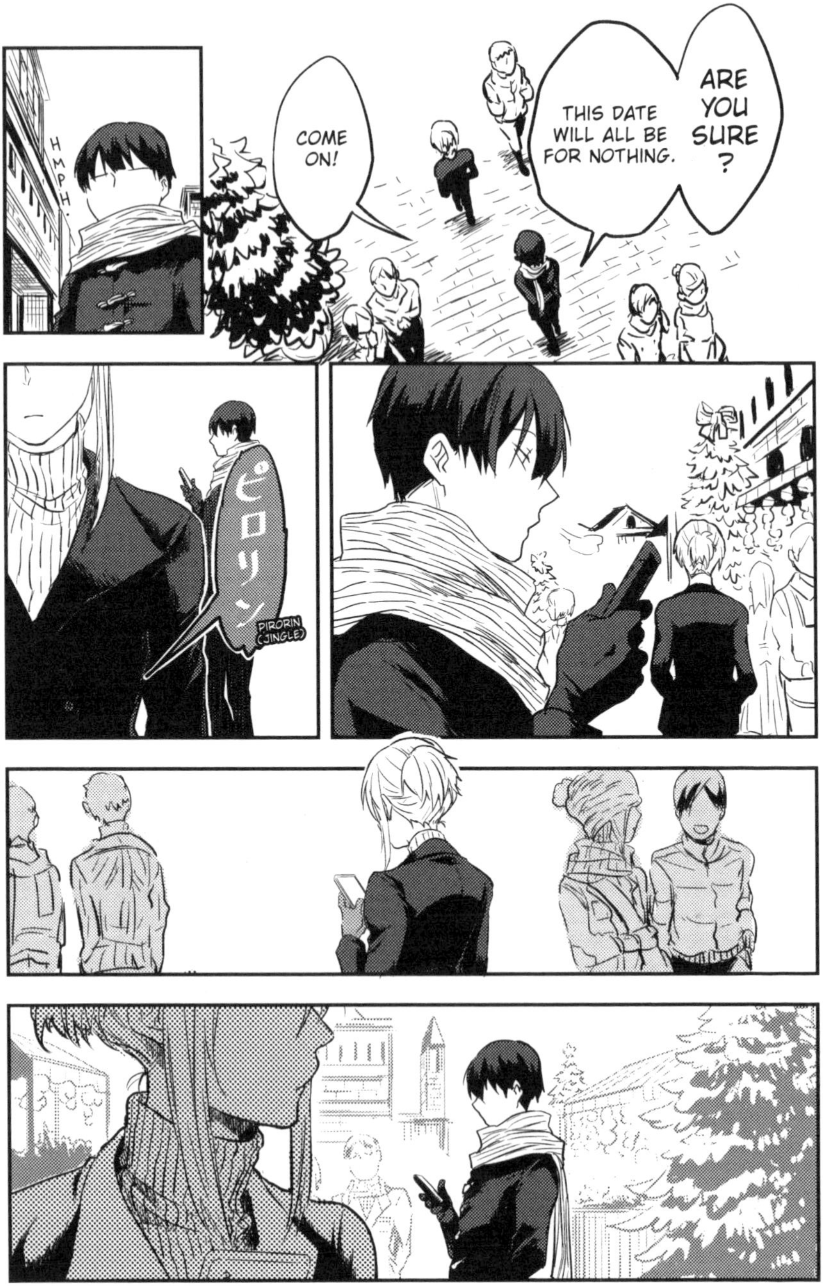
ARE YOU SURE?
THIS DATE WILL ALL BE FOR NOTHING.
COME ON!
HMPH.
ピロリン
PIRORIN (JINGLE)

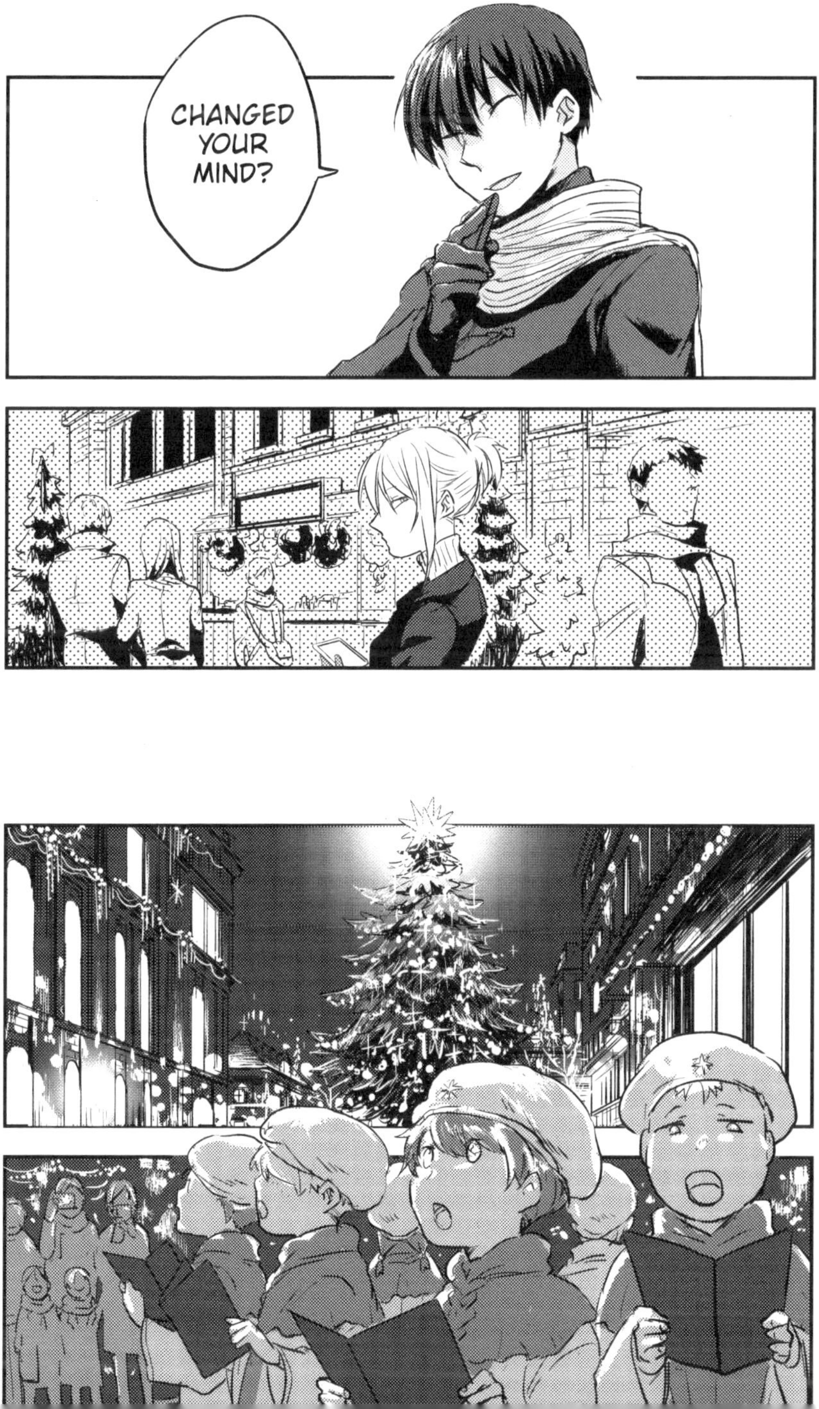
CHANGED YOUR MIND?

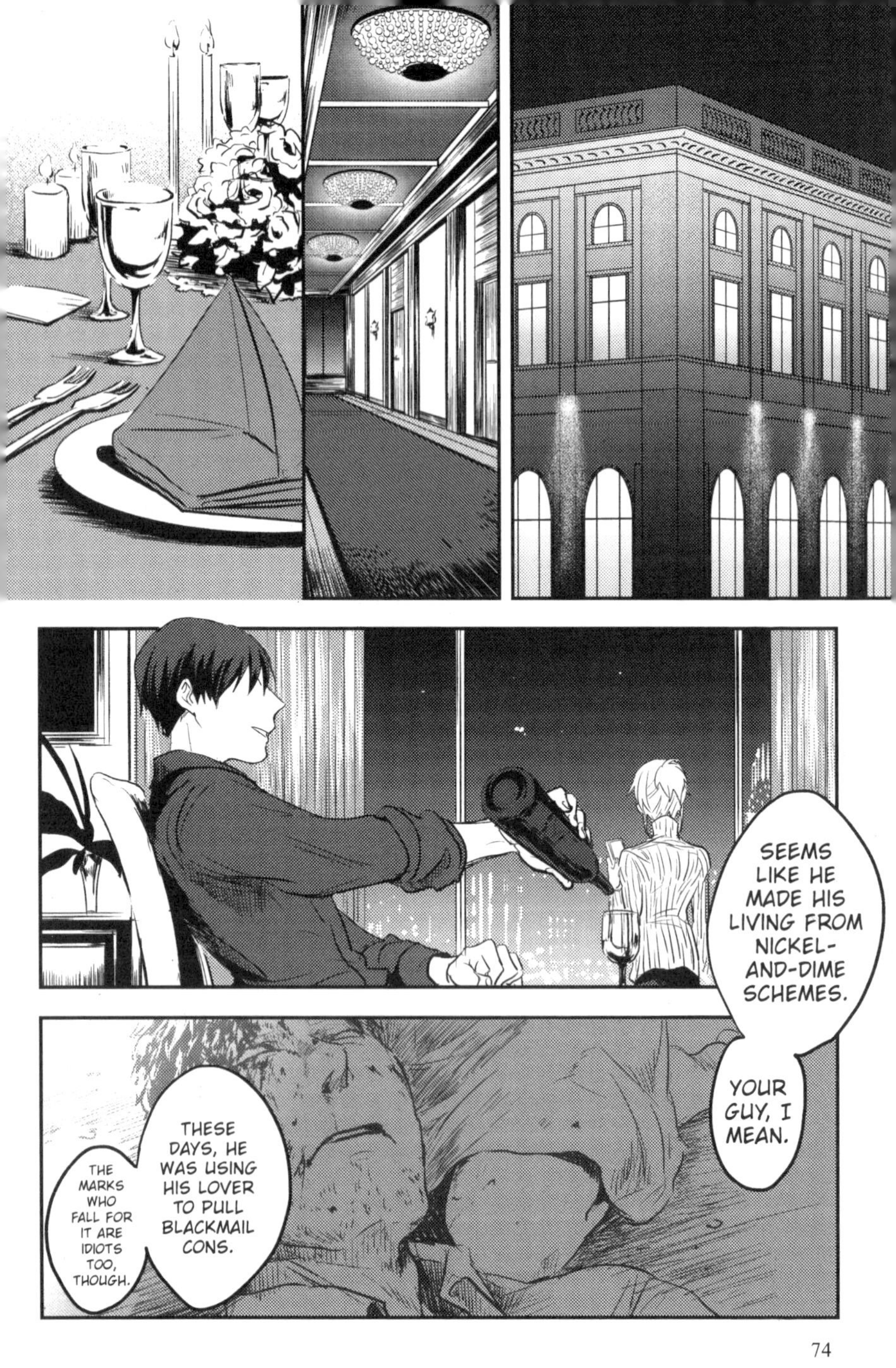
SEEMS LIKE HE MADE HIS LIVING FROM NICKEL-AND-DIME SCHEMES.
YOUR GUY, I MEAN.
THESE DAYS, HE WAS USING HIS LOVER TO PULL BLACKMAIL CONS.
THE MARKS WHO FALL FOR IT ARE IDIOTS TOO, THOUGH.

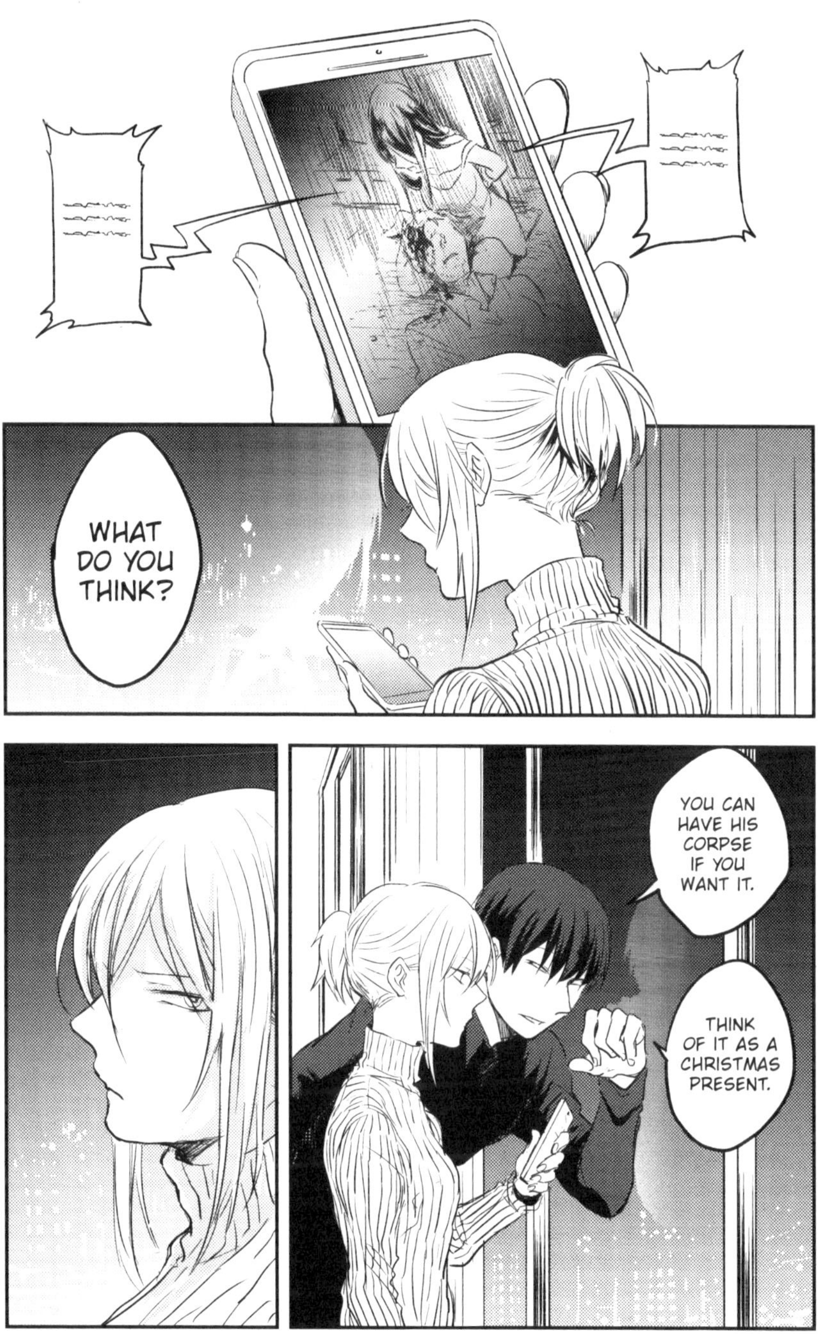
WHAT DO YOU THINK?
YOU CAN HAVE HIS CORPSE IF YOU WANT IT.
THINK OF IT AS A CHRISTMAS PRESENT.

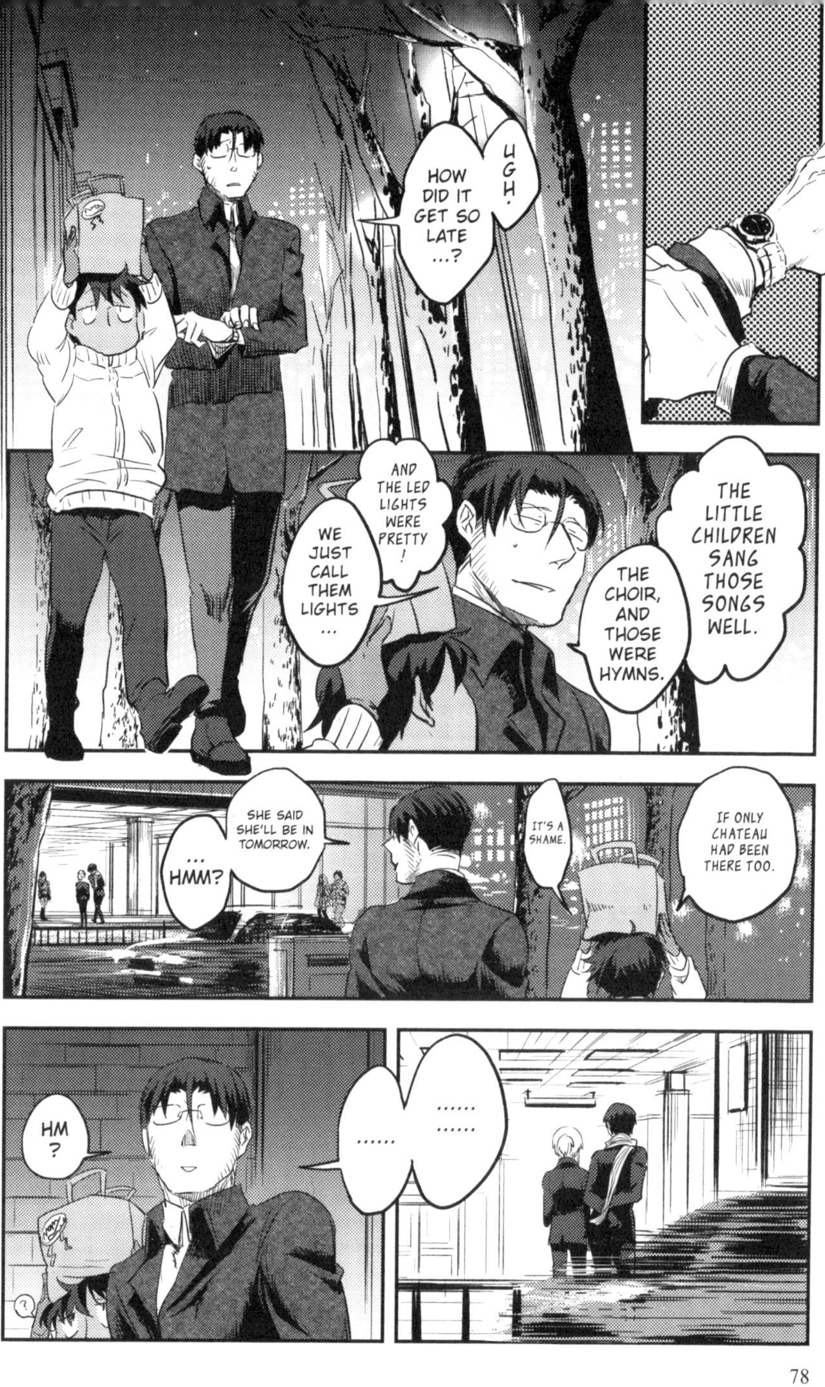
UGH.
HOW DID IT GET SO LATE ...?
THE LITTLE CHILDREN SANG THOSE SONGS WELL.
THE CHOIR, AND THOSE WERE HYMNS.
AND THE LED LIGHTS WERE PRETTY!
WE JUST CALL THEM LIGHTS ...
IF ONLY CHATEAU HAD BEEN THERE TOO.
IT'S A SHAME.
SHE SAID SHE'LL BE IN TOMORROW.
... HMM?
....
......
HM?
?

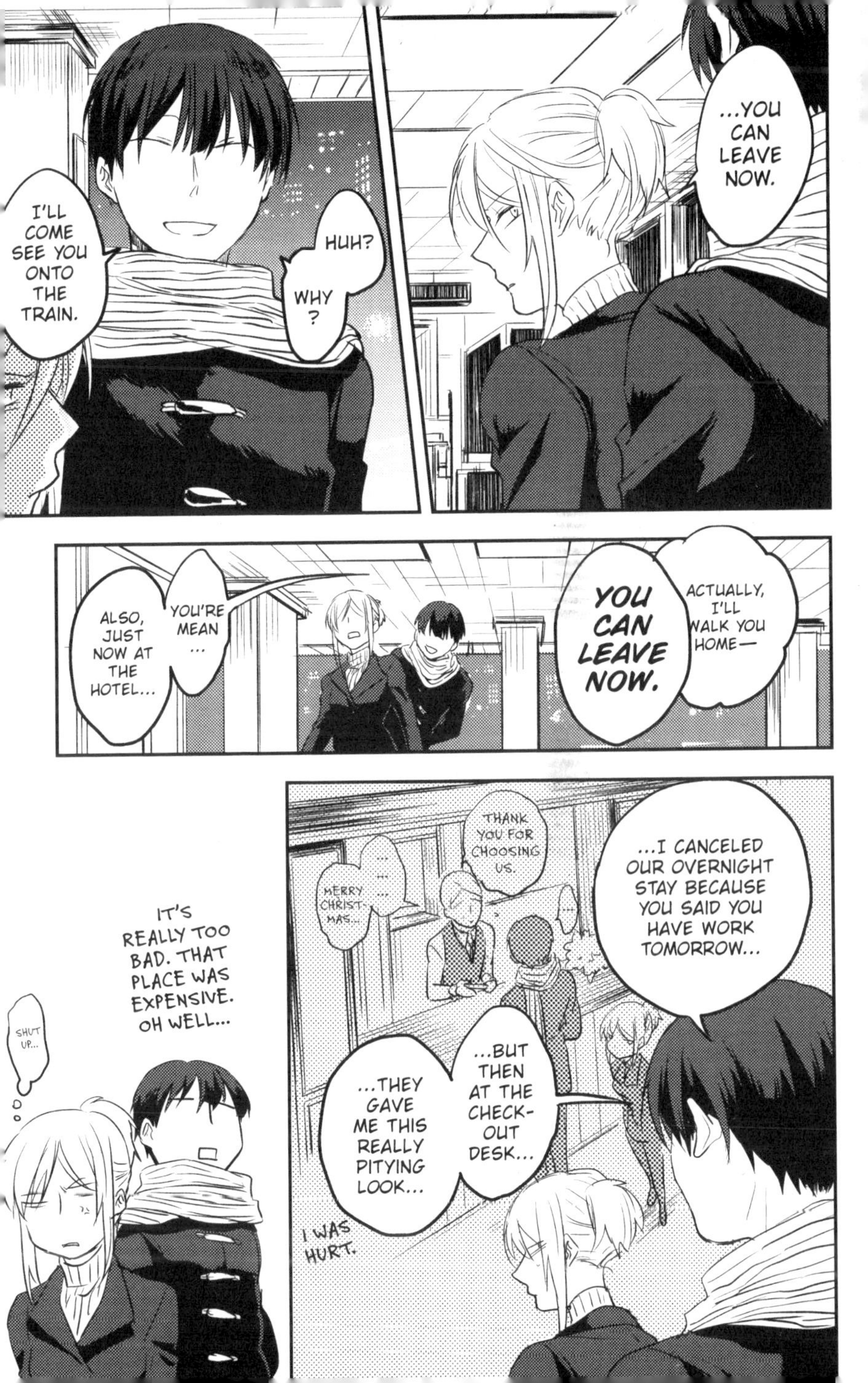
...YOU CAN LEAVE NOW.
HUH? WHY?
I'LL COME SEE YOU ONTO THE TRAIN.
ACTUALLY, I'LL WALK YOU HOME—
YOU CAN LEAVE NOW.
YOU'RE MEAN...
ALSO, JUST NOW AT THE HOTEL...
...I CANCELED OUR OVERNIGHT STAY BECAUSE YOU SAID YOU HAVE WORK TOMORROW...
THANK YOU FOR CHOOSING US.
... ...
MERRY CHRISTMAS...
...BUT THEN AT THE CHECK-OUT DESK...
...THEY GAVE ME THIS REALLY PITYING LOOK...
I WAS HURT.
IT'S REALLY TOO BAD. THAT PLACE WAS EXPENSIVE. OH WELL...
SHUT UP...

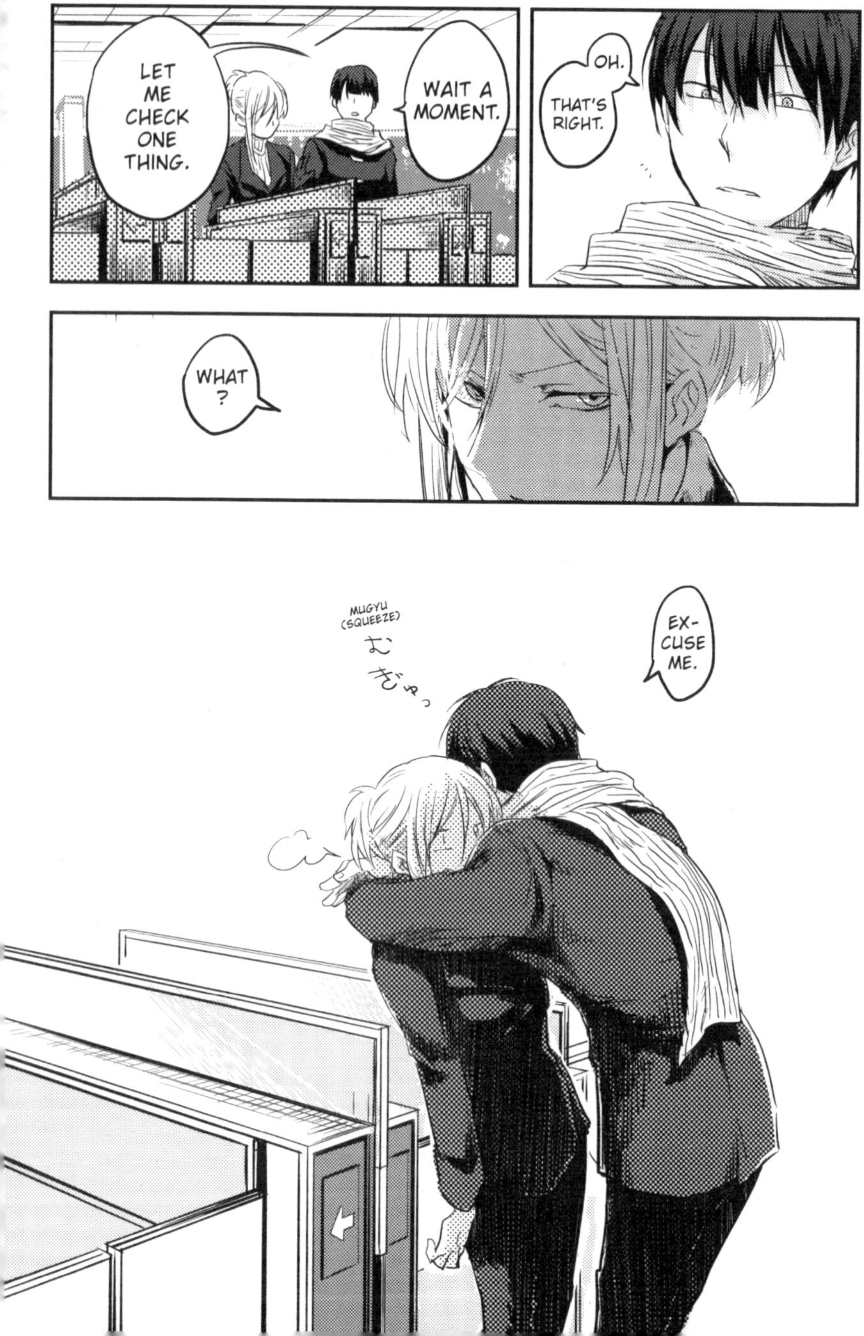
OH.
THAT'S RIGHT.
WAIT A MOMENT.
LET ME CHECK ONE THING.
WHAT?
EX-CUSE ME.
MUGYU (SQUEEZE)
むぎゅっ

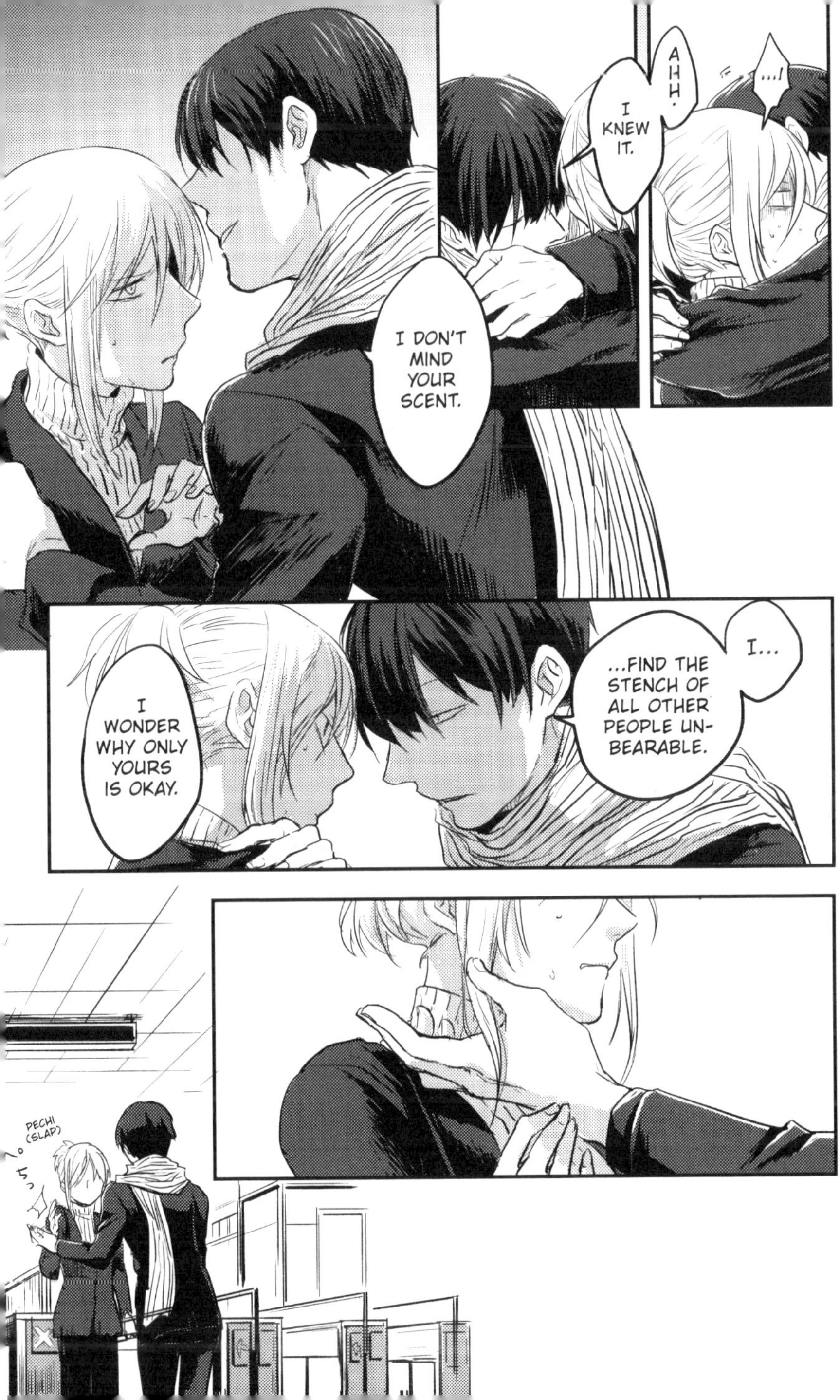
...!
AHH. I KNEW IT.
I DON'T MIND YOUR SCENT.
I...
...FIND THE STENCH OF ALL OTHER PEOPLE UN-BEARABLE.
I WONDER WHY ONLY YOURS IS OKAY.
PECHI (SLAP)
ぺちっ

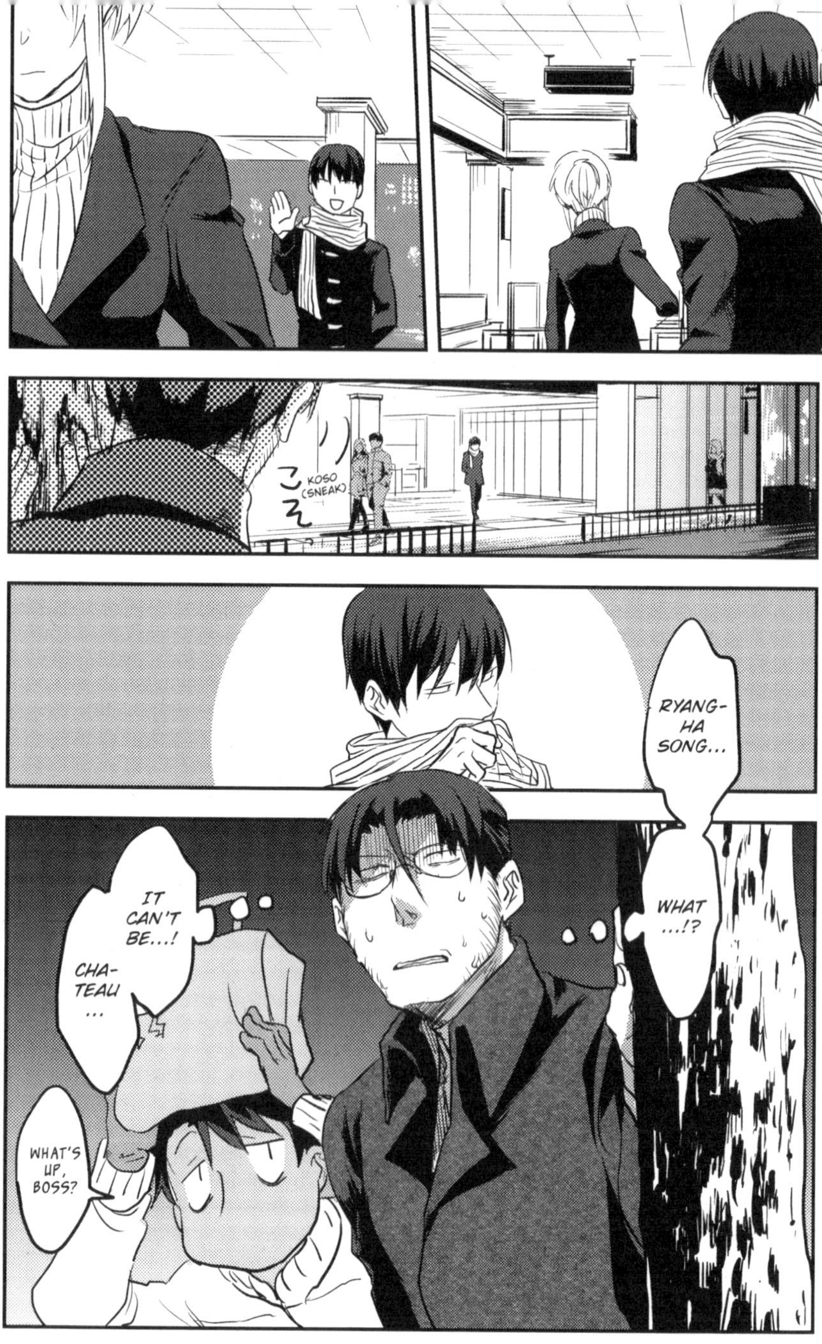
KOSO (SNEAK)
RYANG-HA SONG...
WHAT ...!?
IT CAN'T BE...! CHATEAU ...
WHAT'S UP, BOSS?

ABOUT THE MAJOR CHARACTERS APPEARING IN *LOVE OF KILL*

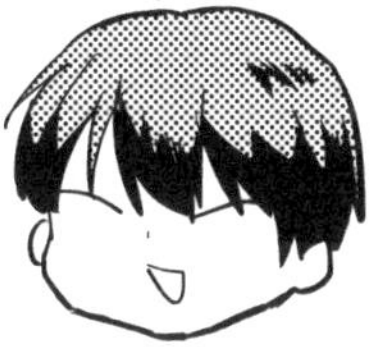

< RYANG-HA SONG >

MAIN CHARACTER #1.
HIS NAME SOUNDS KOREAN. ACCORDING TO HIS FAMILY REGISTER, HE IS ABOUT 32.
HE GIVES THE IMPRESSION OF BEING EASILY LIKED AND, AT THE SAME TIME, EASILY HATED BY OTHER PEOPLE.
I CAME UP WITH HIM AFTER DECIDING THAT I WANTED TO DRAW A CHARACTER WITH FOX-LIKE UPTURNED EYES.

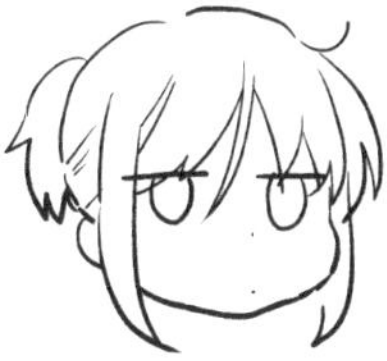

< CHATEAU DANKWORTH >

MAIN CHARACTER #2.
SHE ACTUALLY HAS THE UNIQUE HISTORY THAT I GOT HER CHARACTER DESIGN AND THE NAME "CHATEAU" FROM SOMEONE I KNOW. (I GOT PERMISSION, OF COURSE.) SHE IS VERY RETICENT AND NOT A LIVELY CONVERSATIONALIST.

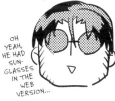

OH YEAH, HE HAD SUNGLASSES IN THE WEB VERSION...

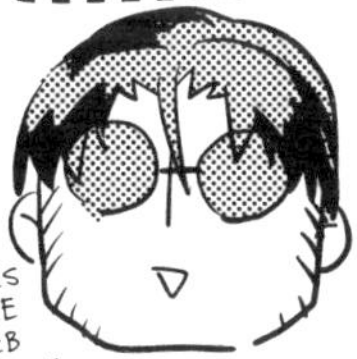

< EURIPIDES RITZLAND >

SUPPORTING CHARACTER. IN THE WEB VERSION, HIS SURNAME WAS HAKKINEN.
I DEVELOPED THIS CHARACTER FOR FUN BEFORE WRITING *LOVE OF KILL*, AND THEN REUSED HIM IN IT OUT OF CONVENIENCE. A NEWLYWED. YOUNGER THAN HE LOOKS.

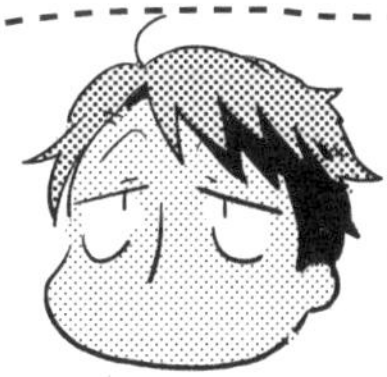

< INDIAN GUY >

SUPPORTING CHARACTER. AN ODDITY IN THIS STORY.
I NEVER FOUND THE RIGHT TIME TO GIVE THIS CHARACTER A NAME OR TO MENTION HIM BY NAME, SO EVEN I NOW CALL HIM "INDIAN GUY." OLDER THAN HE LOOKS.

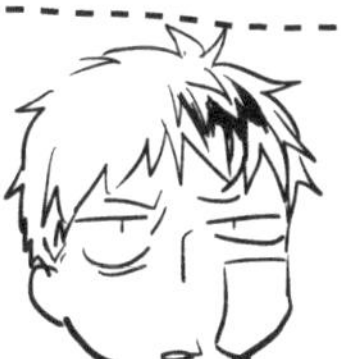

< ? ? ? >

EVEN THOUGH HIS NAME IS EVERYWHERE IN THE WEB VERSION, LOL.
OUT OF ALL THE CHARACTERS, HE WAS THE ONE WHO CHANGED THE MOST WHEN THIS BECAME SERIALIZED...
PERSONALLY, HE IS THE CHARACTER WHOSE WORDS AND ACTIONS I CAN MOST SYMPATHIZE WITH.

MUNCH

MUNCH

CATEAU
AND
NYAN-HA

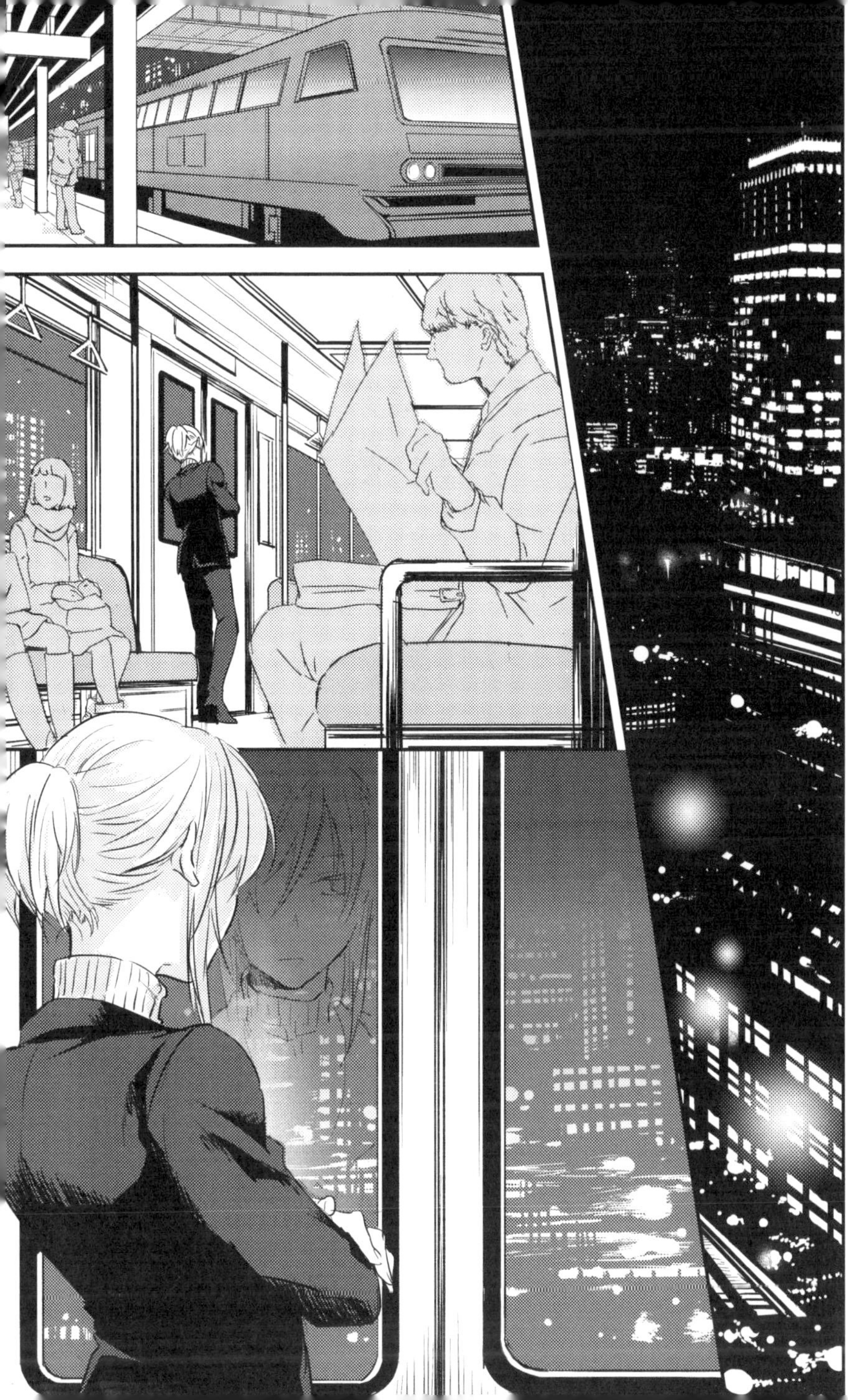

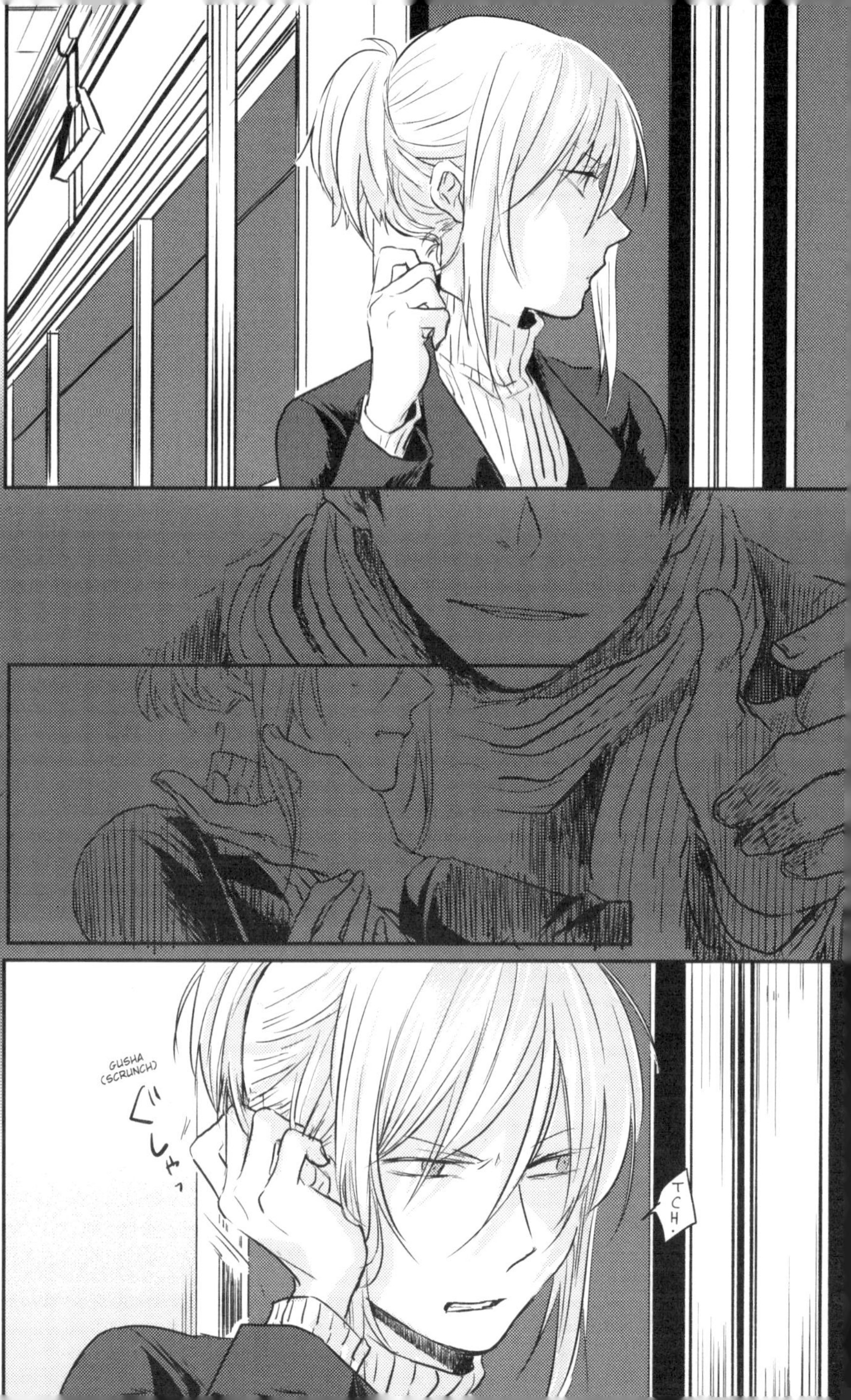
GUSHA (SCRUNCH)
ぐしゃっ
TCH!

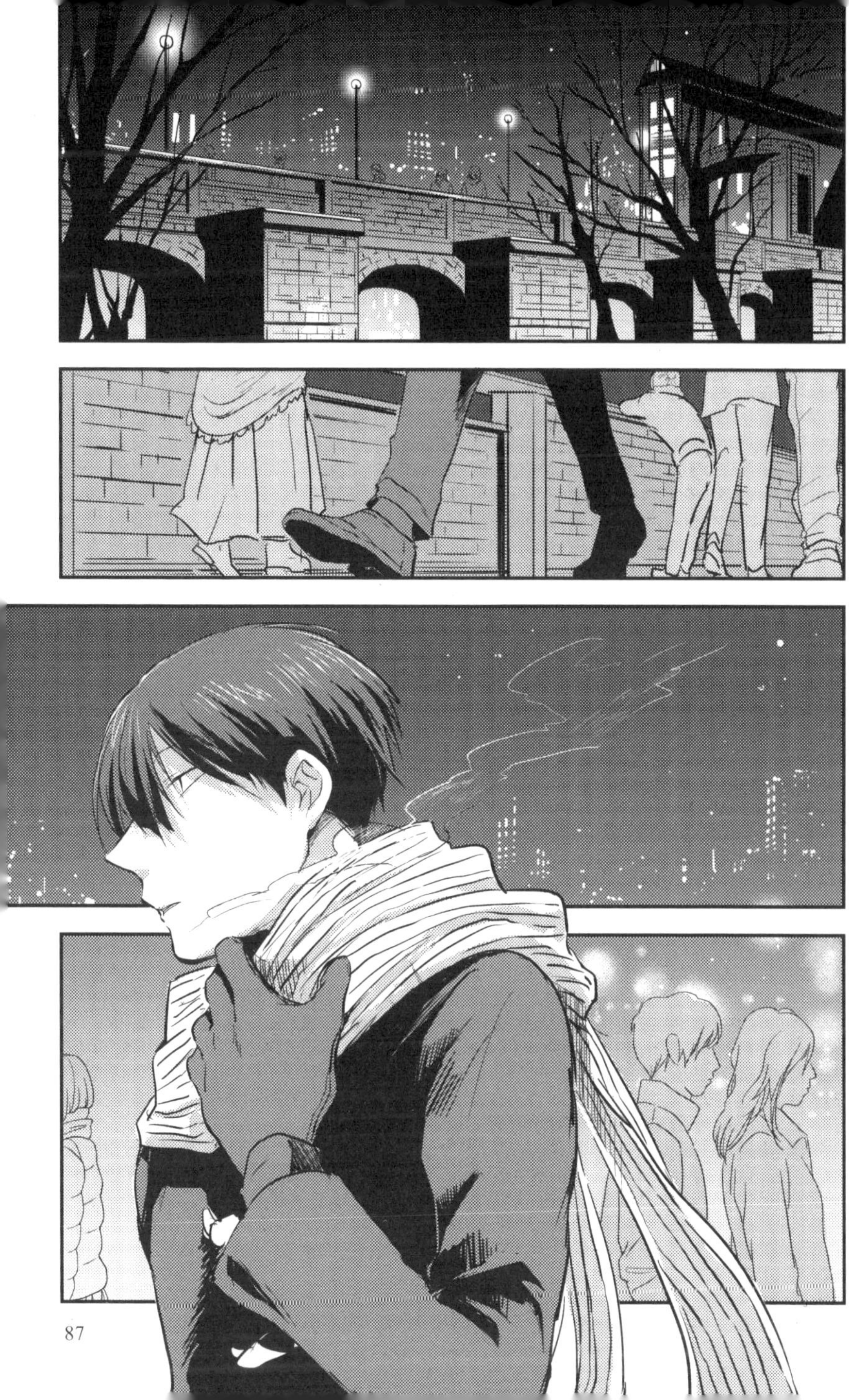

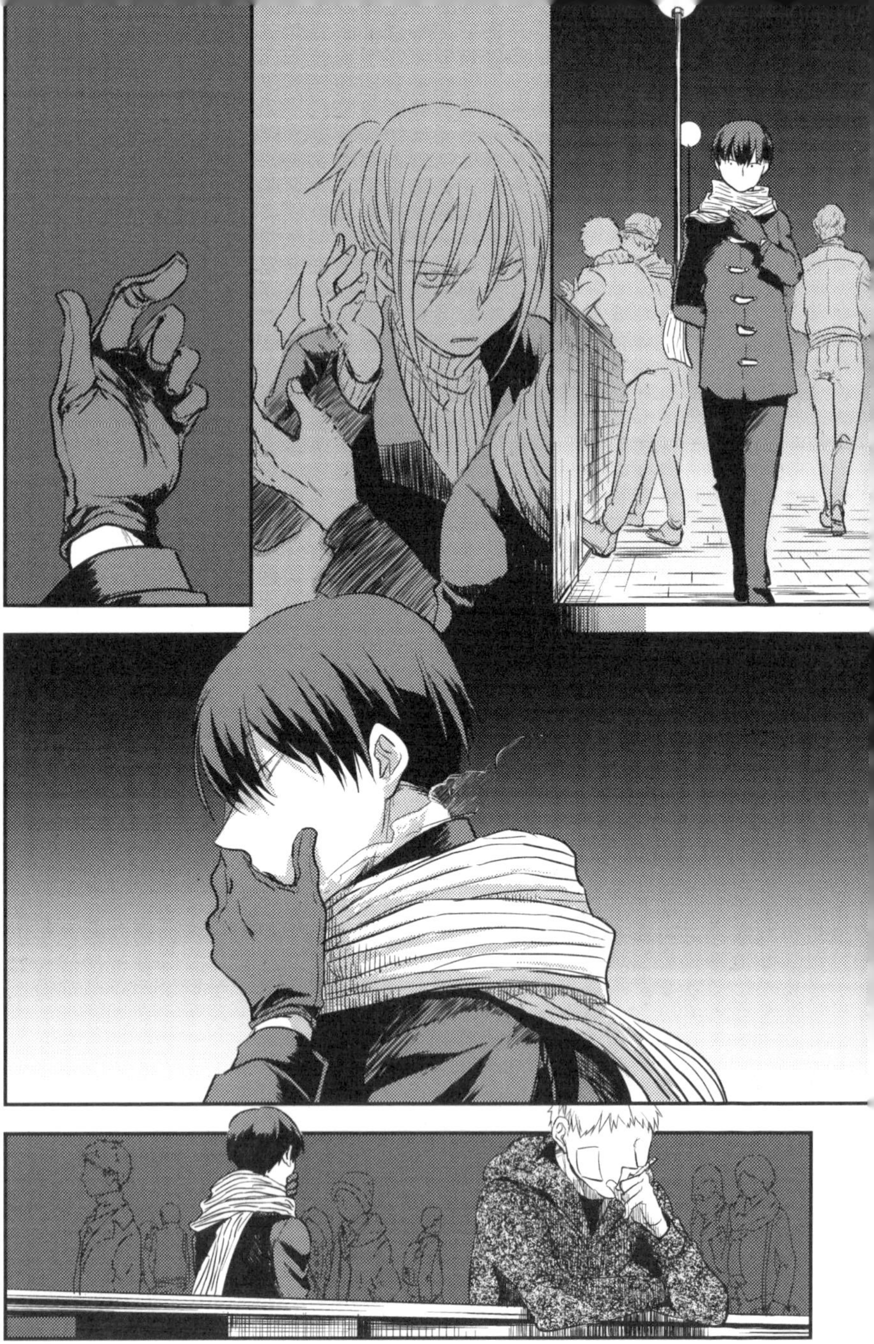

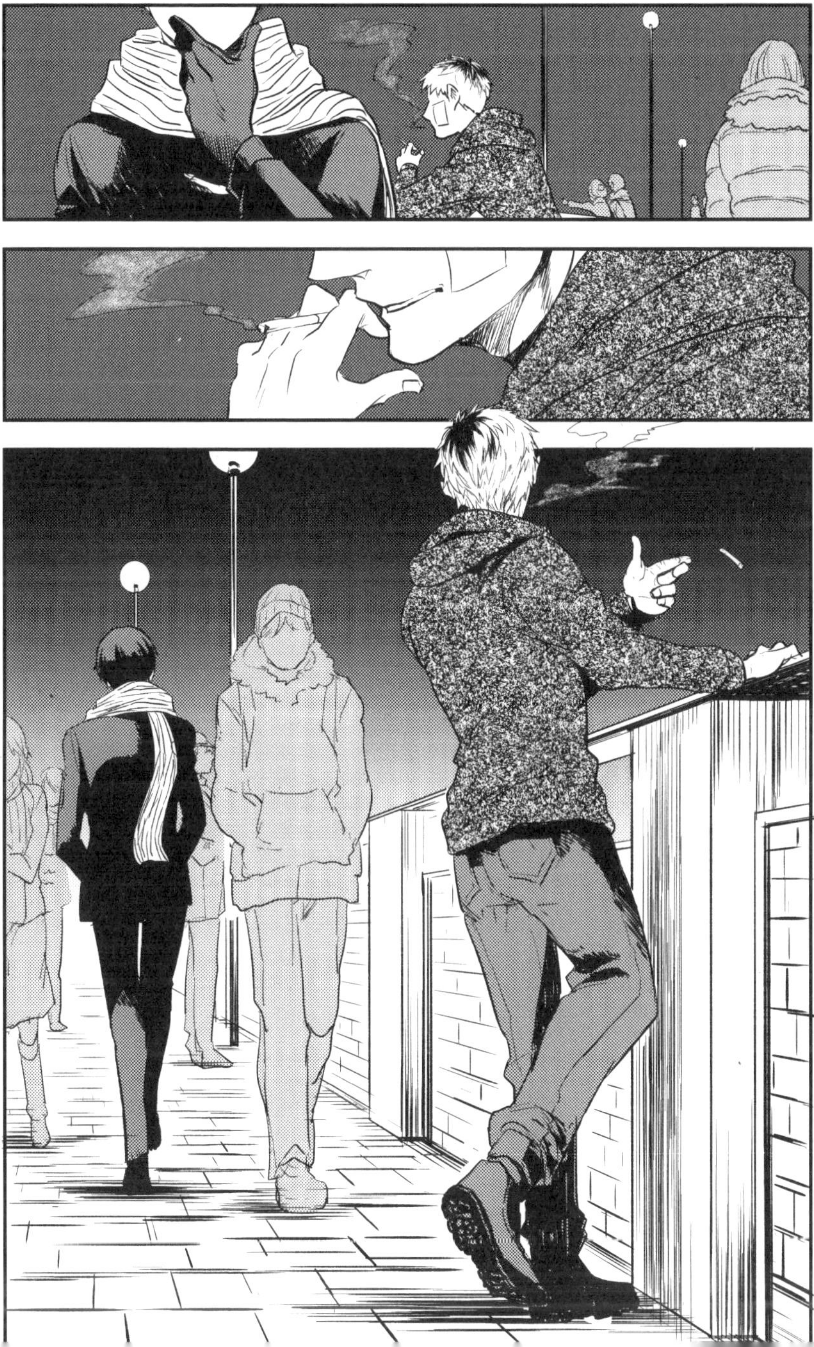

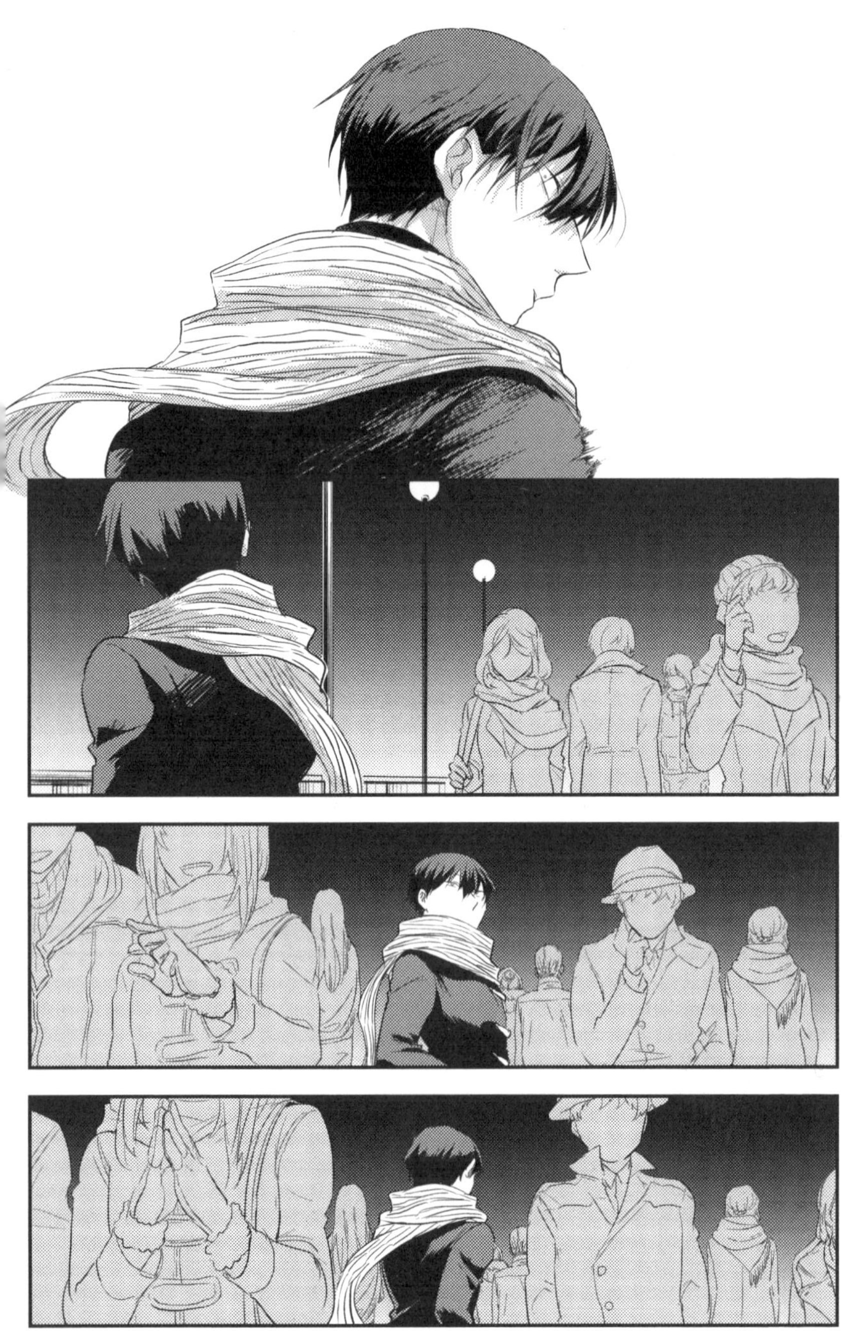

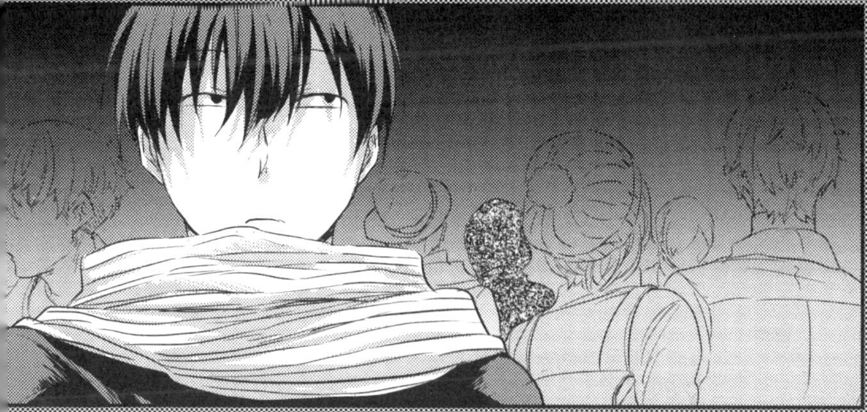

FILE 04 TARGET

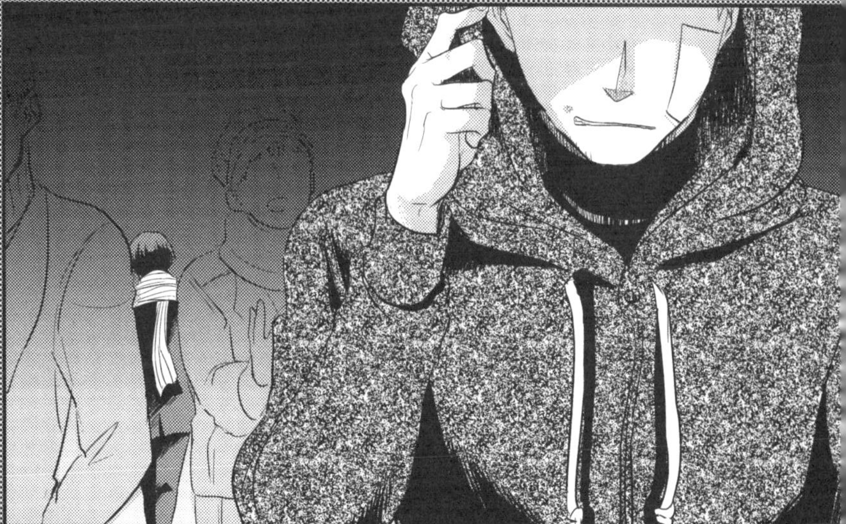

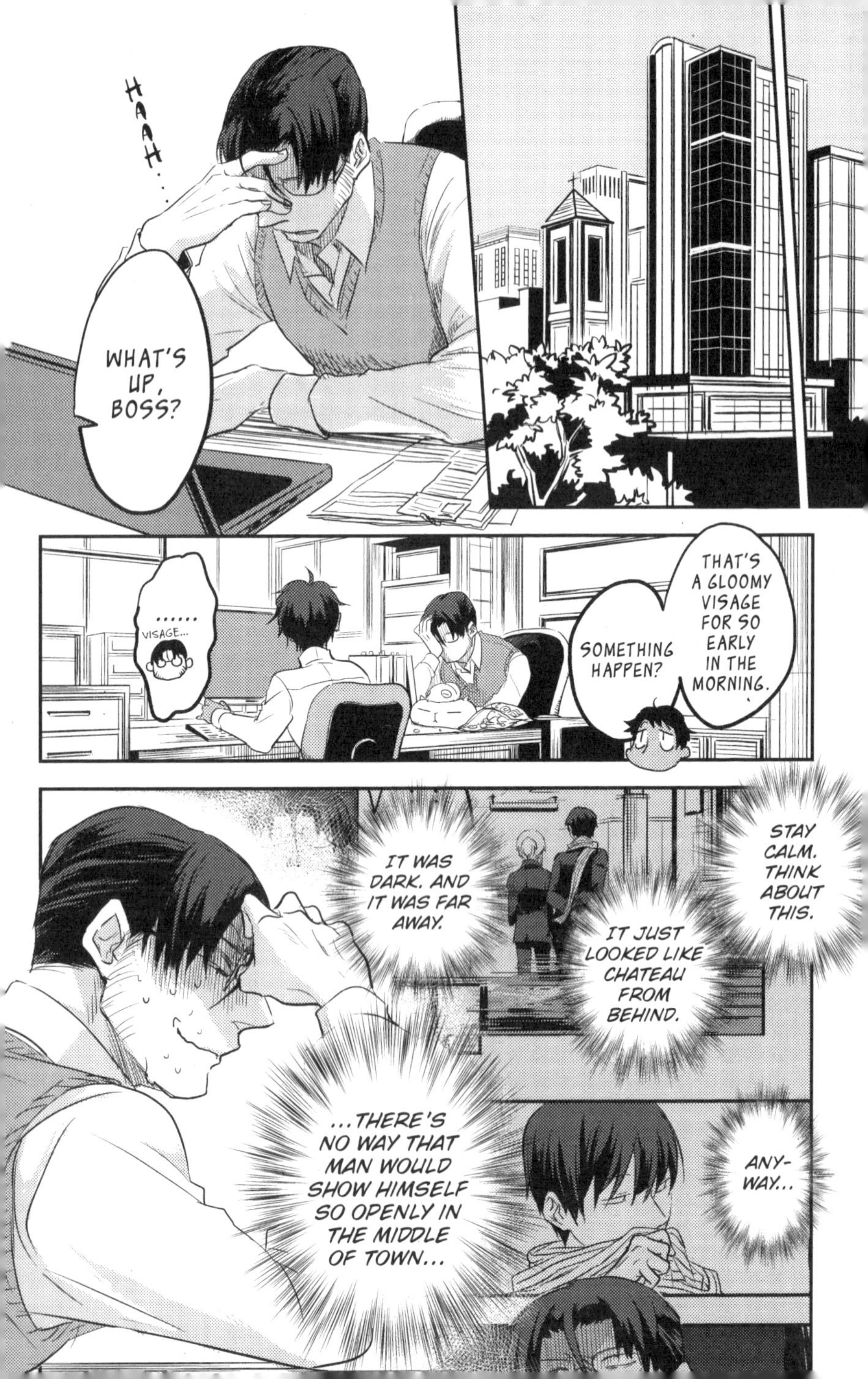
HAAAH...
WHAT'S UP, BOSS?
THAT'S A GLOOMY VISAGE FOR SO EARLY IN THE MORNING.
SOMETHING HAPPEN?
......
VISAGE...
STAY CALM. THINK ABOUT THIS.
IT WAS DARK. AND IT WAS FAR AWAY.
IT JUST LOOKED LIKE CHATEAU FROM BEHIND.
ANY-WAY...
...THERE'S NO WAY THAT MAN WOULD SHOW HIMSELF SO OPENLY IN THE MIDDLE OF TOWN...

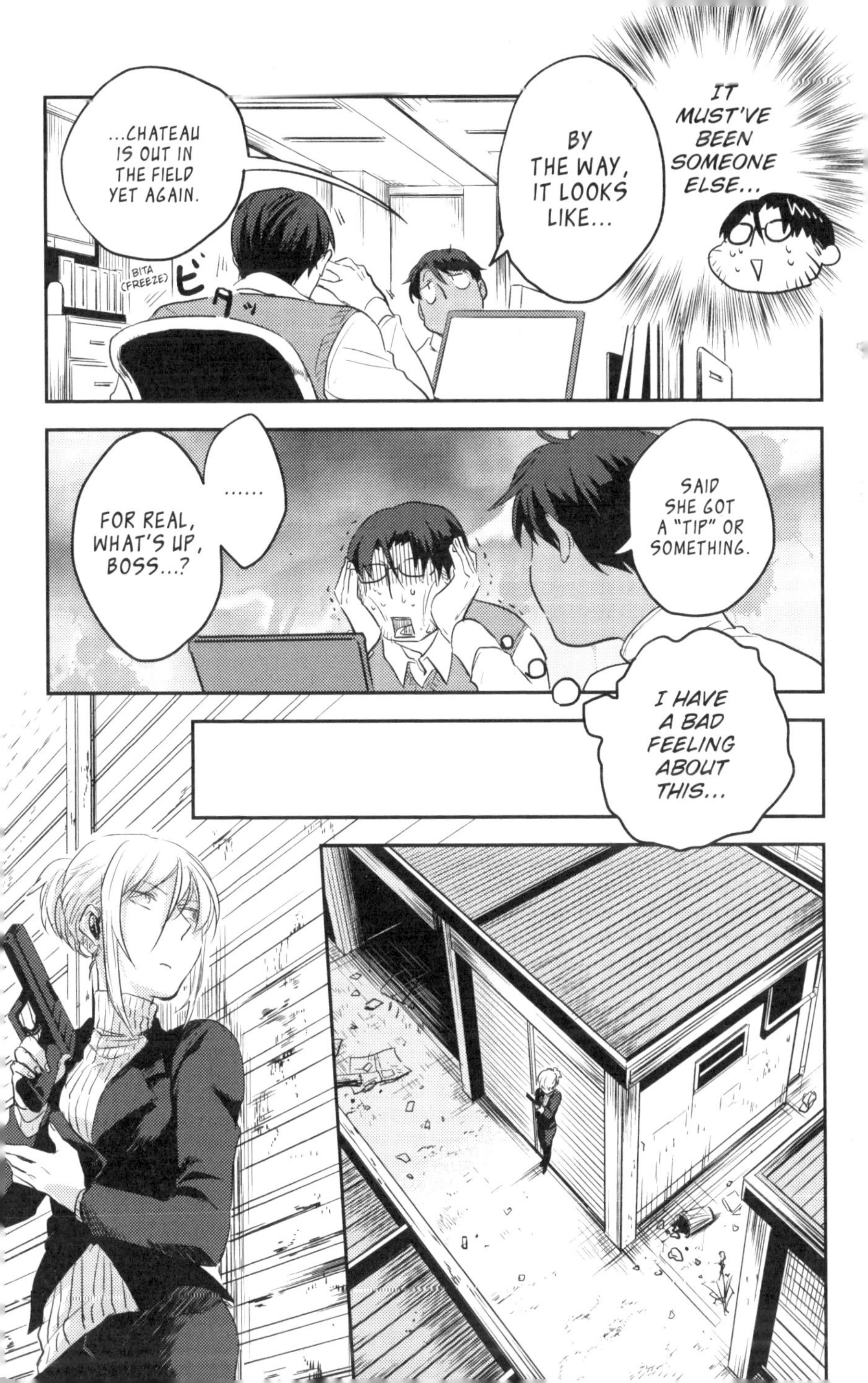
IT MUST'VE BEEN SOMEONE ELSE...
BY THE WAY, IT LOOKS LIKE...
...CHATEAU IS OUT IN THE FIELD YET AGAIN.
ビタッ
BITA (FREEZE)
SAID SHE GOT A "TIP" OR SOMETHING.
......
FOR REAL, WHAT'S UP, BOSS...?
I HAVE A BAD FEELING ABOUT THIS...

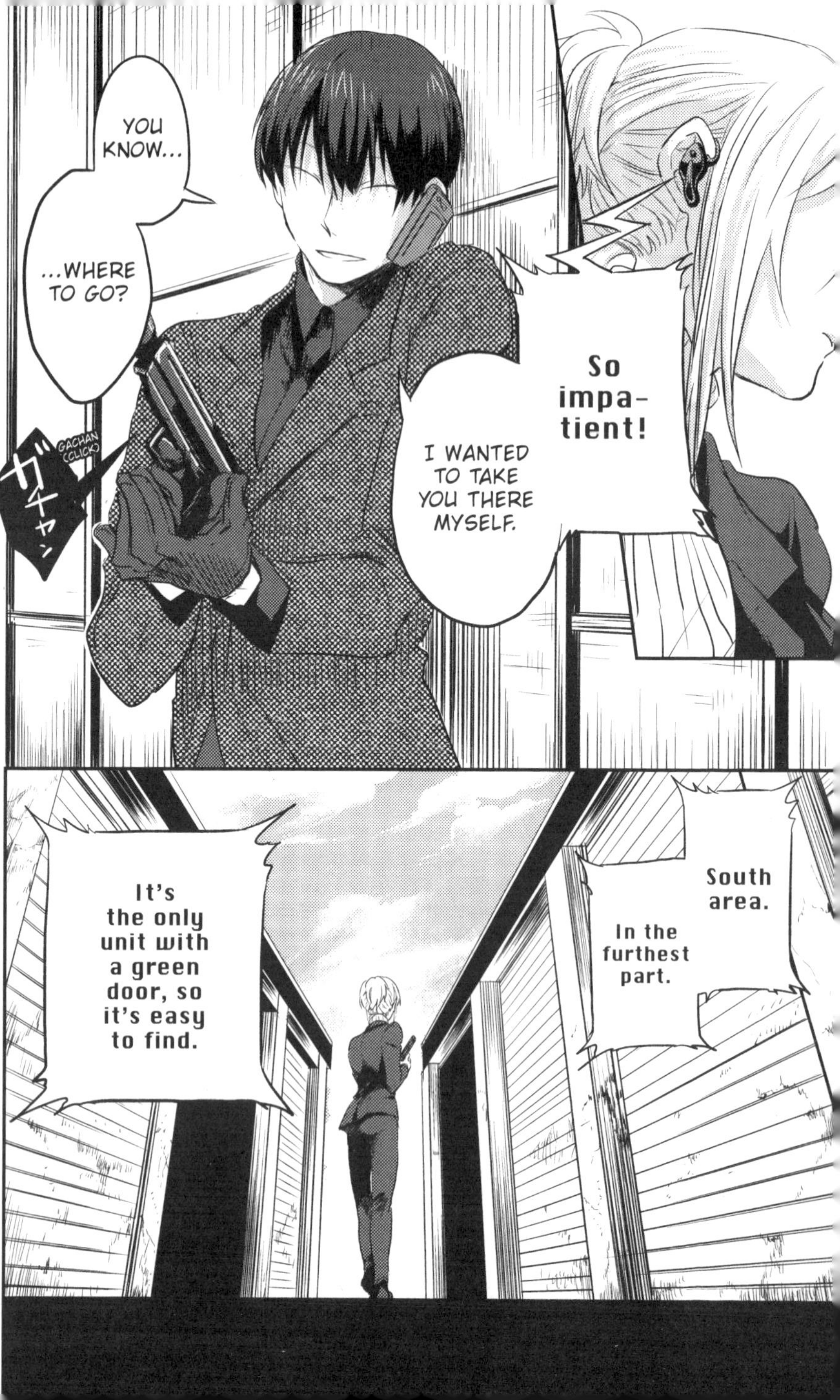
So impatient!
I WANTED TO TAKE YOU THERE MYSELF.
YOU KNOW...
...WHERE TO GO?
ガチャン
GACHAN (CLICK)
South area.
In the furthest part.
It's the only unit with a green door, so it's easy to find.

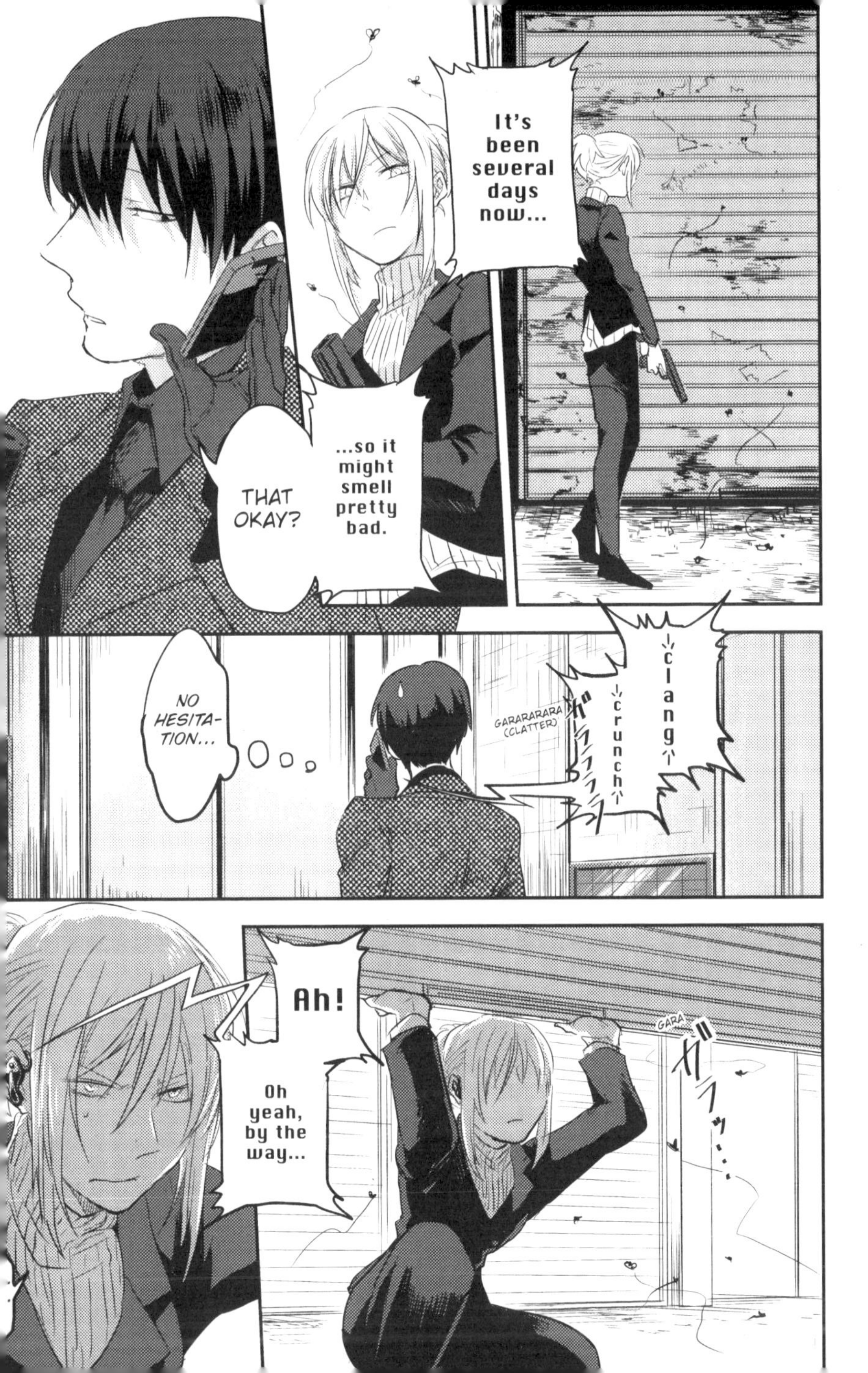
It's been several days now...
...so it might smell pretty bad.
THAT OKAY?
clang
crunch
GARARARARA (CLATTER)
NO HESITATION...
GARA
Ah!
Oh yeah, by the way...

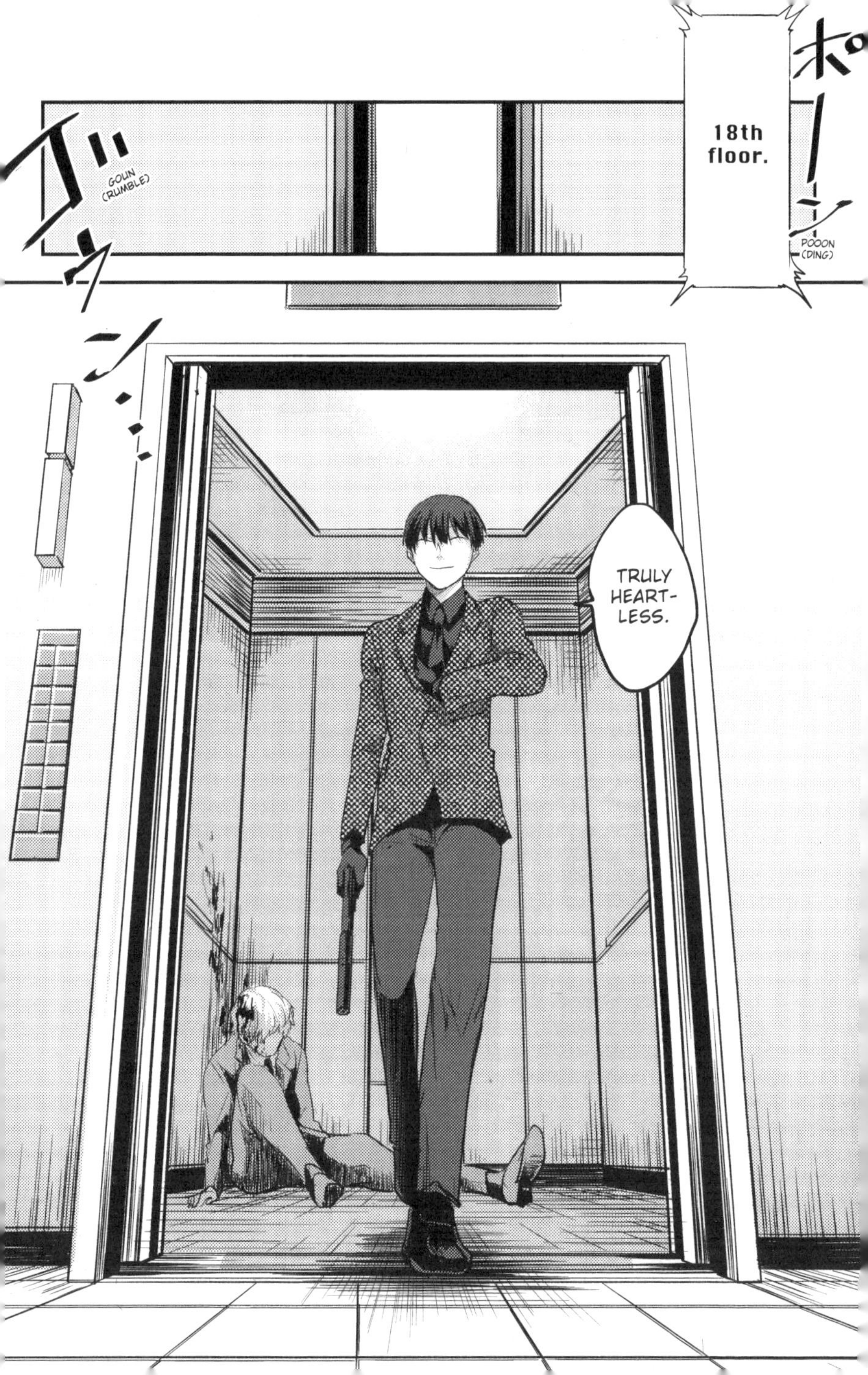
ポーン
18th floor.
POOON (DING)
ゴウン
GOUN (RUMBLE)
TRULY HEART-LESS.

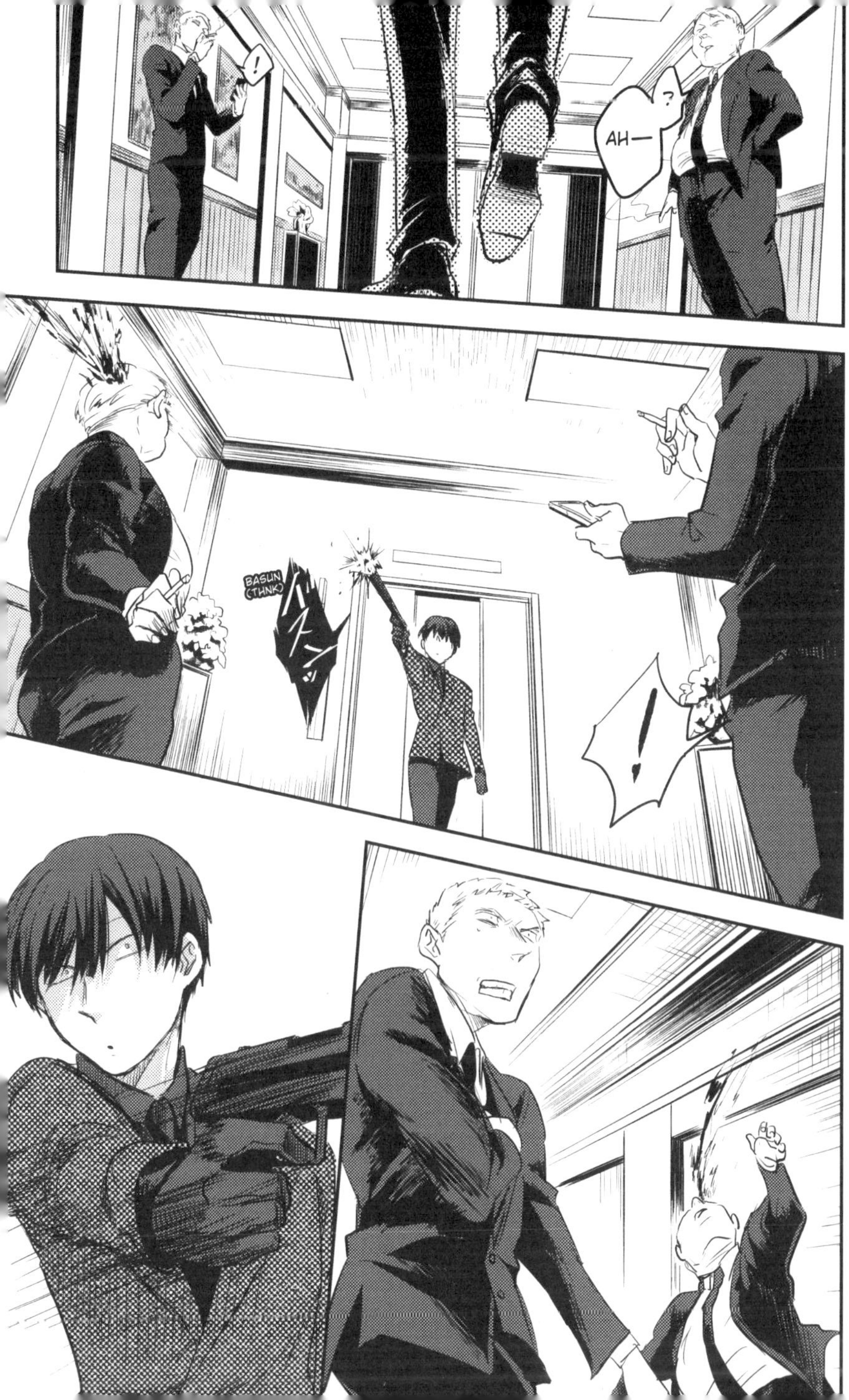
?
AH—
!
BASUN (THNK)
!

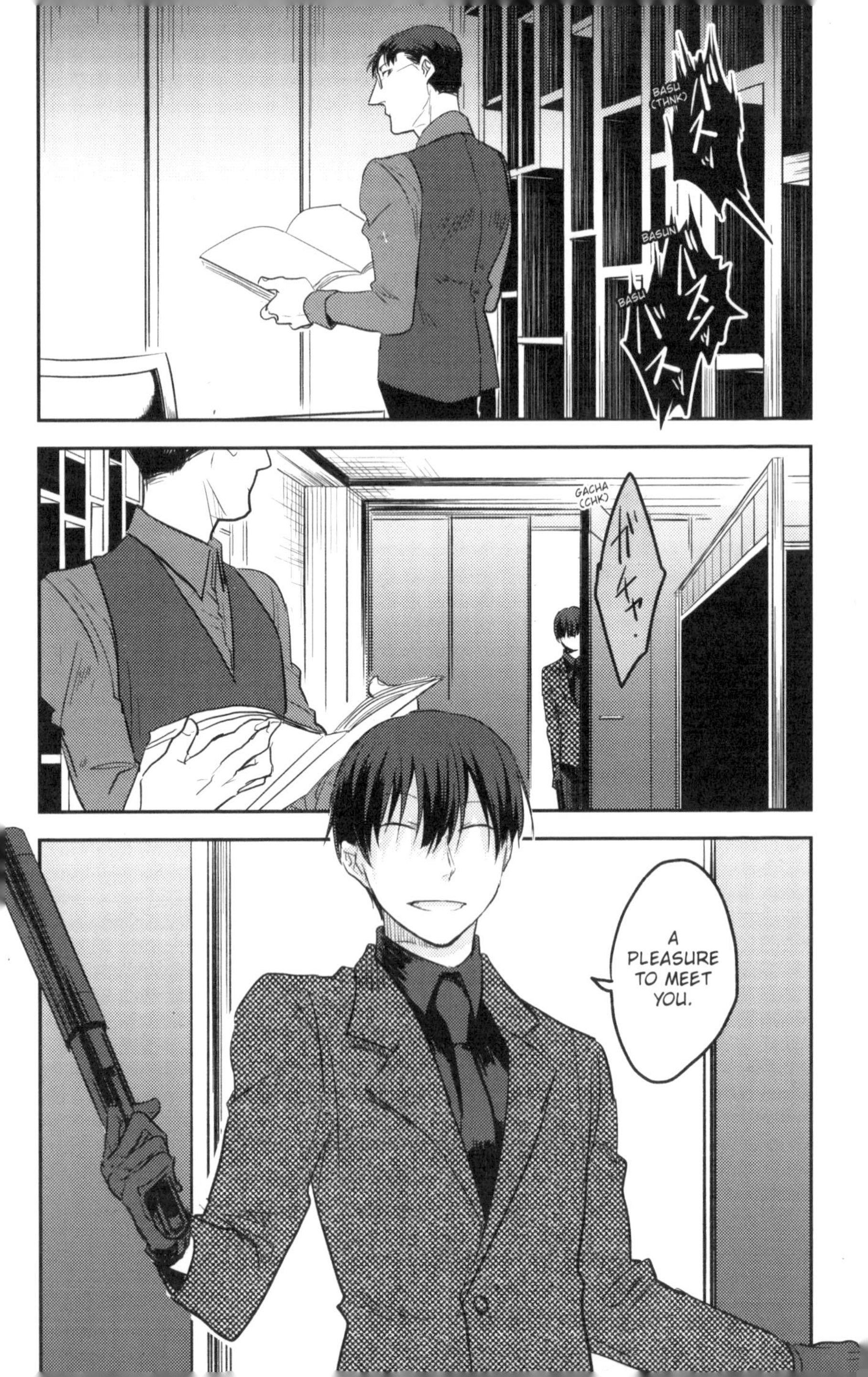
BASU (THNK)
バスッ
BASUN
バスンッ
BASU
バスッ
GACHA (CHK)
ガチャ
A PLEASURE TO MEET YOU.

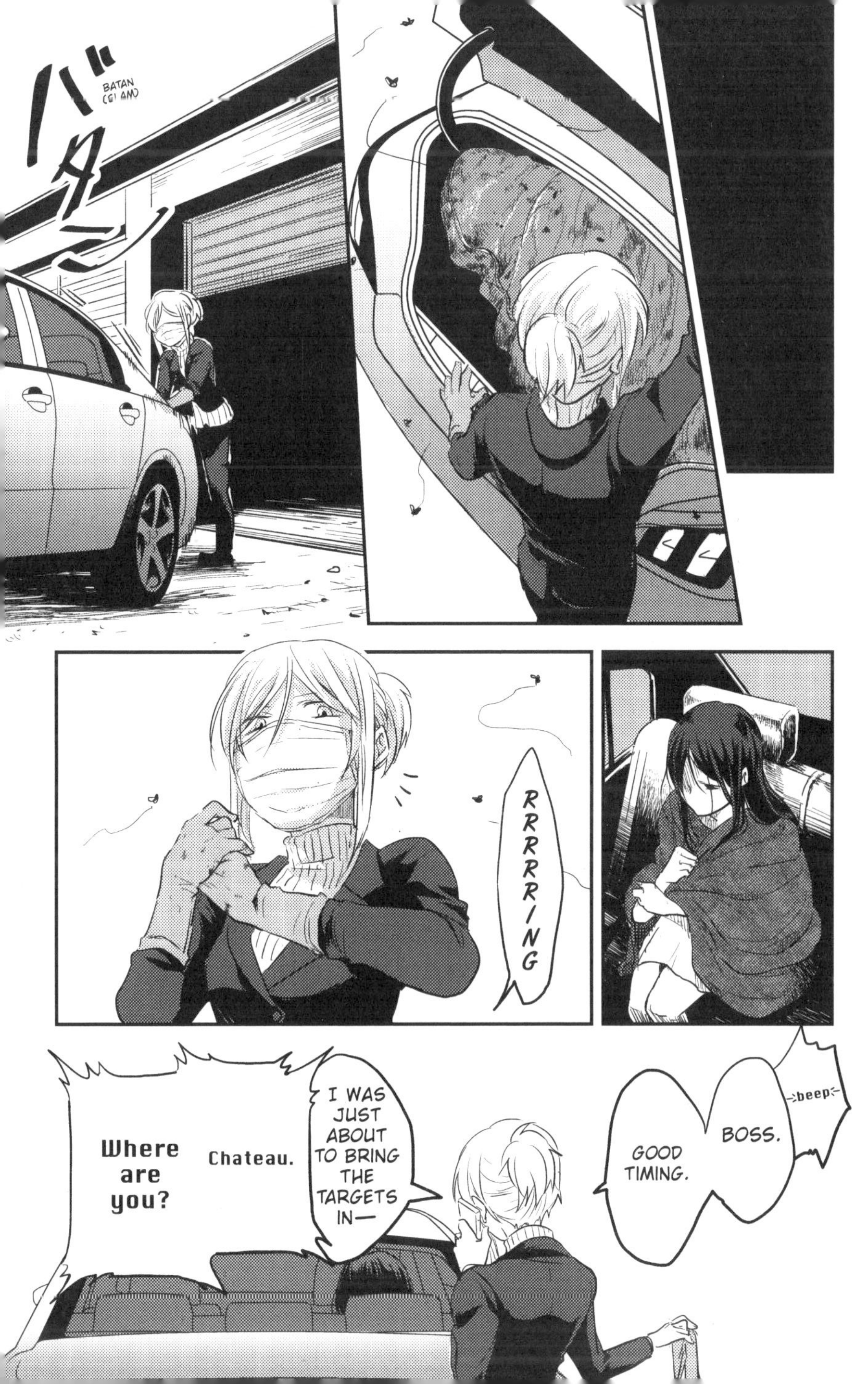
バタン
BATAN (SLAM)
RRRRRING
beep
BOSS.
GOOD TIMING.
I WAS JUST ABOUT TO BRING THE TARGETS IN—
Chateau.
Where are you?

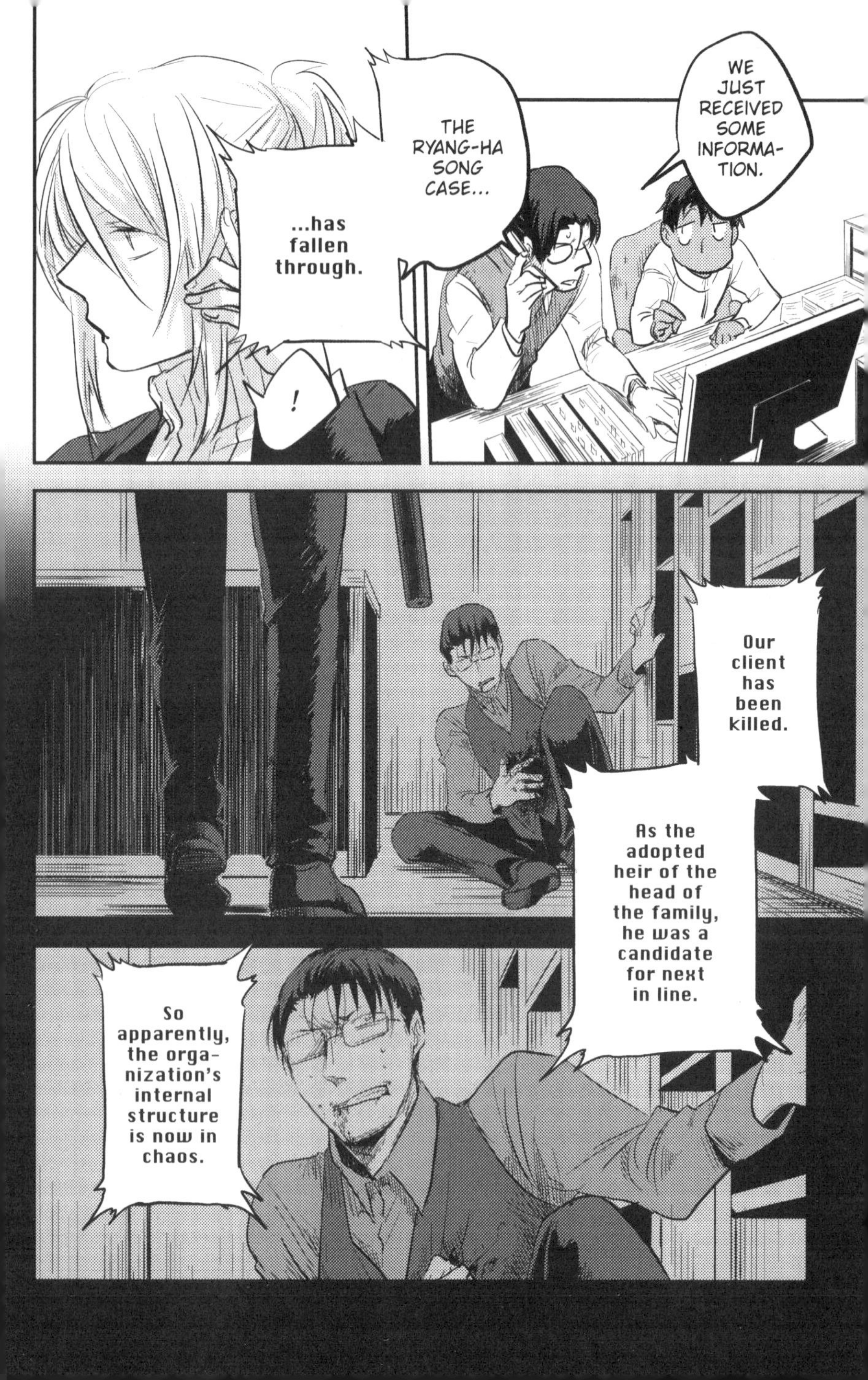
WE JUST RECEIVED SOME INFORMATION.
THE RYANG-HA SONG CASE...
...has fallen through.
!
Our client has been killed.
As the adopted heir of the head of the family, he was a candidate for next in line.
So apparently, the organization's internal structure is now in chaos.

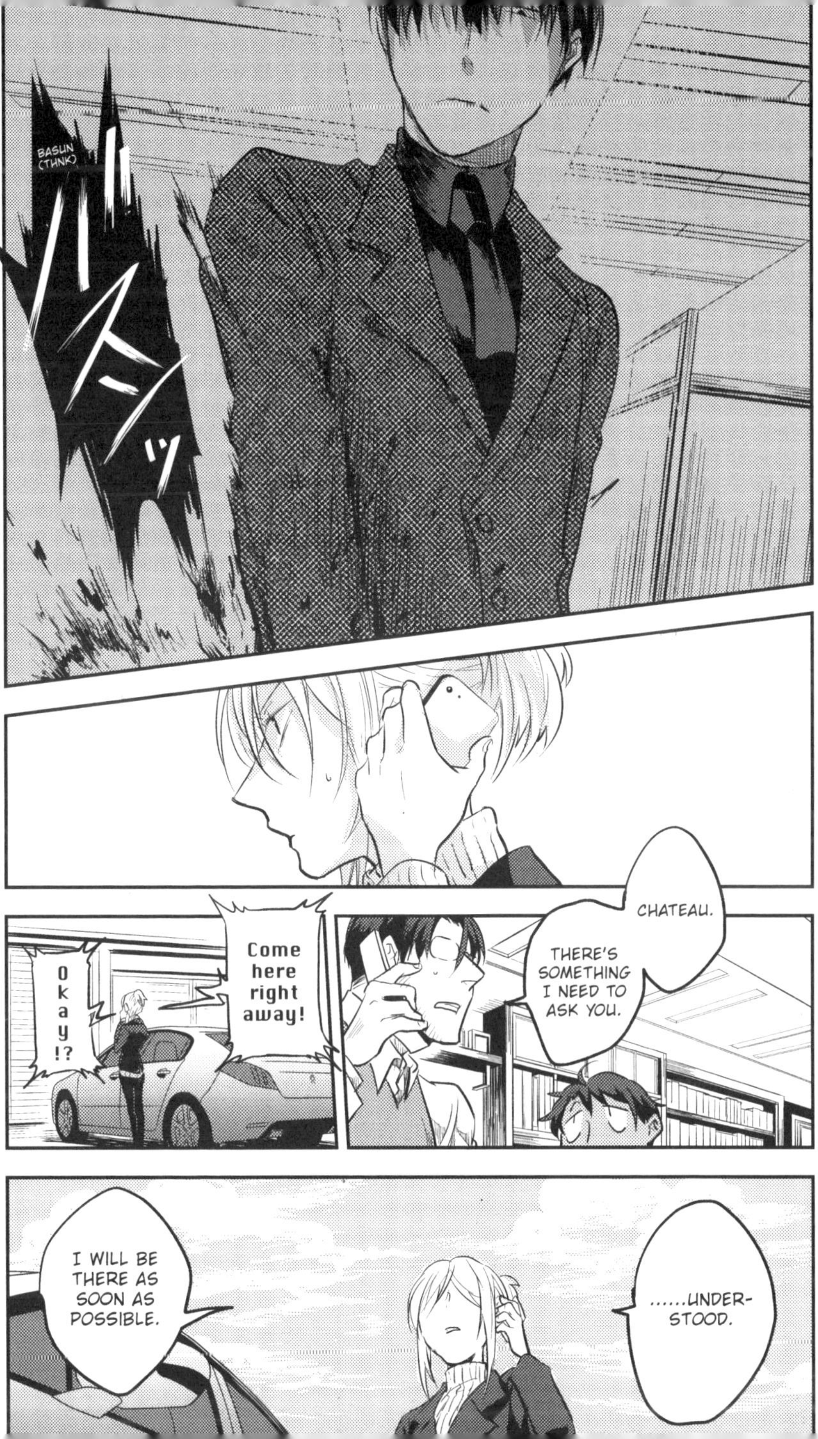
BASUN (THNK)
バスンッ
CHATEAU.
THERE'S SOMETHING I NEED TO ASK YOU.
Come here right away!
Okay!?
......UNDER-STOOD.
I WILL BE THERE AS SOON AS POSSIBLE.

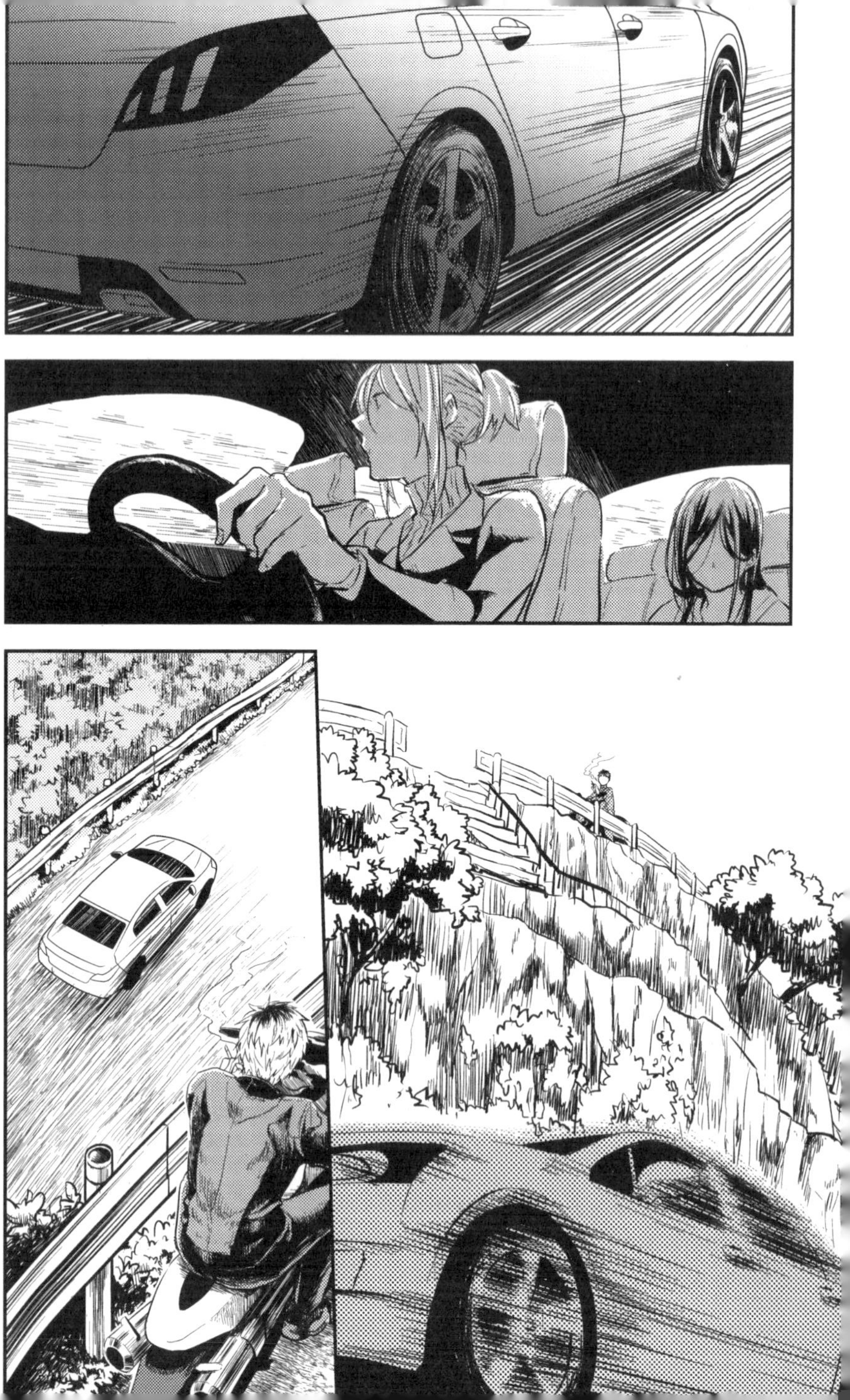

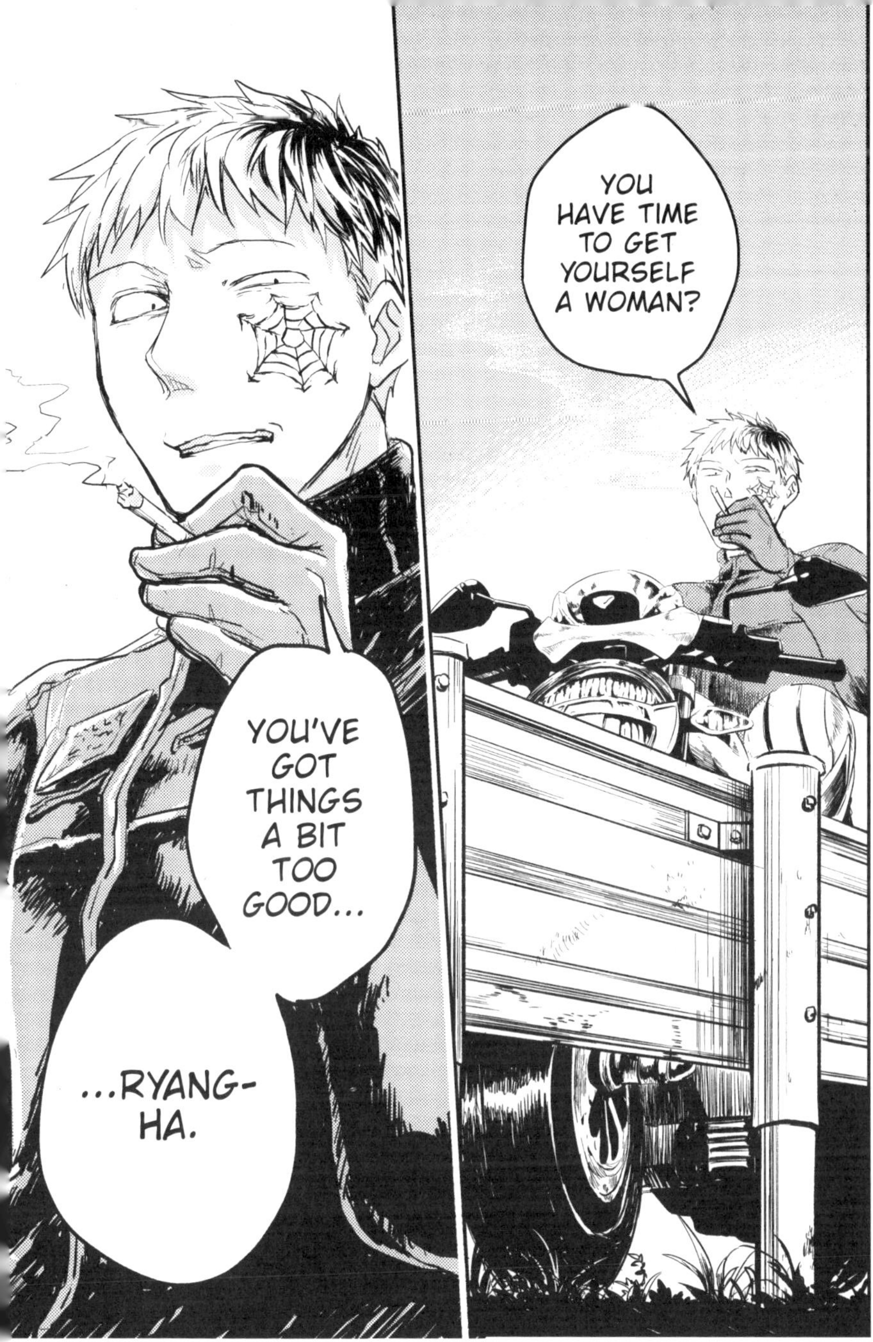
YOU HAVE TIME TO GET YOURSELF A WOMAN?
YOU'VE GOT THINGS A BIT TOO GOOD...
...RYANG-HA.

C'MON.
YOU CAN JUST TELL ME YOUR NAME.
TELL ME YOUR NAME.
HEY.
HEY.
TELL ME.
UGH!

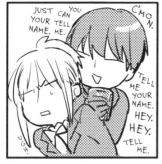

FILE 1: WHAT'S YOUR NAME?

"*LOVE OF KILL*? THAT'S A HELL OF A TITLE THIS MANGA'S GOT..." I THINK THAT'S WHAT I WOULD THINK IF I WERE A READER, LOL. IT DOES LOOK OMINOUS...I FEEL LIKE IT TOOK ME MORE THAN A FULL DAY TO LOOK DIRECTLY AT MY PAGES WHEN THEY APPEARED IN THE MANGA MAGAZINE. I WAS HALF-EXCITED AND HALF-NERVOUS.

FILE 2: TRADE

THIS CHAPTER HAD A LOT OF EXPOSITION. DUE TO THE NATURE OF THE SETTING, A LOT OF THE MINOR CHARACTERS IN THIS MANGA ARE MIDDLE-AGED MEN OR THUGS, BUT SINCE I CAN'T DRAW THEM SO YOU CAN ACTUALLY TELL THEM APART, YOU OFTEN GET A SENSE OF DÉJÀ VU, THINKING "I FEEL LIKE THIS GUY TURNED UP BEFORE..." I'M SORRY.

AND... ACTION!

I DON'T WANT THIS.

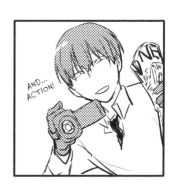

FILE 3: WITNESS

FOR THE RELATIVELY COMPELLING REASONS THAT THIS ISSUE OF THE MAGAZINE WOULD BE GOING ON SALE IN DECEMBER AND THAT I THOUGHT IT QUITE POSSIBLE I WOULDN'T BE IN THE MAGAZINE THIS TIME NEXT YEAR, I SQUEEZED IN A CHRISTMAS CHAPTER, LOL. I WANTED TO TRY MATCHING THE SEASON TO THE RELEASE DATE JUST ONCE. GOAL ACHIEVED! THE EIGHT-PAGE BONUS COMIC AT THE END OF THIS VOLUME TAKES PLACE A FEW HOURS BEFORE THE EVENTS OF THIS CHAPTER.

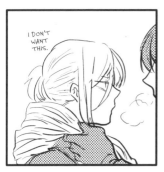

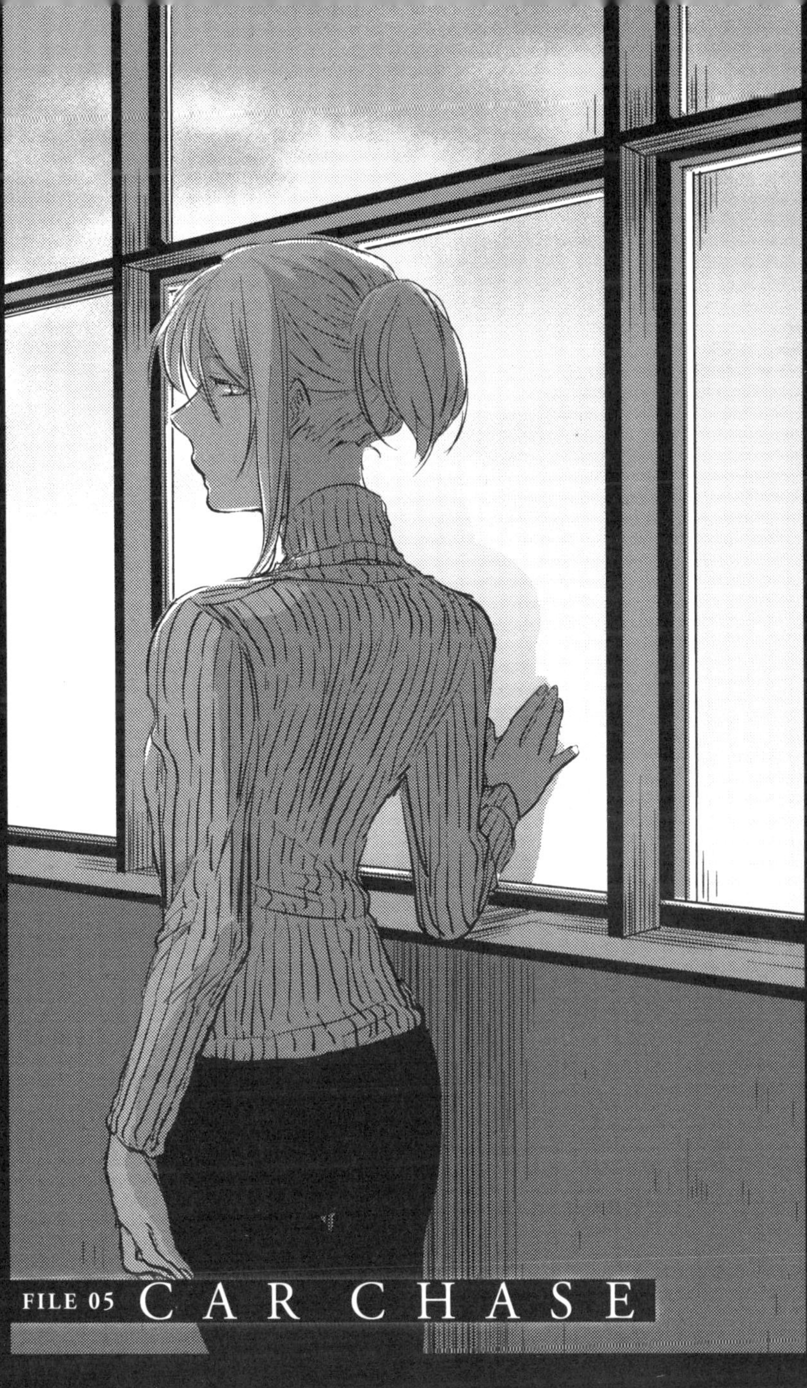

FILE 05 CAR CHASE

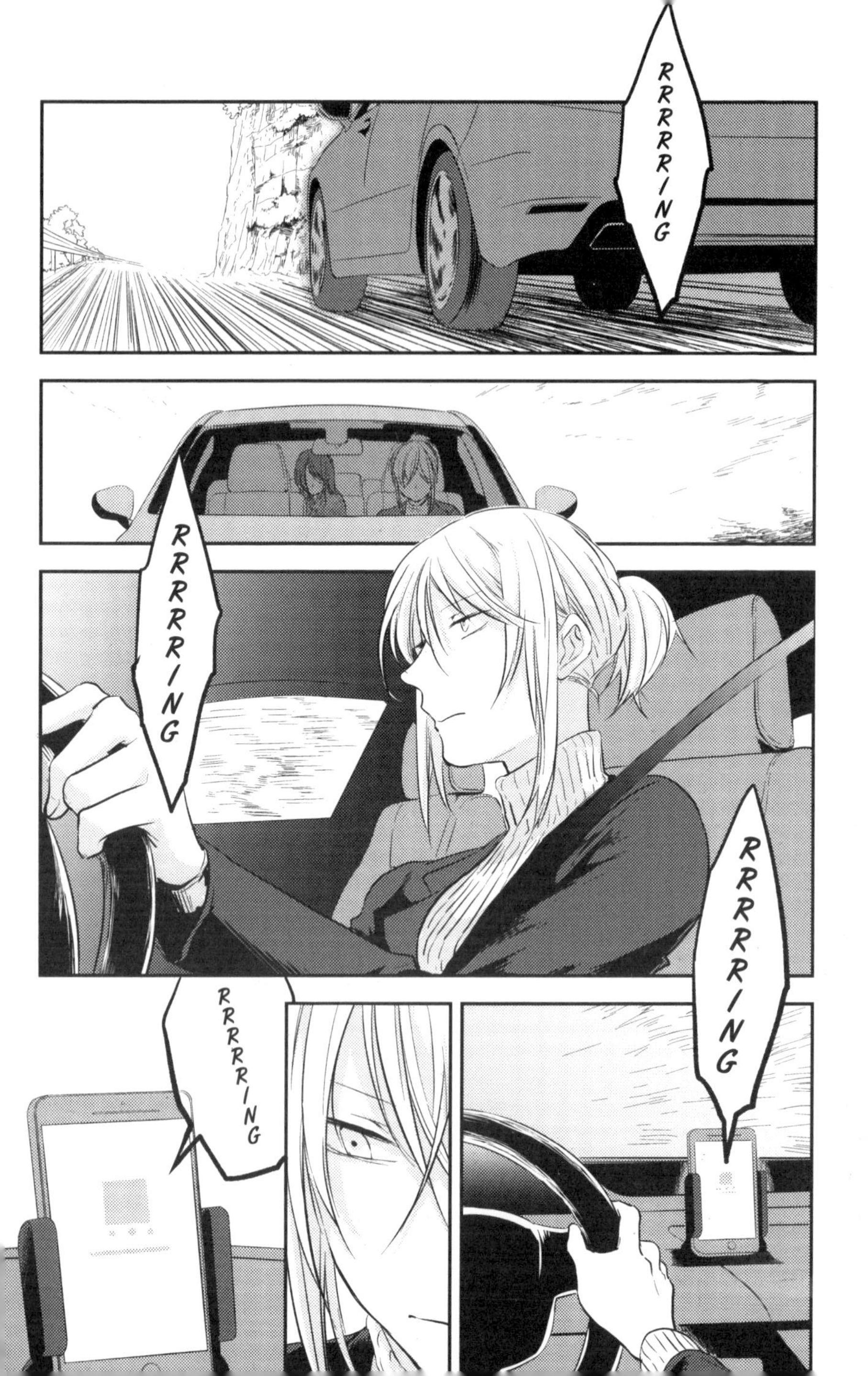
RRRRRING
RRRRRING
RRRRRING
RRRRRING

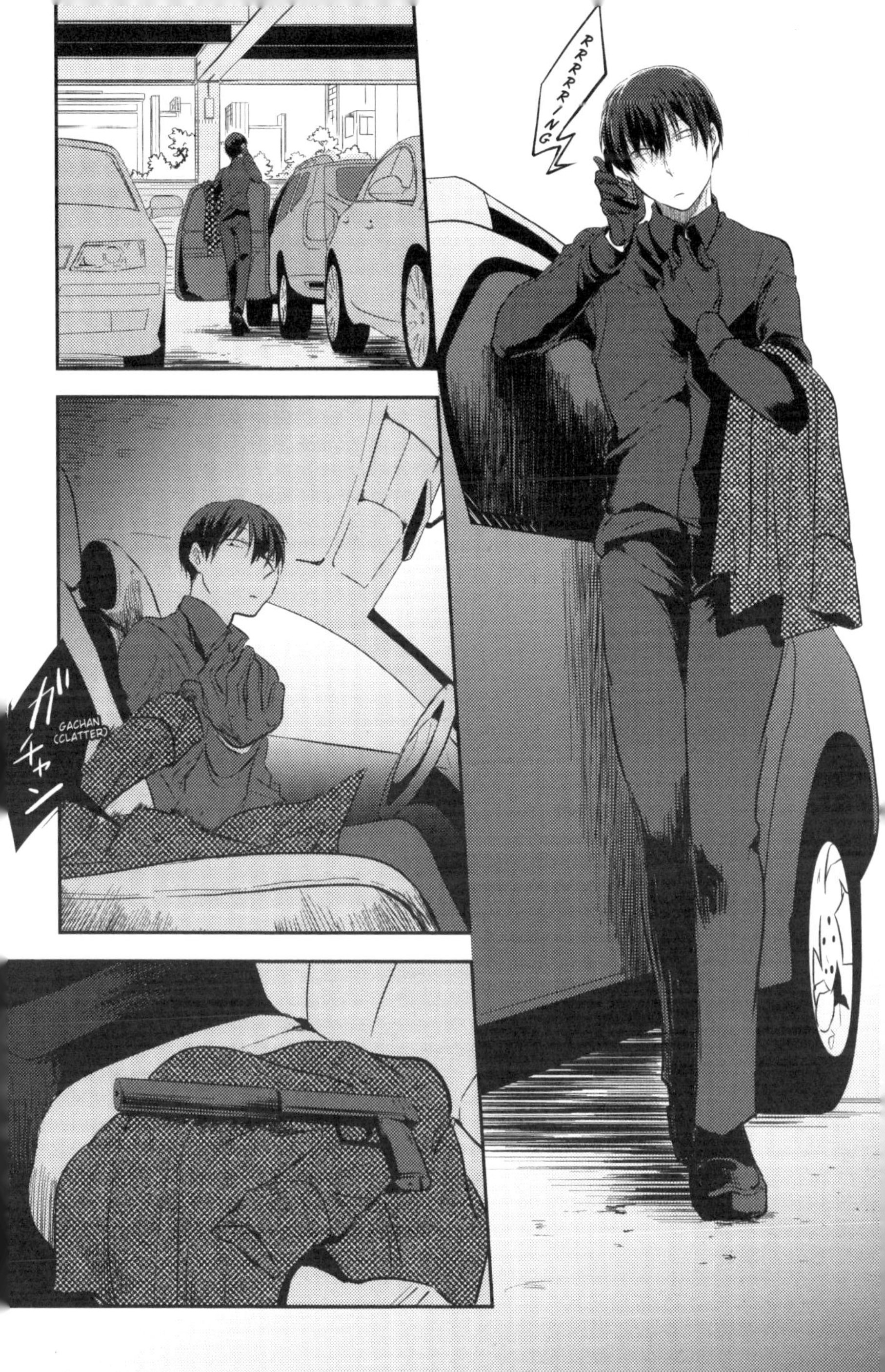
RRRRRING
ガチャン
GACHAN (CLATTER)

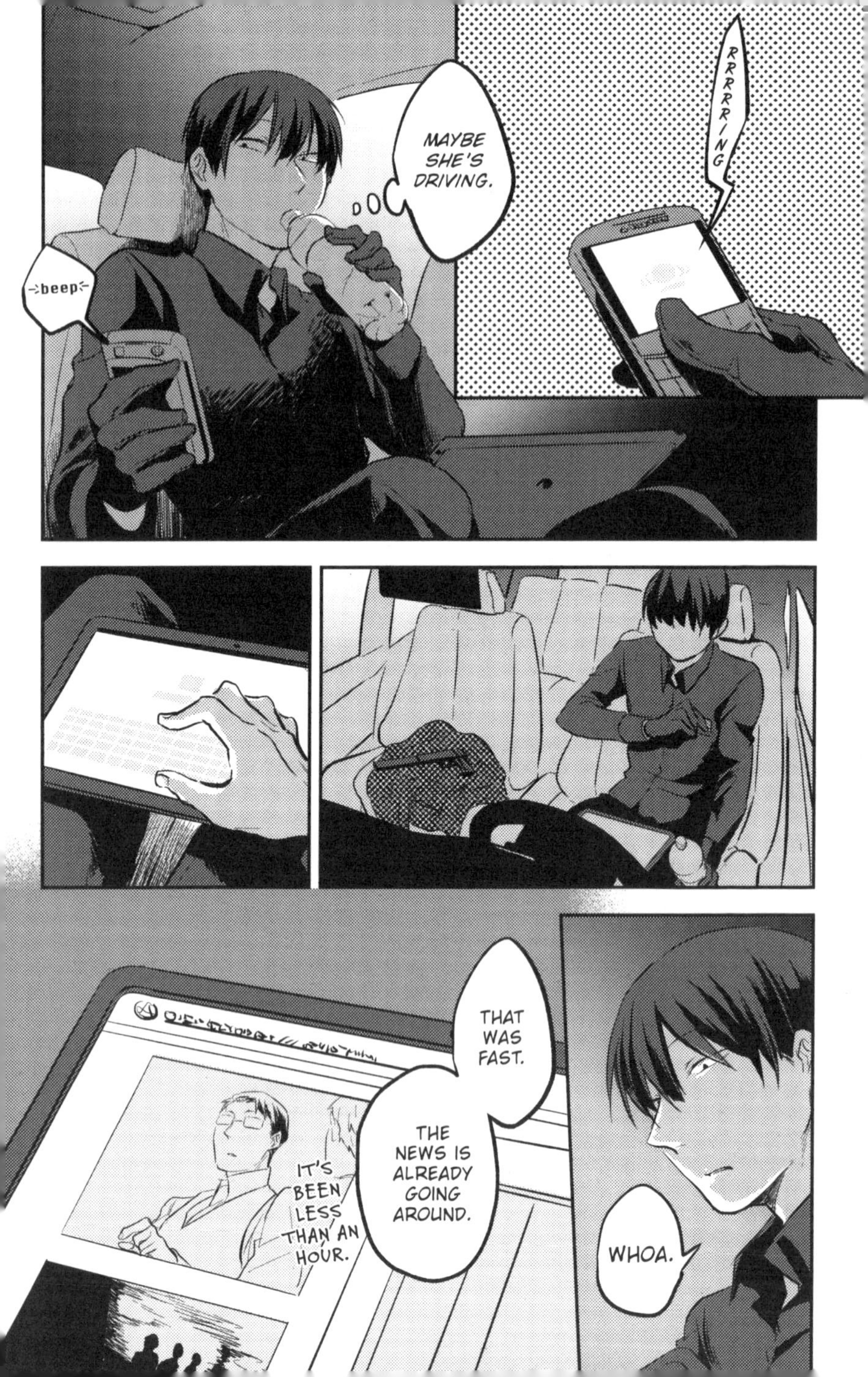
RRRRRING
MAYBE SHE'S DRIVING.
beep
WHOA.
THAT WAS FAST.
THE NEWS IS ALREADY GOING AROUND.
IT'S BEEN LESS THAN AN HOUR.

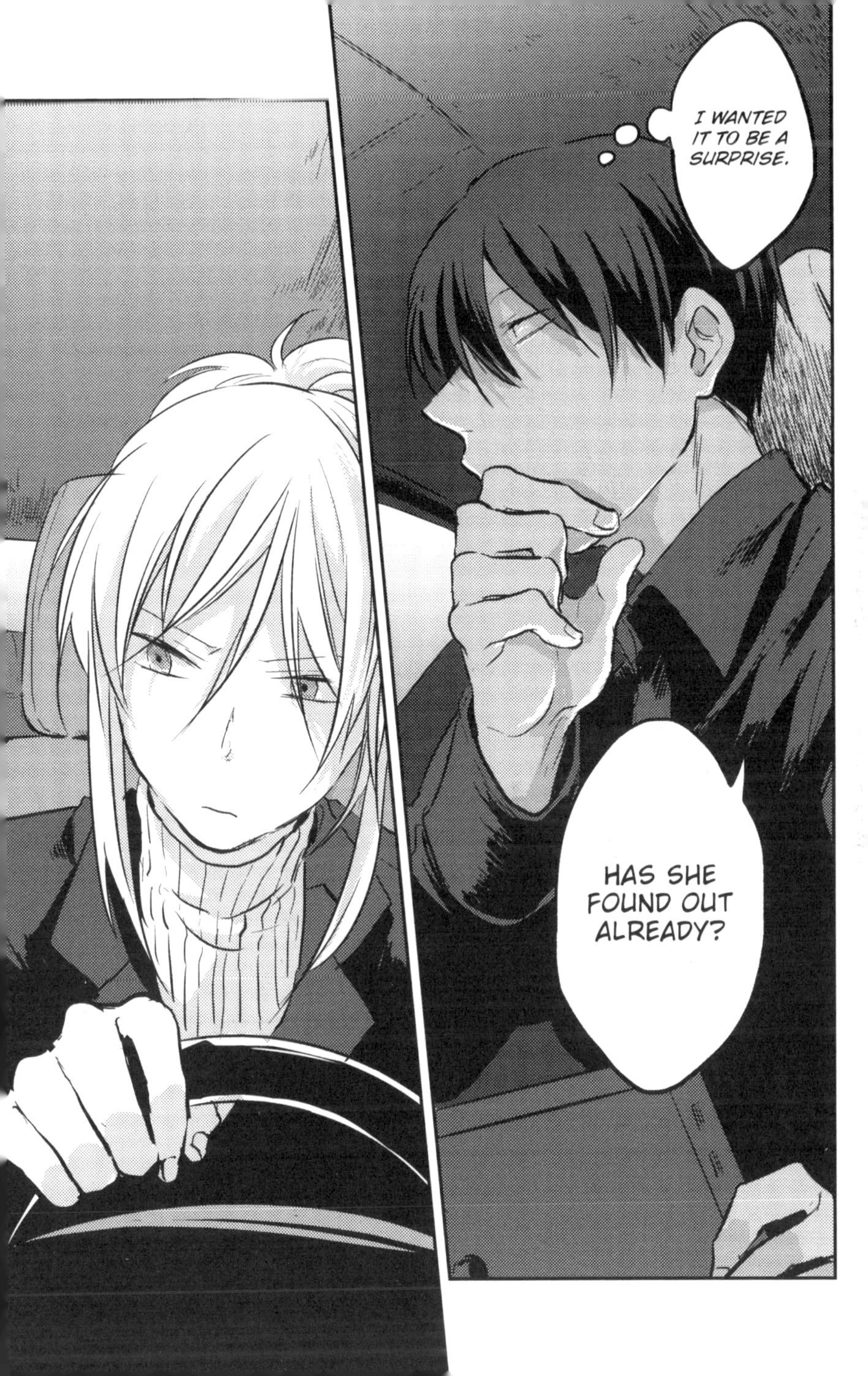
I WANTED IT TO BE A SURPRISE.
HAS SHE FOUND OUT ALREADY?

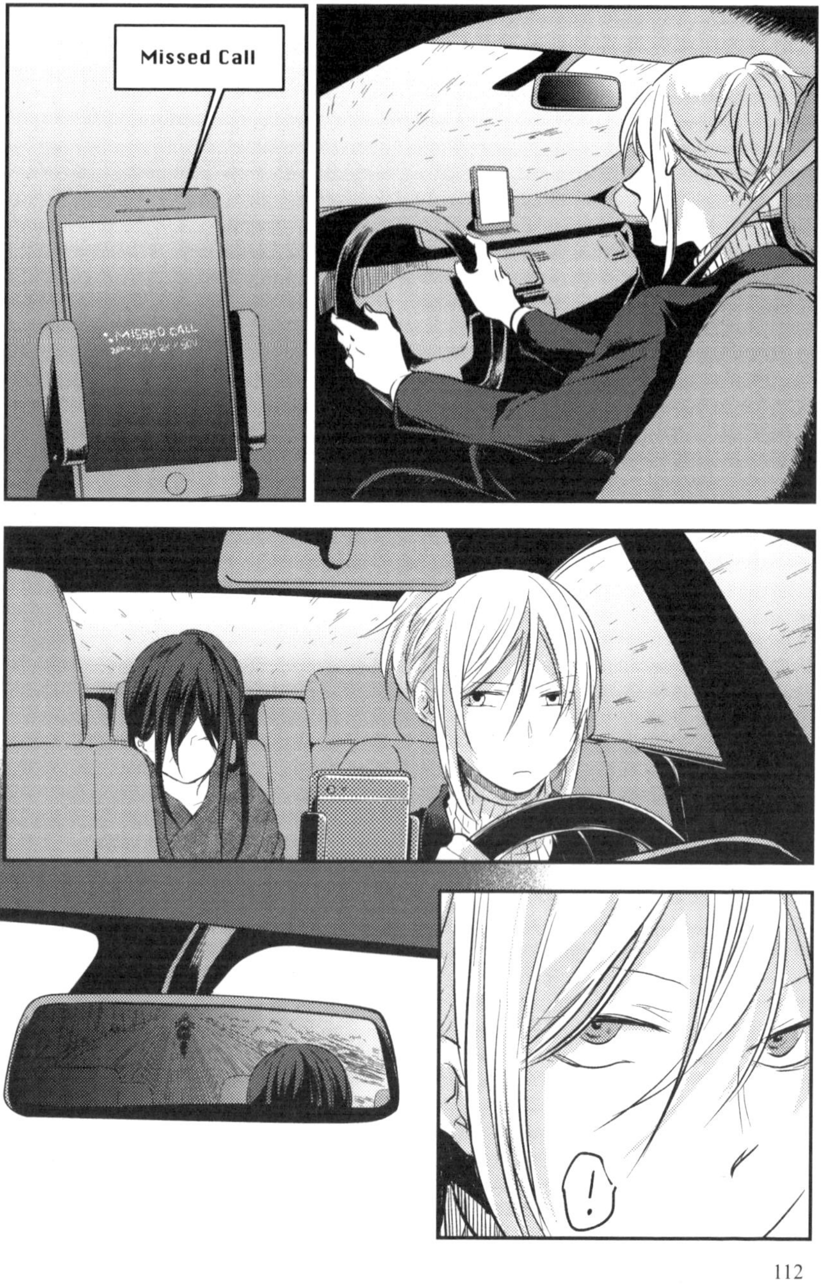
Missed Call
MISSED CALL
!

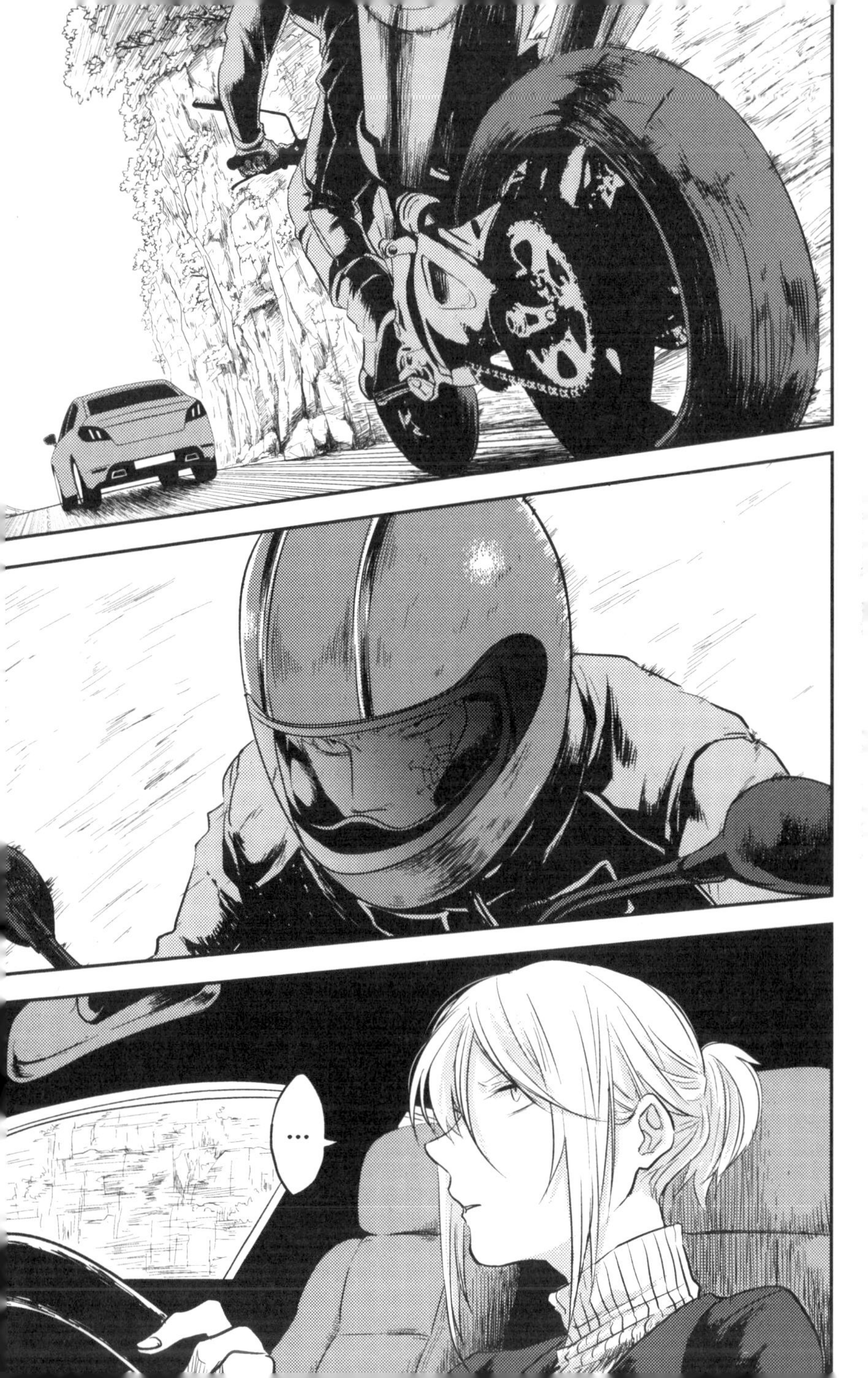
...

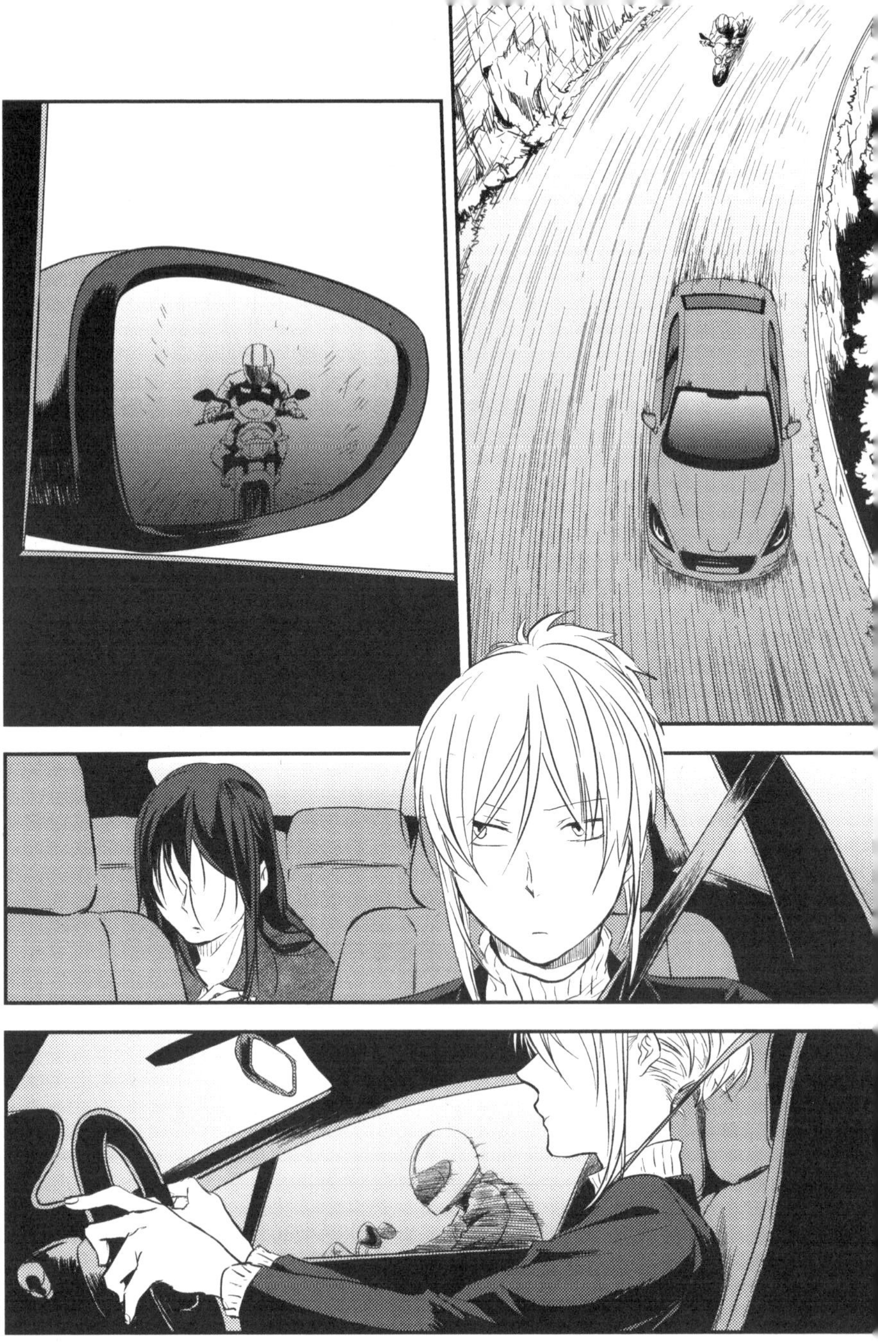

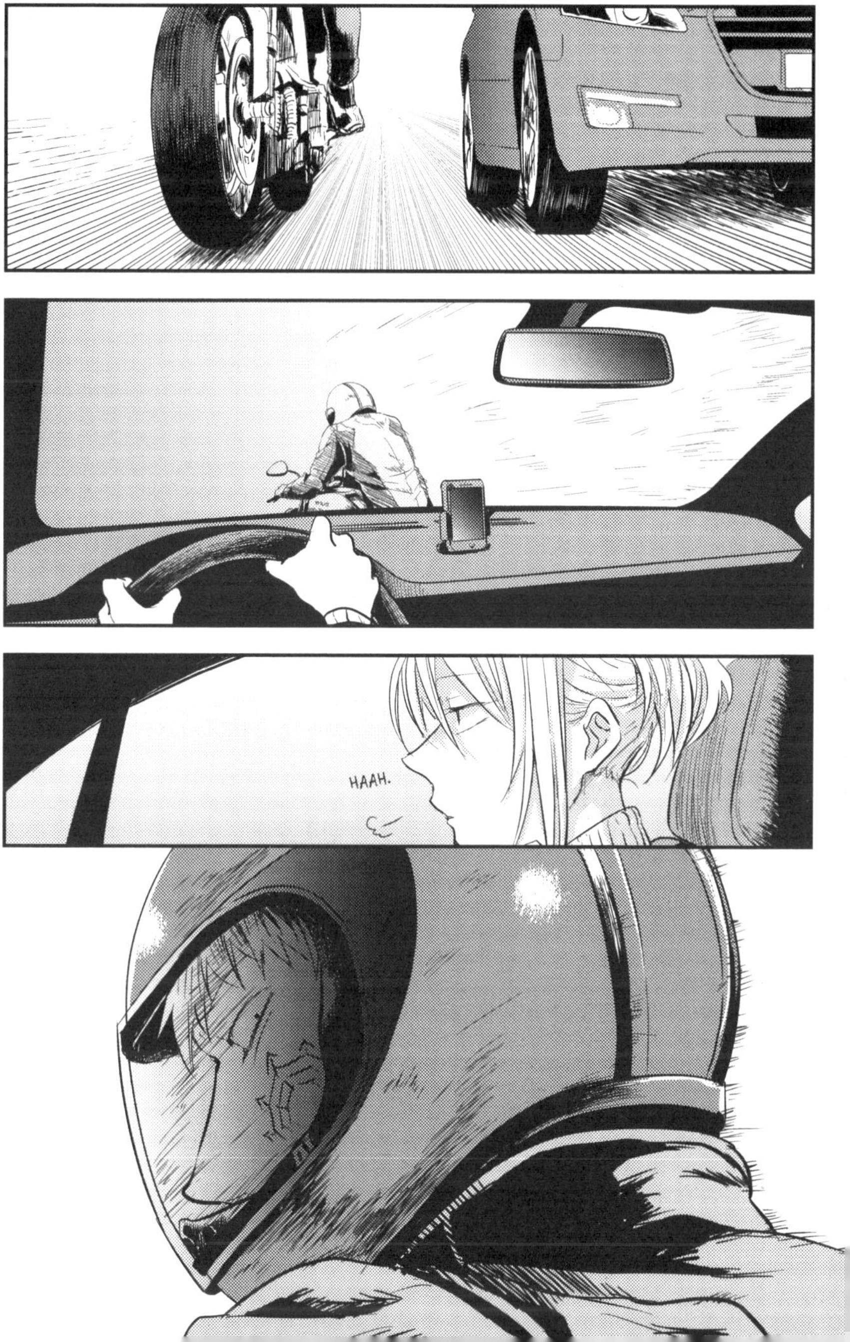
HAAH.

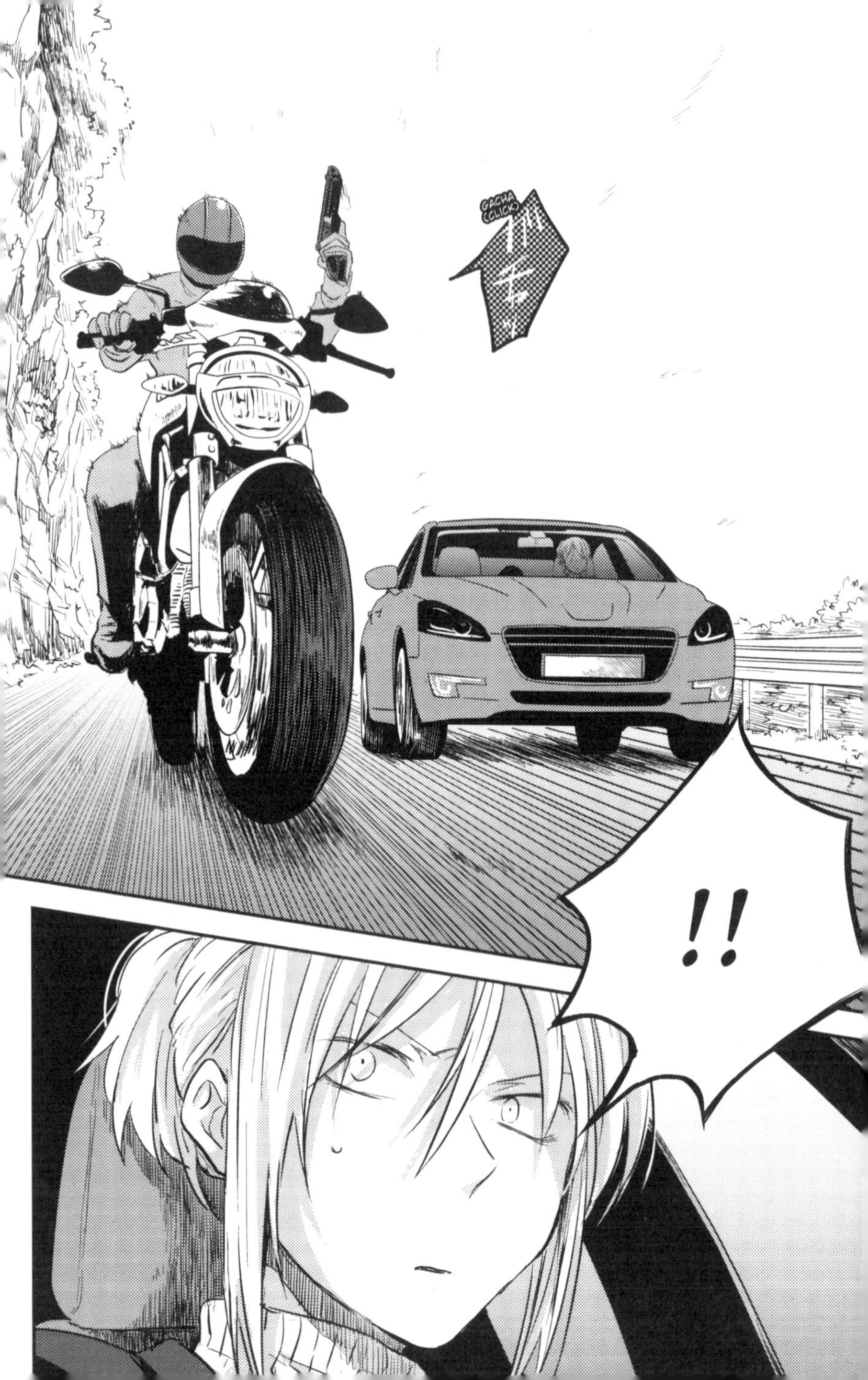
GACHA (CLICK)
ガチャッ
!!

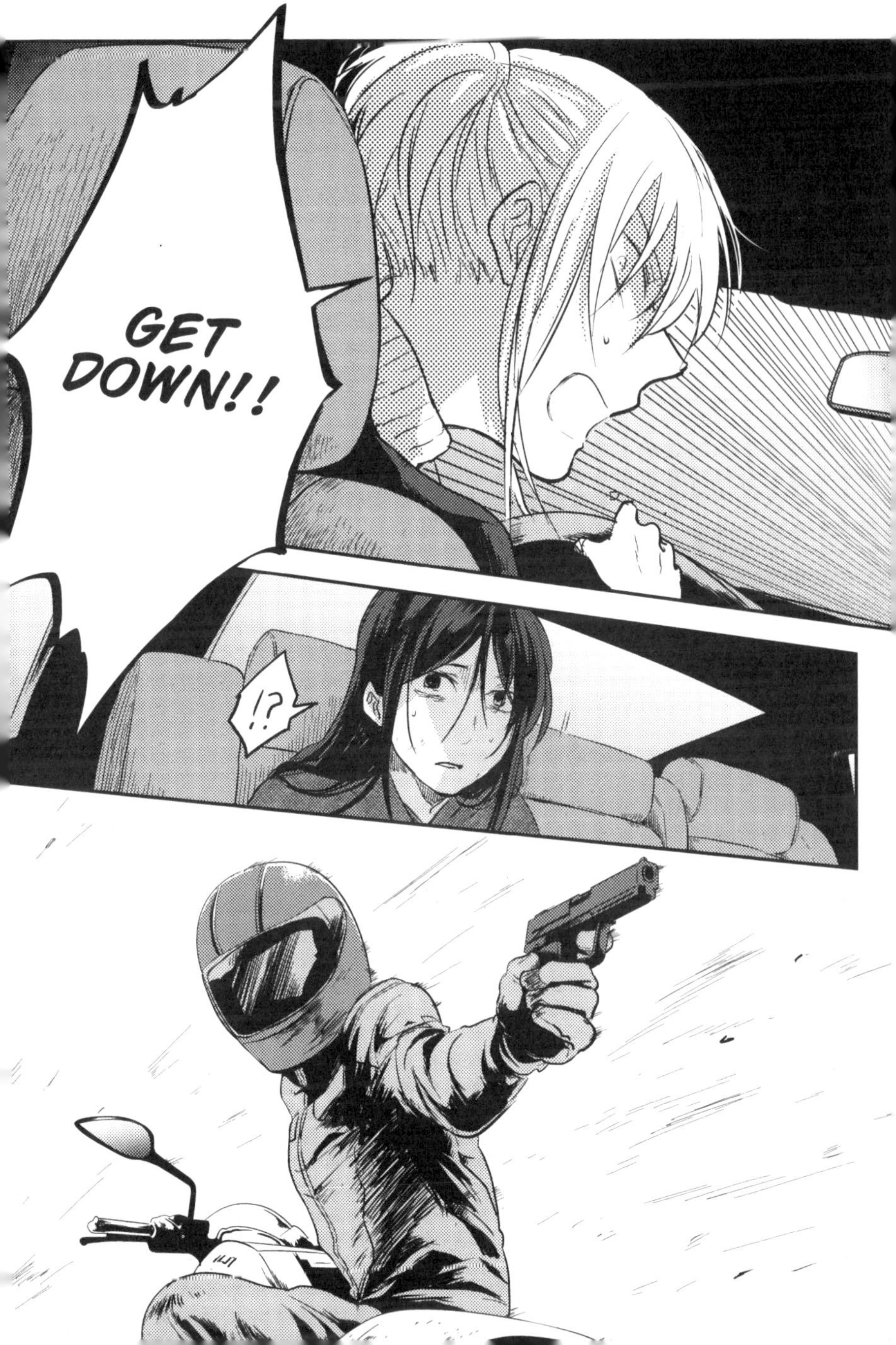
GET DOWN!!
!?

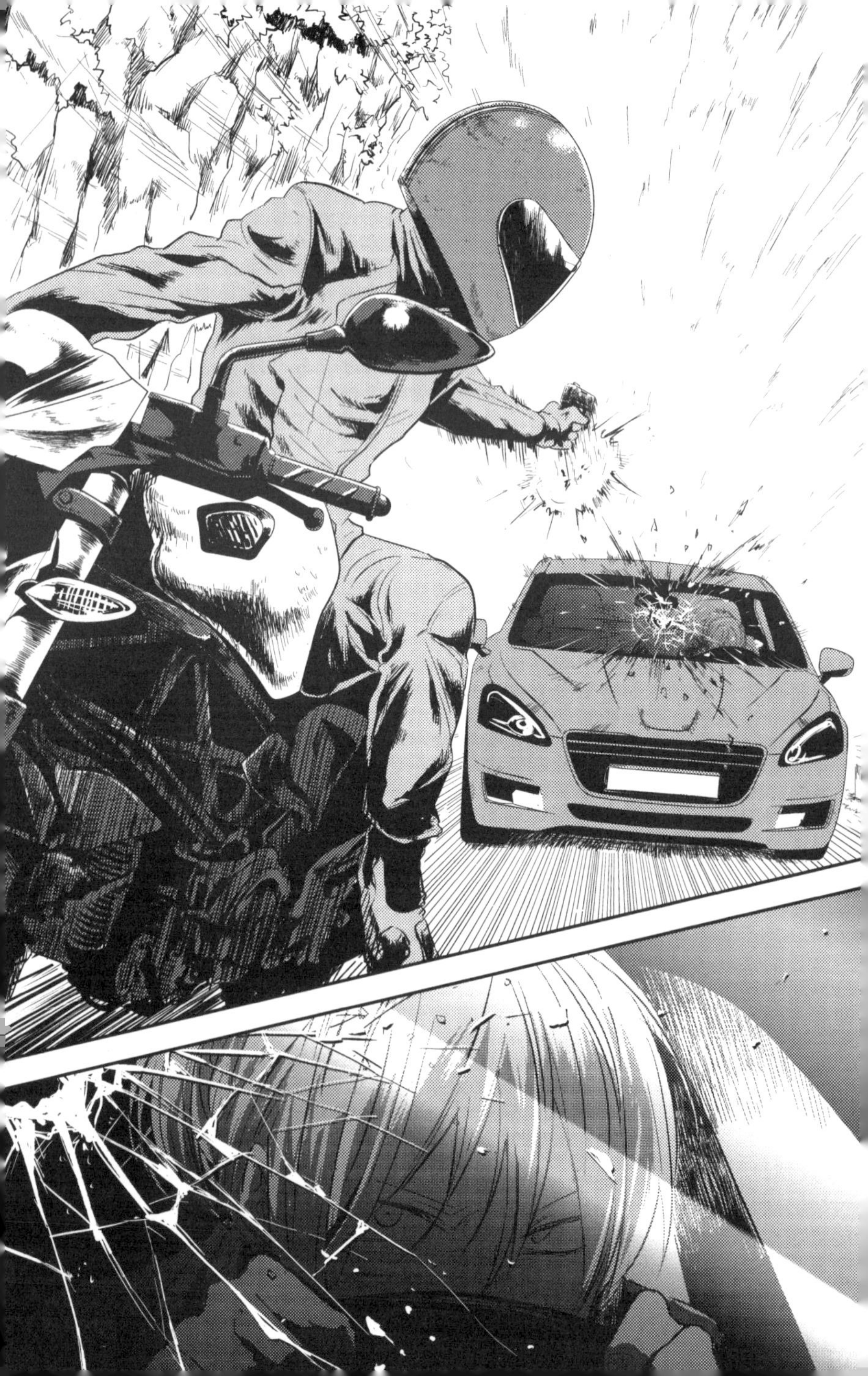

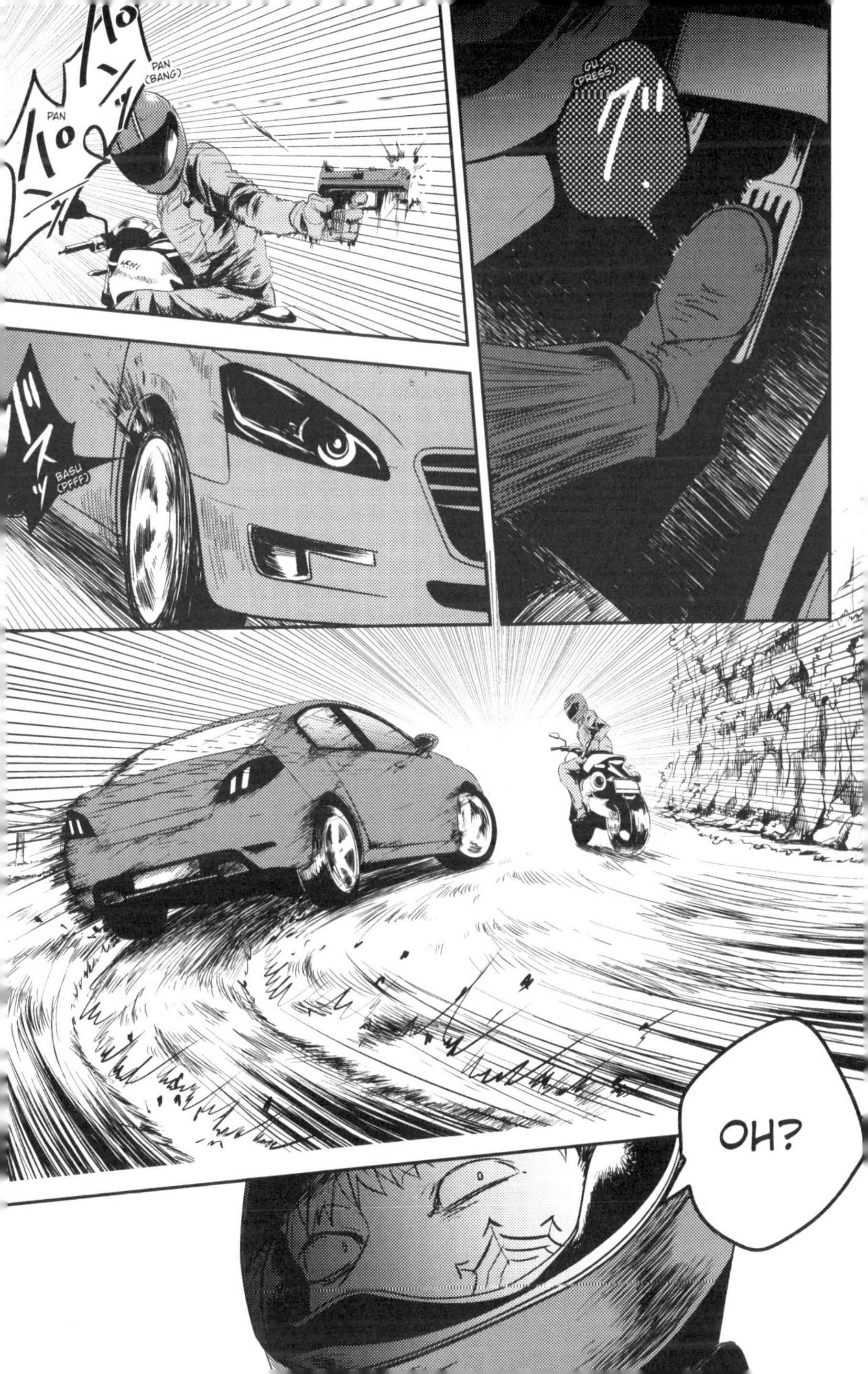
GU
(PRESS)
PAN
(BANG)
PAN
BASU
(PFFF)
OH?

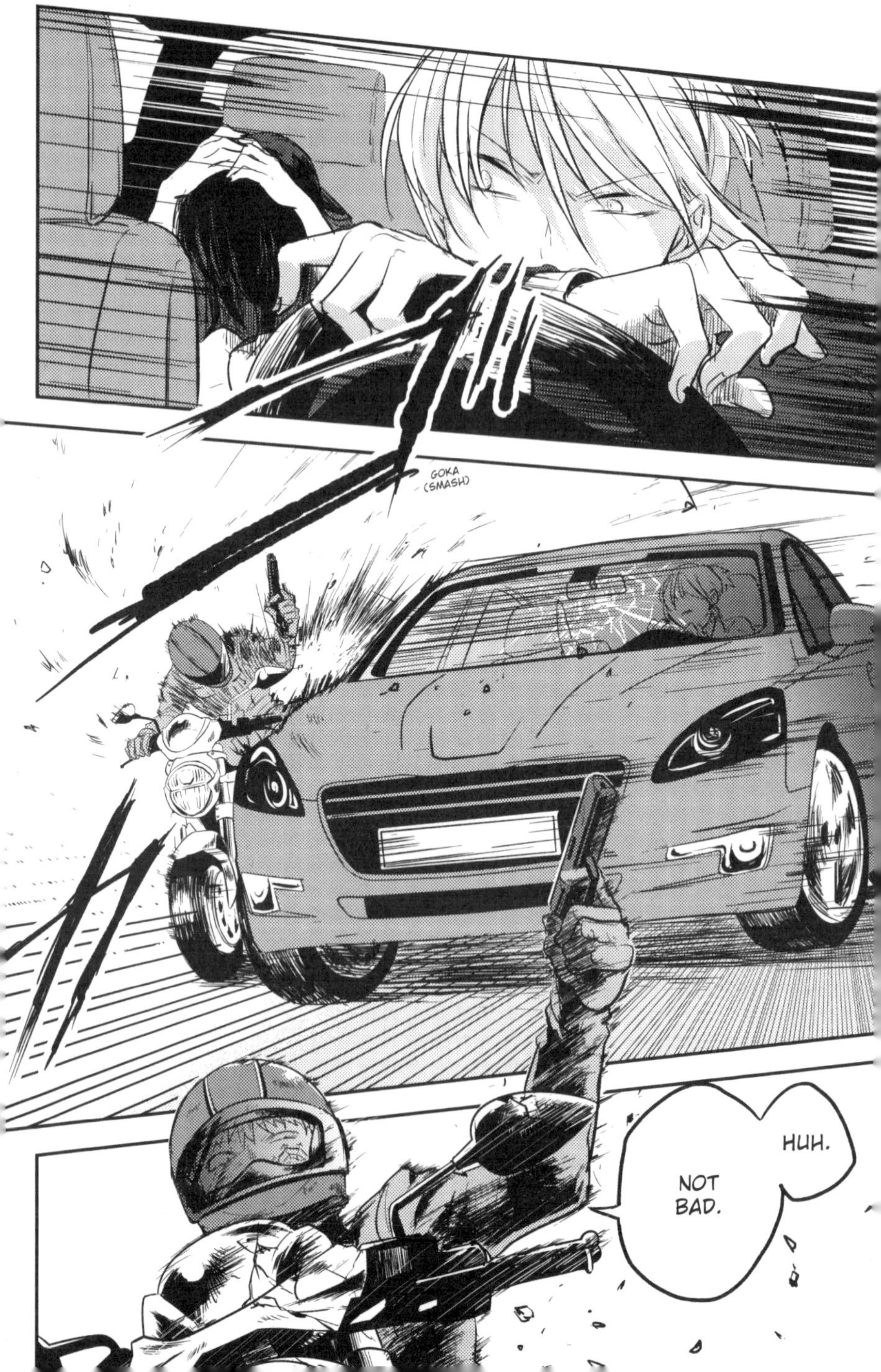
GOKA
(SMASH)
HUH.
NOT BAD.

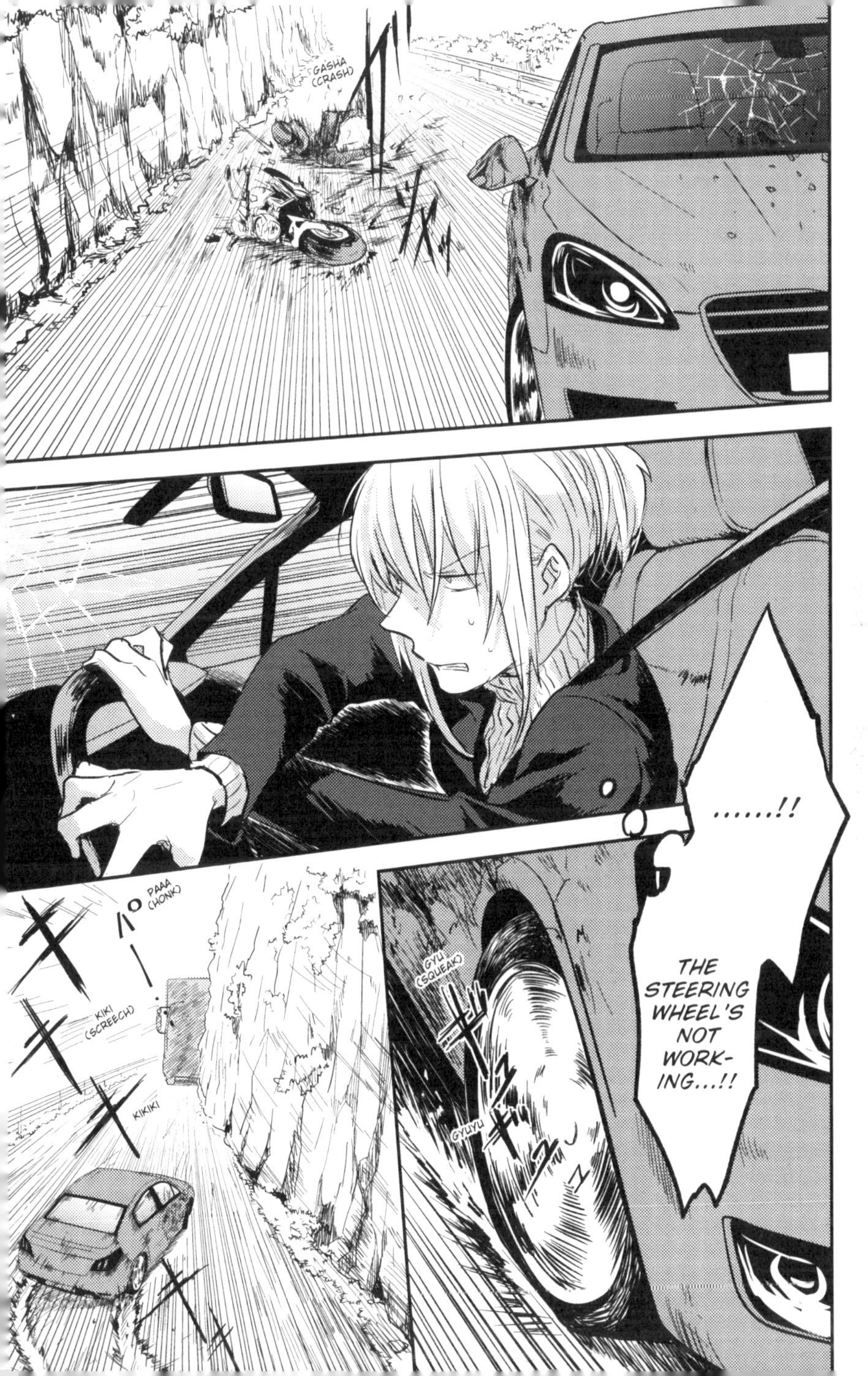
GASHA (CRASH)
......!!
THE STEERING WHEEL'S NOT WORKING...!!
GYU (SQUEAK)
GYUYU
PAAA (HONK)
KIKI (SCREECH)
KIKIKI

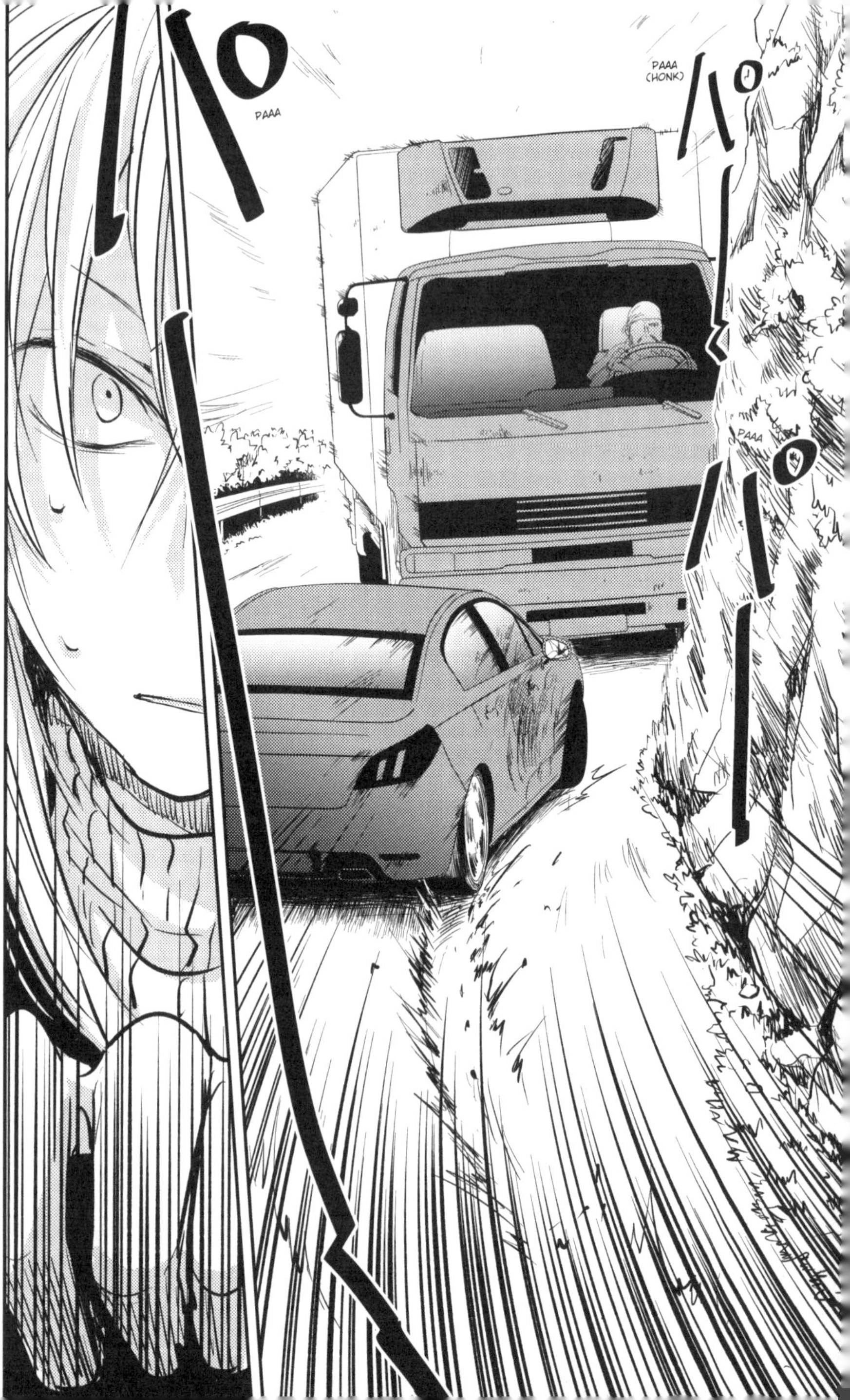
PAAA
(HONK)
PAAA
PAAA

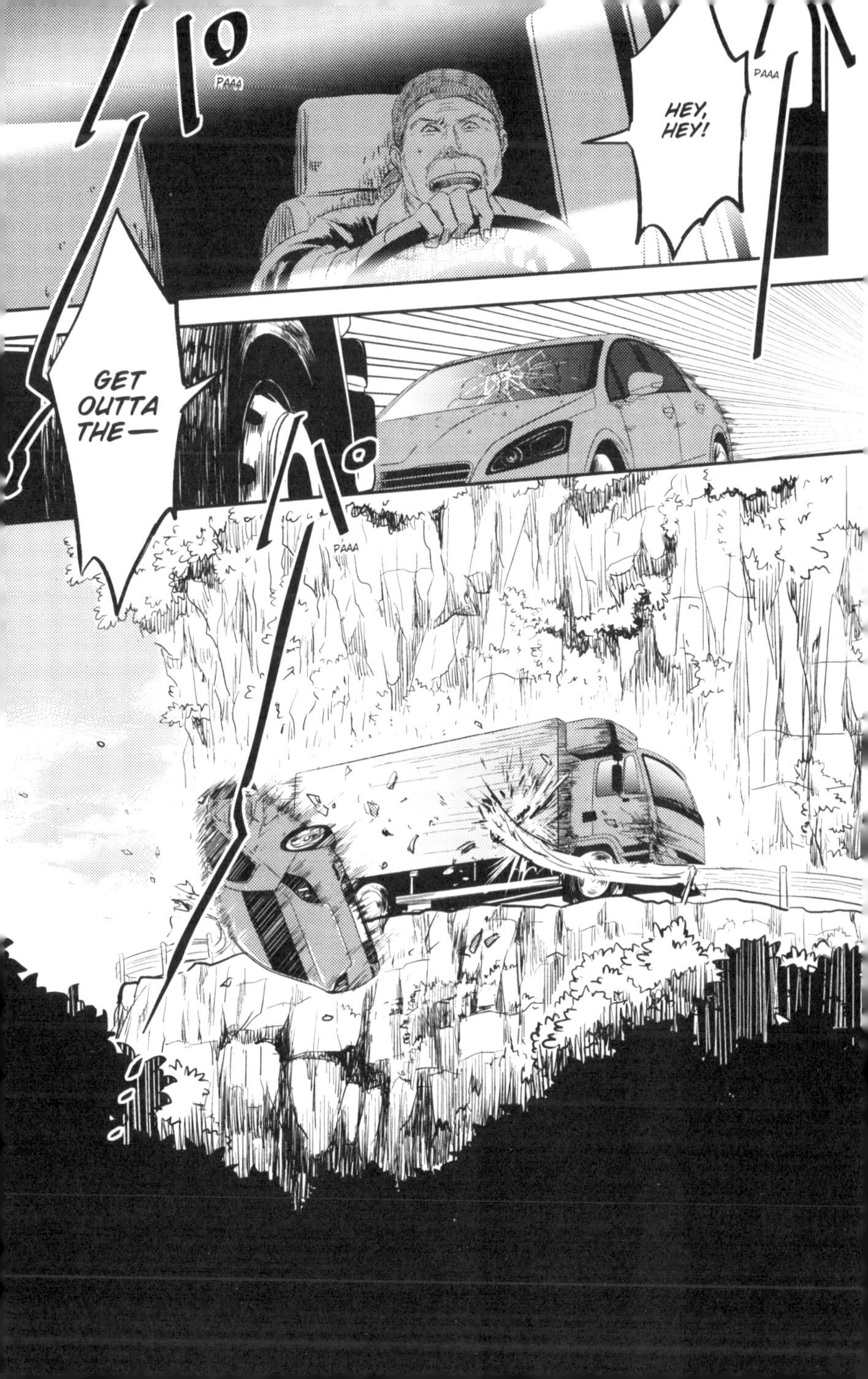
PAAA
HEY, HEY!
PAAA
GET OUTTA THE—
PAAA

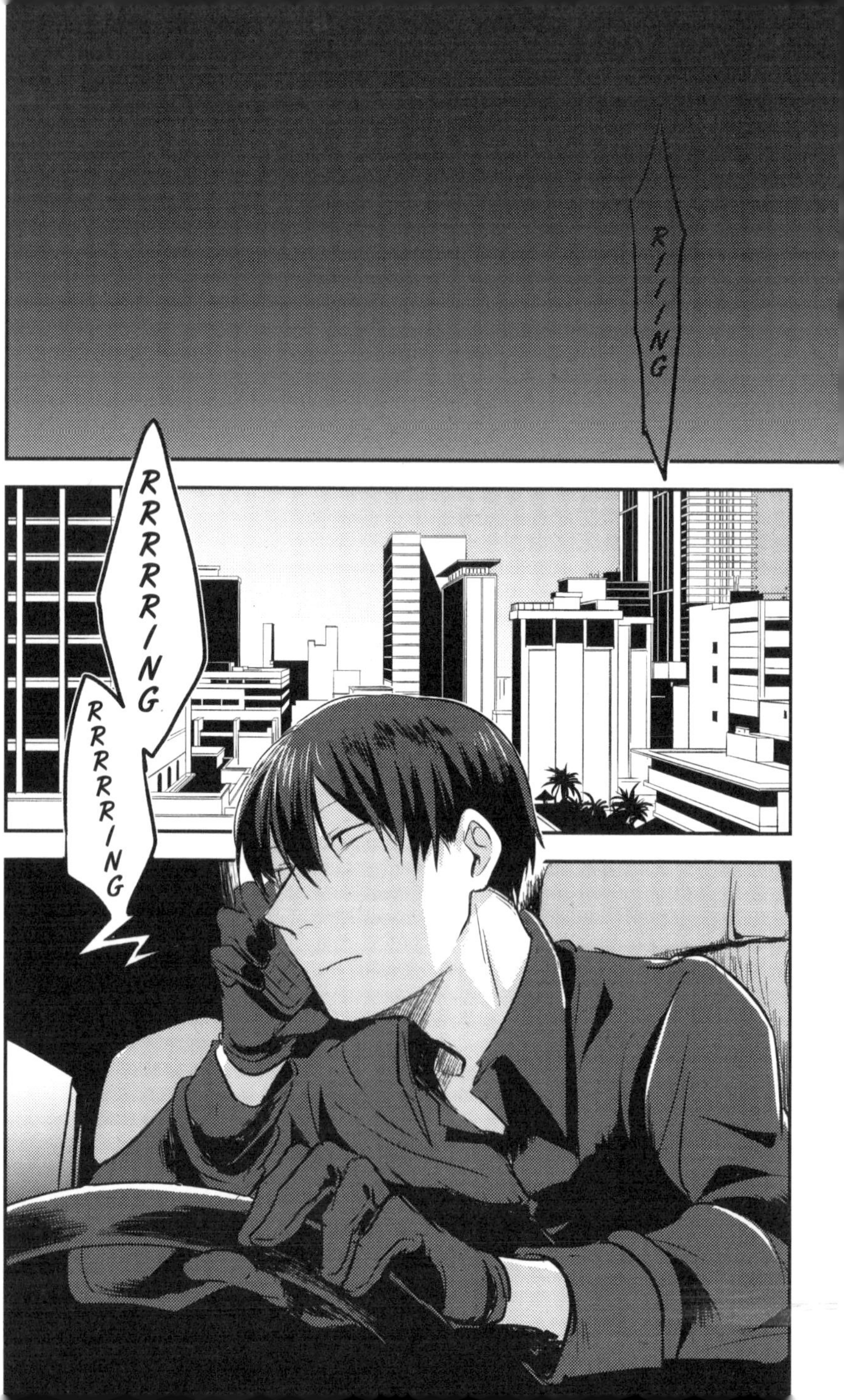
RIIING
RRRRRING
RRRRRING

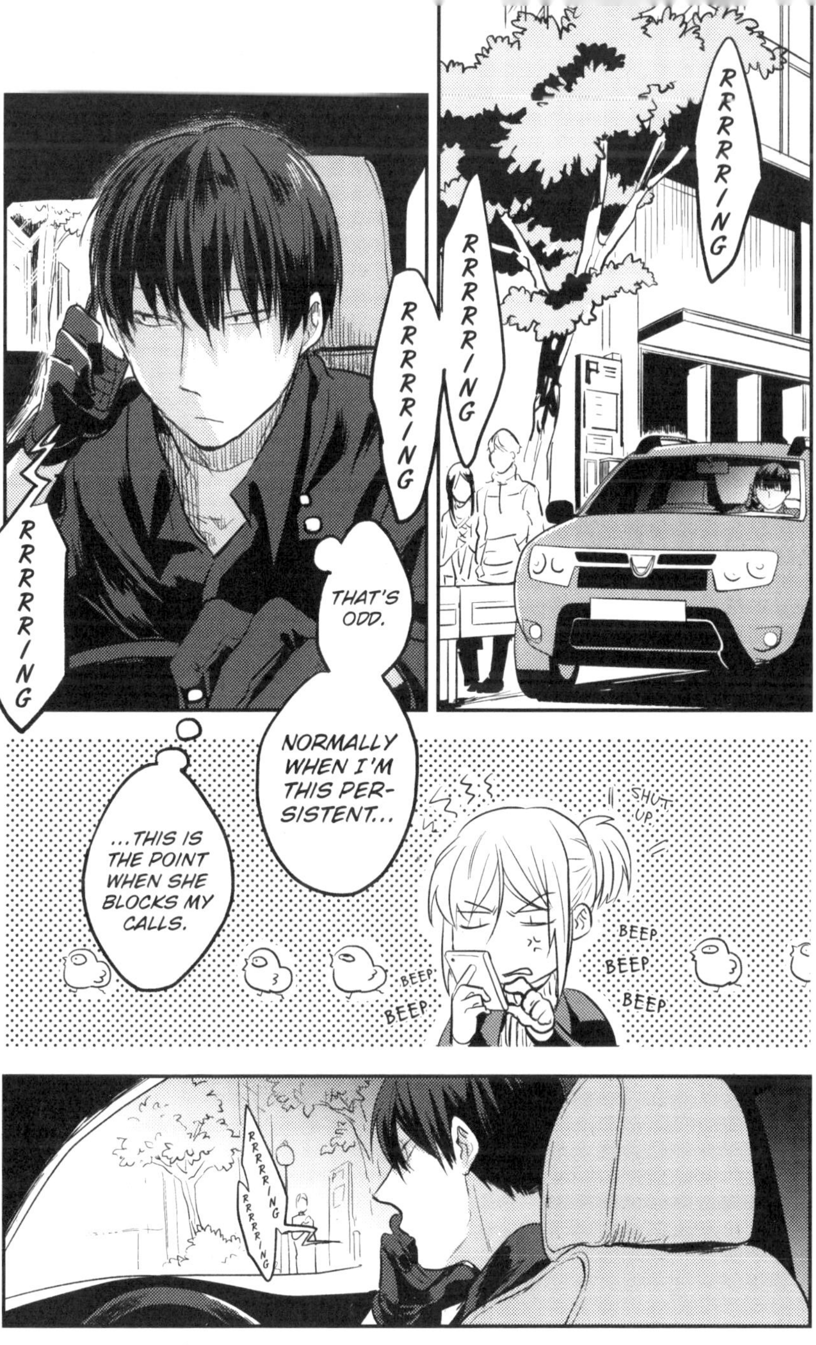

RRRRRING
RRRRRING
RRRRRING
RRRRRING
THAT'S ODD.
NORMALLY WHEN I'M THIS PER-SISTENT...
...THIS IS THE POINT WHEN SHE BLOCKS MY CALLS.
SHUT UP
BEEP
BEEP
BEEP
BEEP
BEEP
RRRRRING
RRRRRING

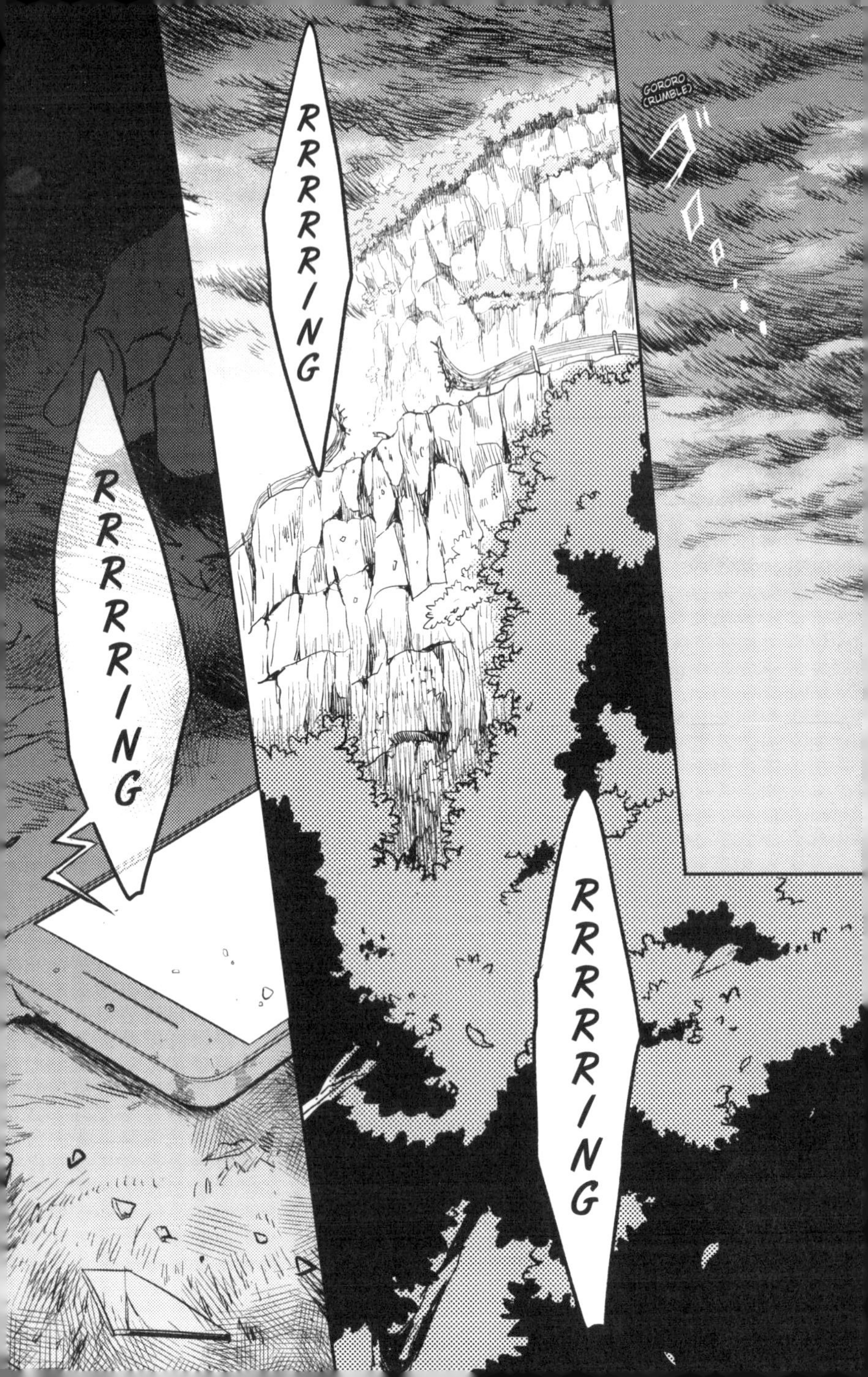
GORORO (RUMBLE)
RRRRRING
RRRRRING
RRRRRING

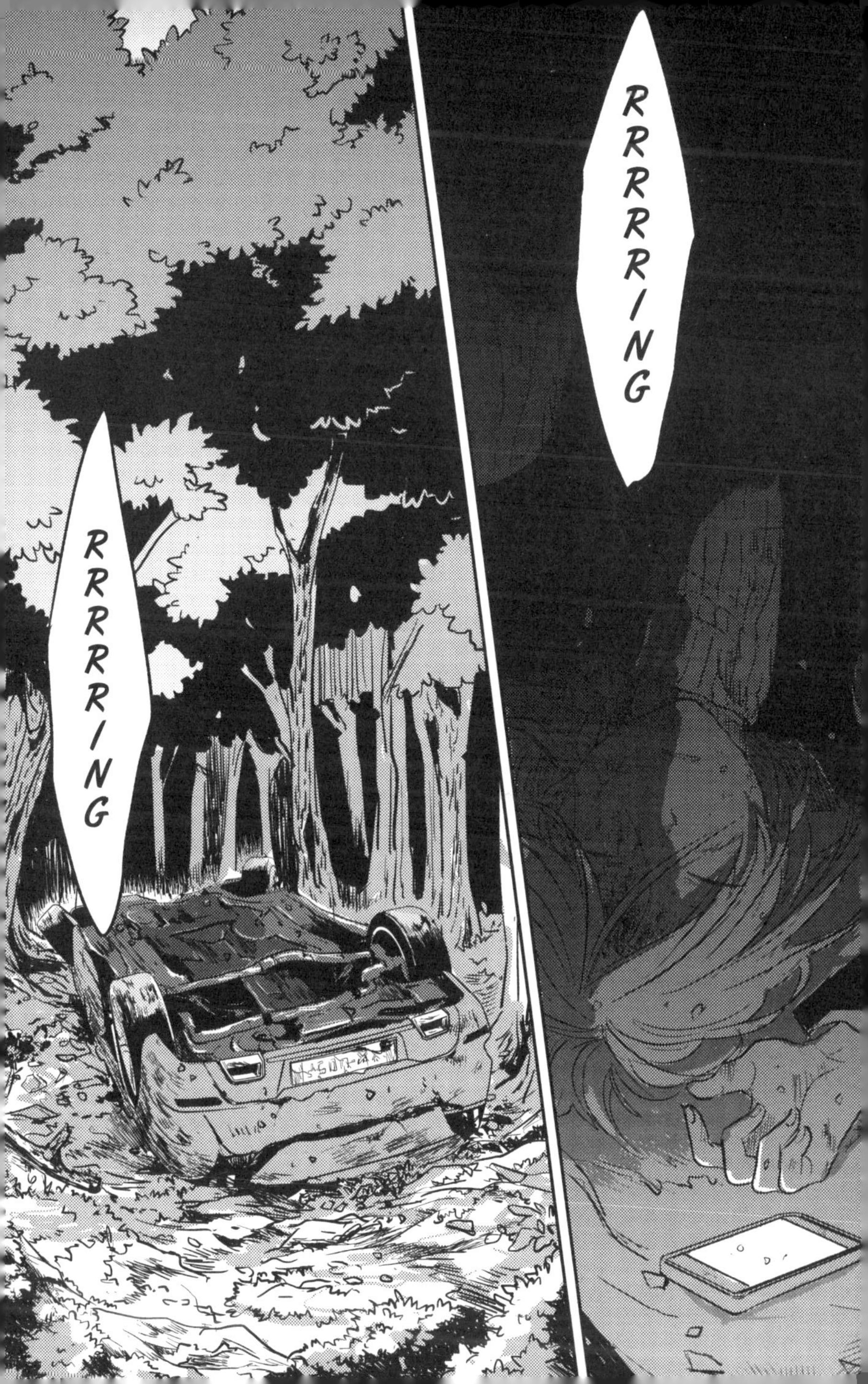
RRRRRING
RRRRRING

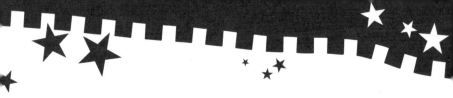

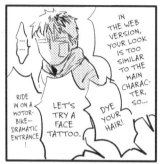

IN THE WEB VERSION, YOUR LOOK IS TOO SIMILAR TO THE MAIN CHARACTER, SO...
DYE YOUR HAIR!
LET'S TRY A FACE TATTOO.
RIDE IN ON A MOTORBIKE—DRAMATIC ENTRANCE!
……

FILE 4: TARGET
A NEW CHARACTER APPEARS AT THE END OF THE CHAPTER, BUT IT TURNS OUT THAT THIS COLLECTED VOLUME ENDS WITHOUT HIS NAME BEING REVEALED...
I SOMEHOW ENDED UP DECIDING TO PUT THIS GUY ON A MOTORCYCLE FOR HIS ENTRANCE. AS A CONSEQUENCE, I SUFFER LATER.

FILE 5: CAR CHASE
IN TERMS OF DRAWING, THIS WAS A TOUGH CHAPTER. FOR THE CAR, I ALREADY HAD A STRONG ALLY KNOWN AS "THE CAR BOSS," SO THAT WORKED OUT ALL RIGHT, BUT UNFORTUNATELY I'D NEVER EVEN DRAWN A MOTORCYCLE BEFORE...LUCKILY, A FRIEND OF MINE GRACIOUSLY ALLOWED ME TO PHOTOGRAPH THEIR MOTORBIKE FOR REFERENCE, SO THAT WORKED OUT TOO.
N. KAWA-SAN, THANK YOU SO MUCH!!

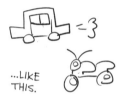

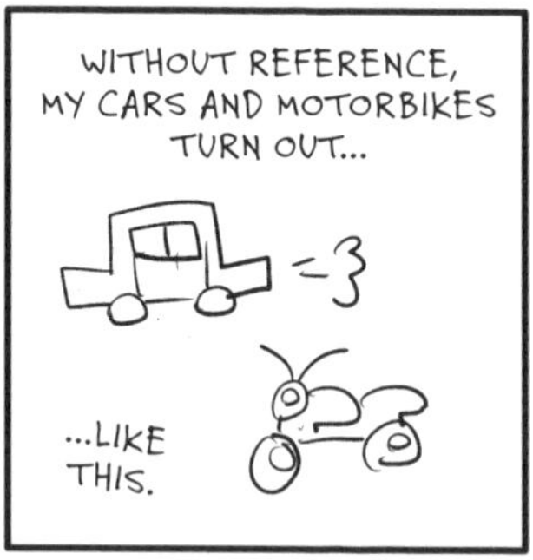

WITHOUT REFERENCE, MY CARS AND MOTORBIKES TURN OUT...
...LIKE THIS.

WHAT'S WITH THIS FANCY BACK-GROUND...?

FILE 6: ? (UNTITLED AS OF 1/3/2016)

BECAUSE MY EDITOR DOES THE CHAPTER TITLES FOR ME.

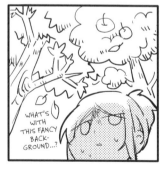

IT FEELS AS THOUGH MY FEMALE CHARACTERS ARE ALWAYS SUFFERING MISFORTUNES...I DON'T KNOW WHY. YOU MAY FEEL INCLINED TO POINT OUT SOME ISSUES, SUCH AS HOW CHATEAU MANAGED TO SURVIVE A FALL FROM THAT HEIGHT, BUT THAT'S THE BEAUTY OF FICTION.
I DON'T FULLY UNDERSTAND HOW TO DRAW A FOREST, SO THAT WAS A STRUGGLE...
THE SUBJECT OF MY DRAWING PROCESS SEEMS TO COME UP EVERY CHAPTER. THAT NEEDS WORK.

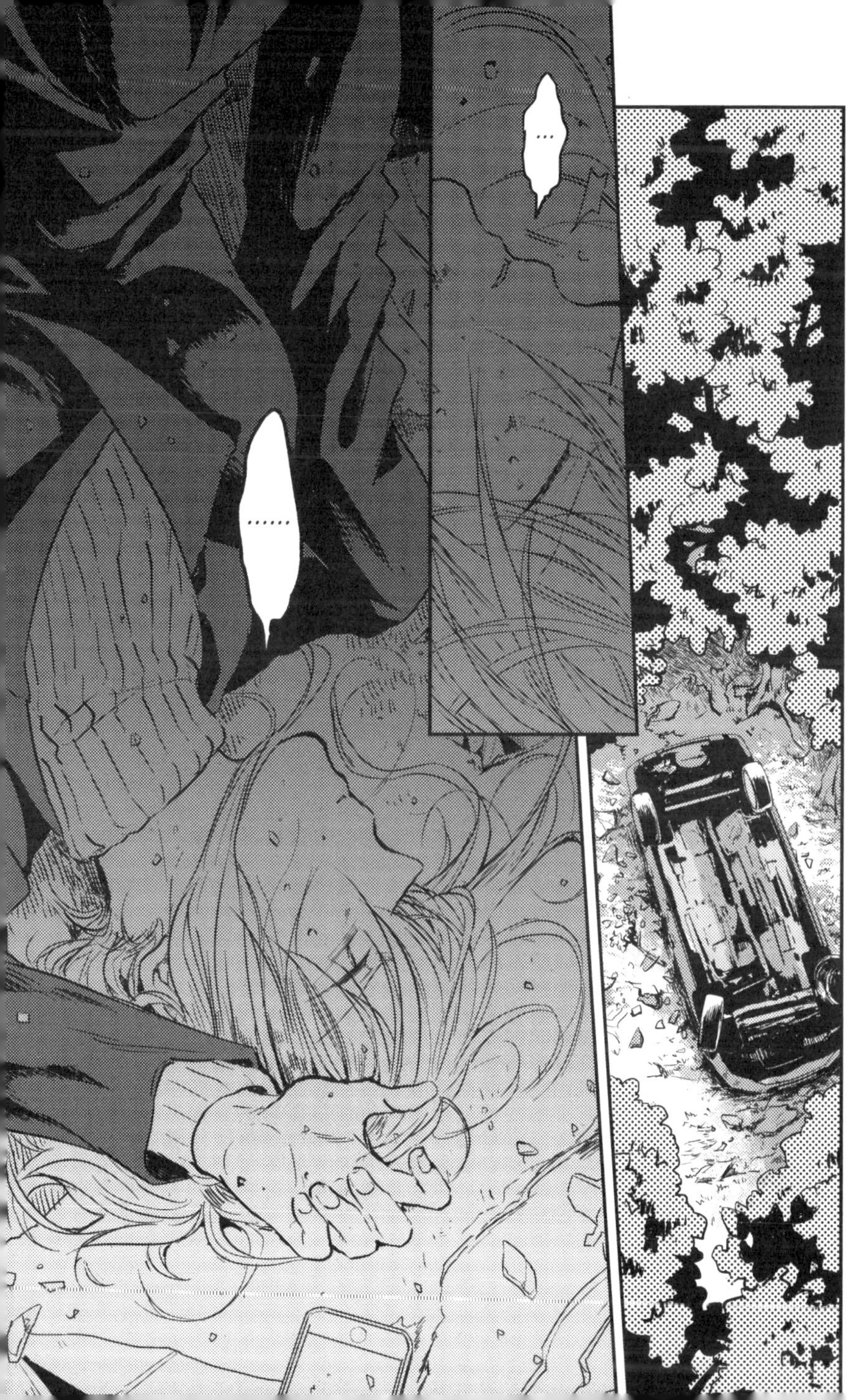
…
……

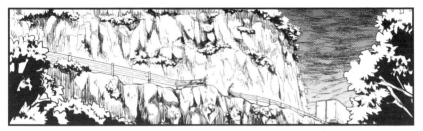

WHAT THE —?

I DON'T BELIEVE THIS...

...HUH?

YOU THERE! YOU ALL RIGHT!?

KOKI (CRACK)

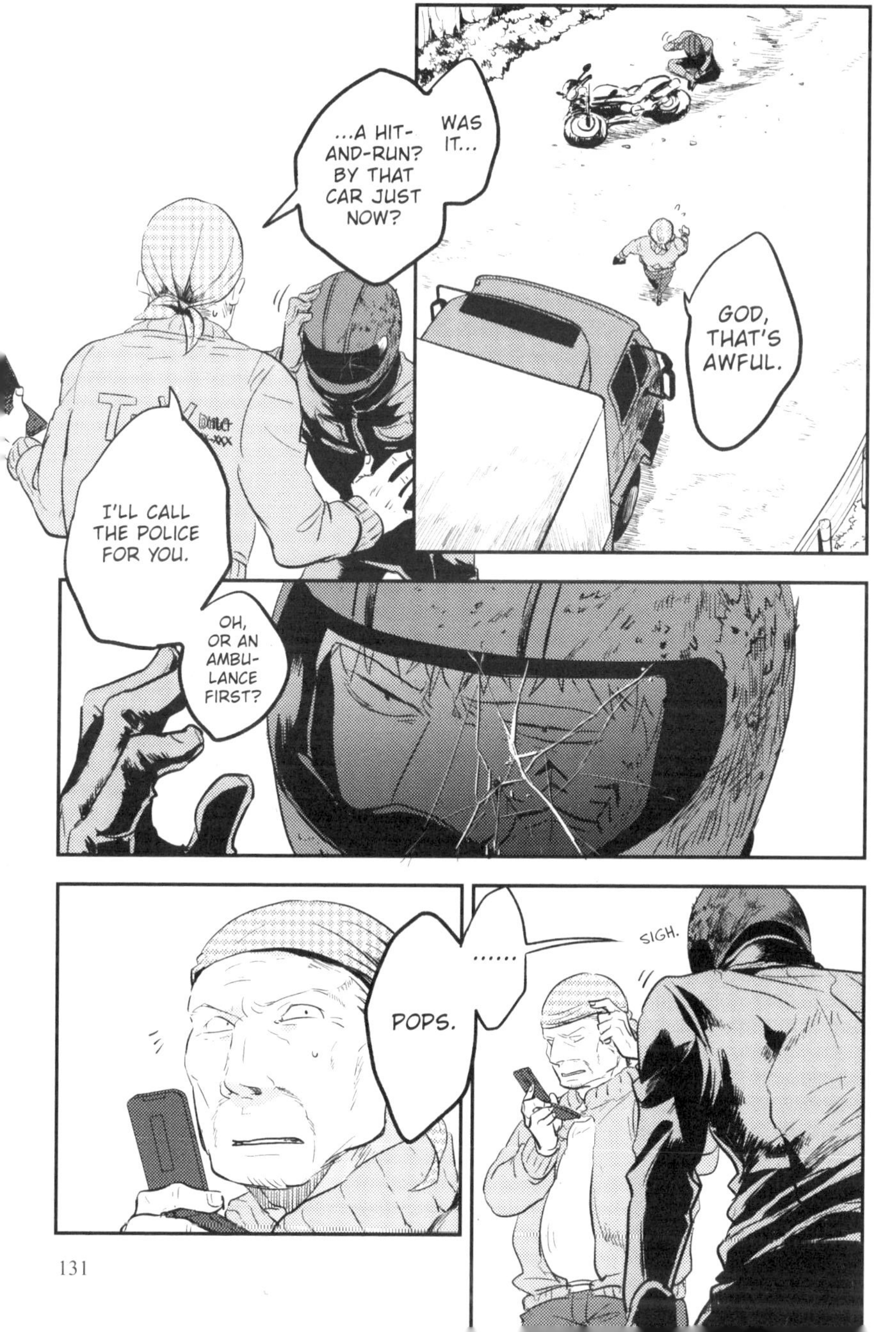
WAS IT... ...A HIT-AND-RUN? BY THAT CAR JUST NOW?
GOD, THAT'S AWFUL.
I'LL CALL THE POLICE FOR YOU.
OH, OR AN AMBULANCE FIRST?
SIGH.
...... POPS.

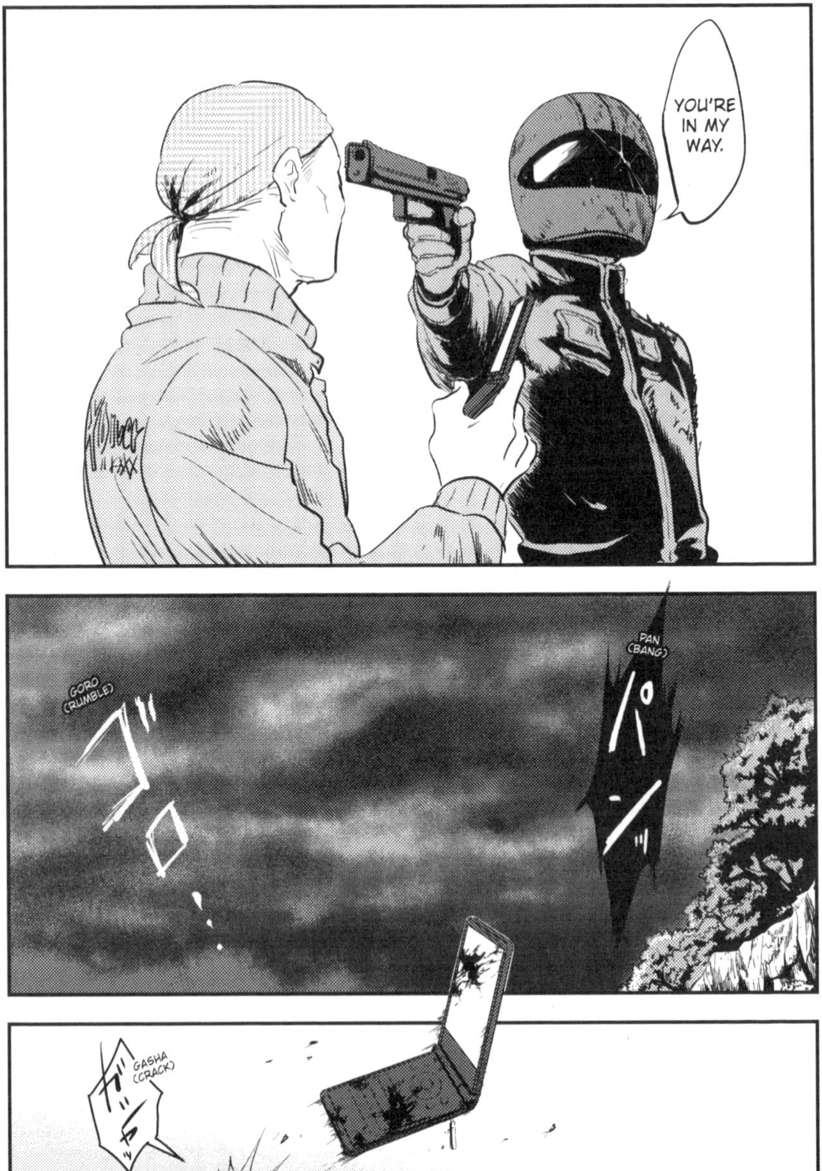
YOU'RE IN MY WAY.
PAN (BANG)
GORO (RUMBLE)
GASHA (CRACK)

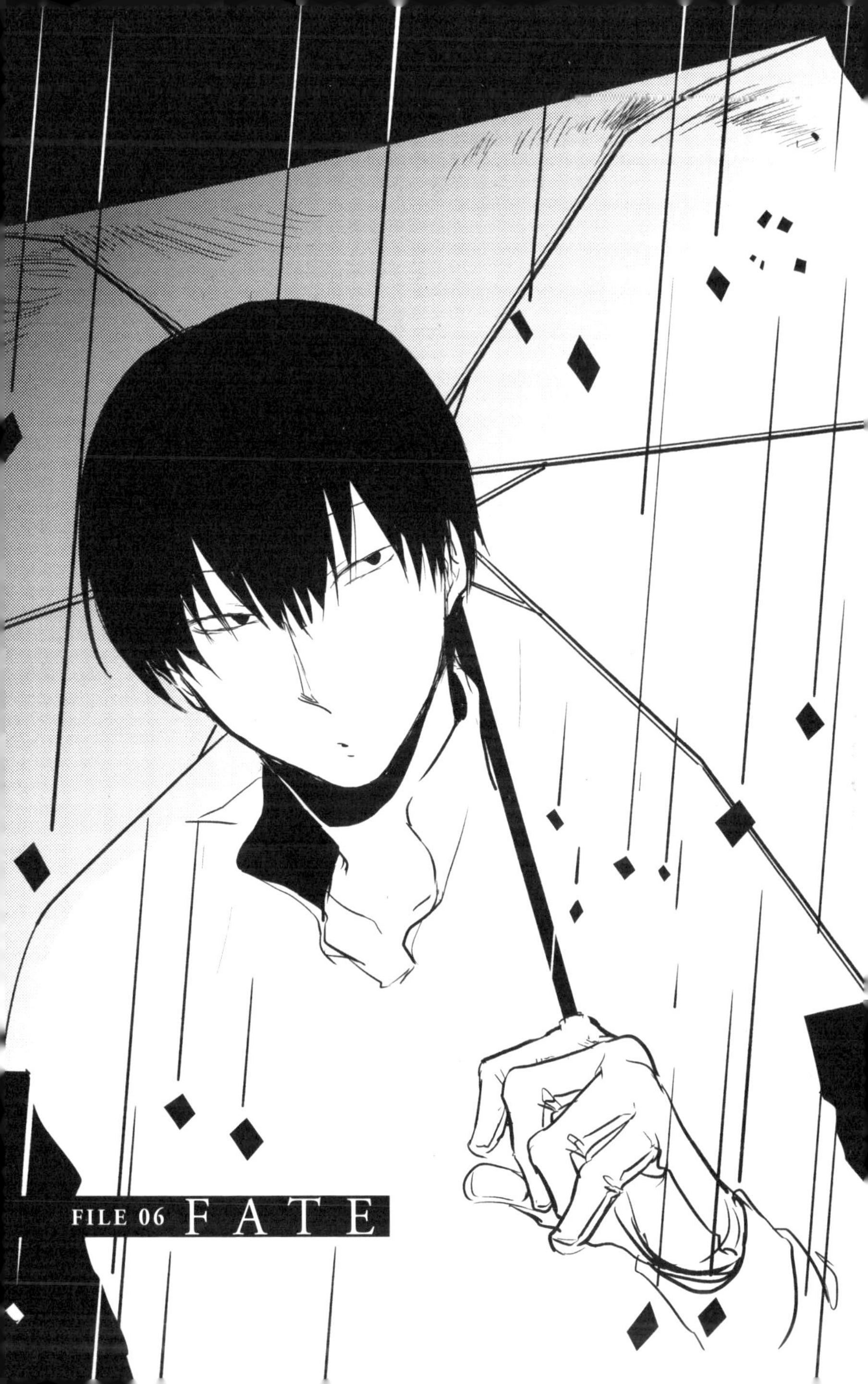
FILE 06 FATE

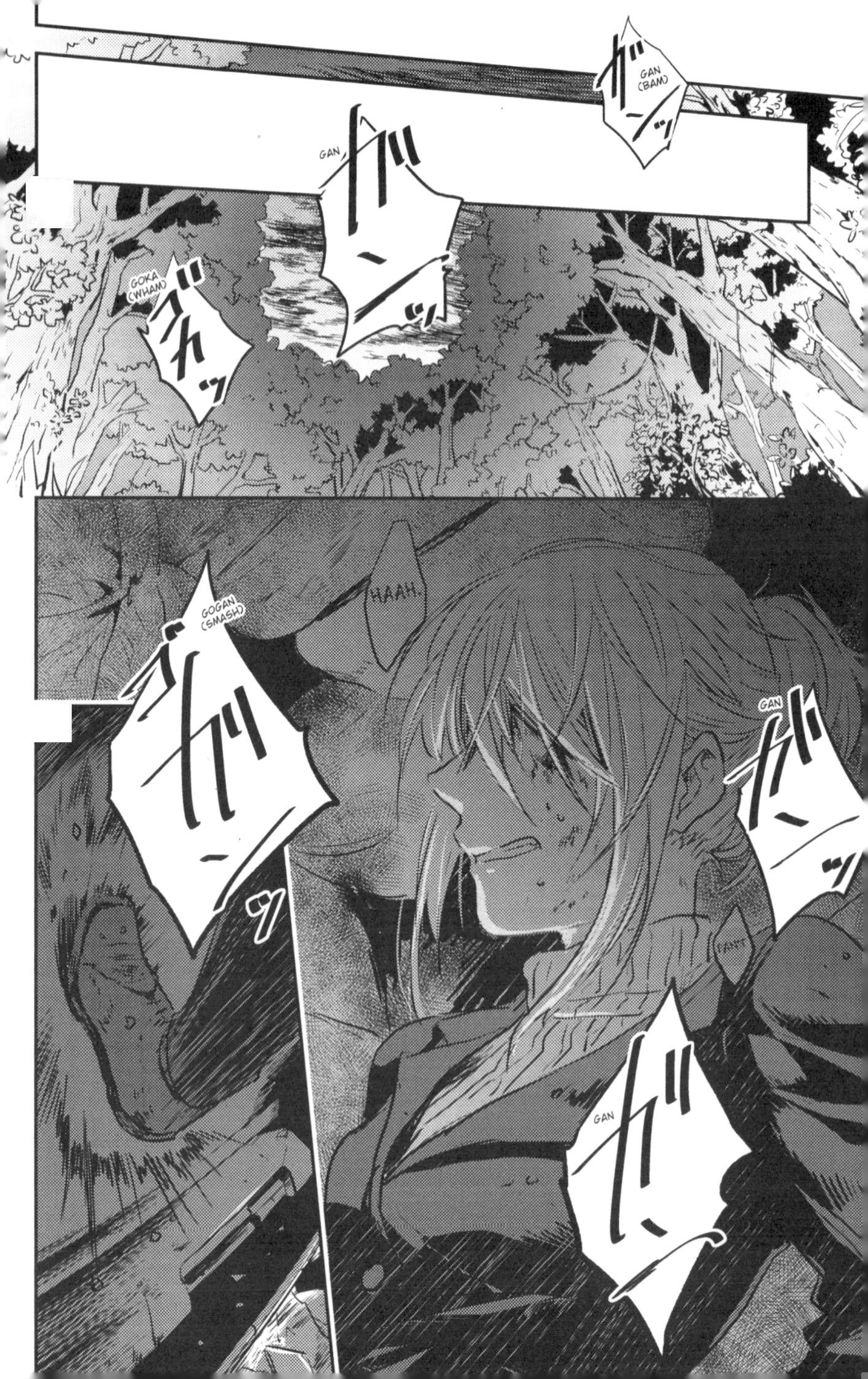
GAN (BAM)
GAN
GOKA (WHAM)
HAAH
GAN
GOGAN (SMASH)
PANT
GAN

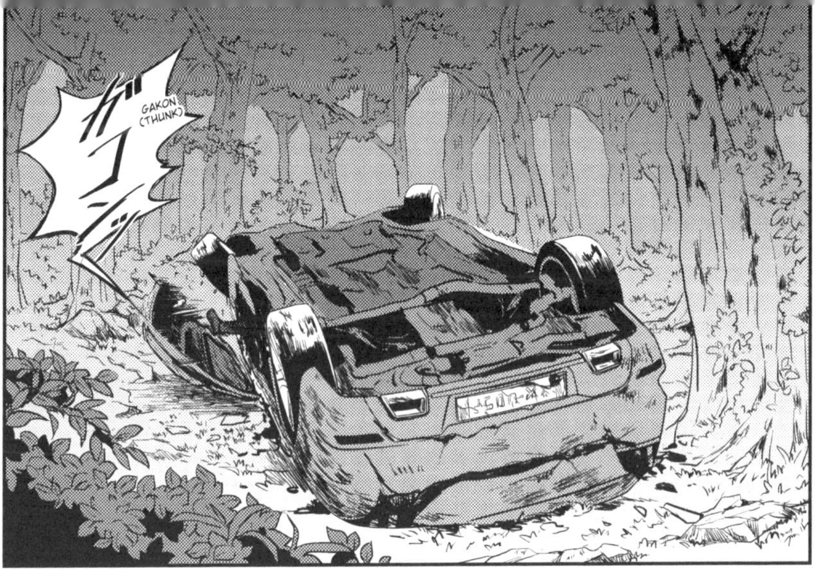
ガコンッ
GAKON (THUNK)
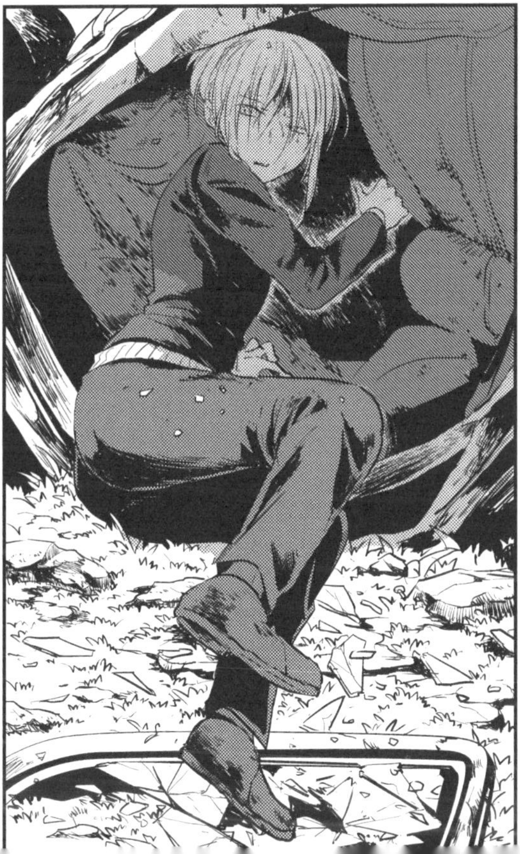
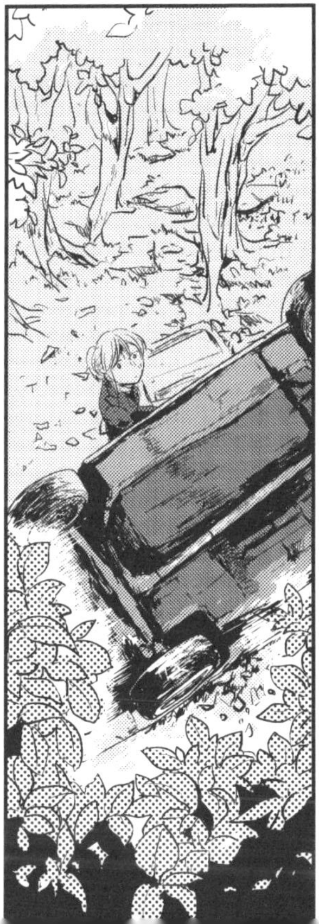

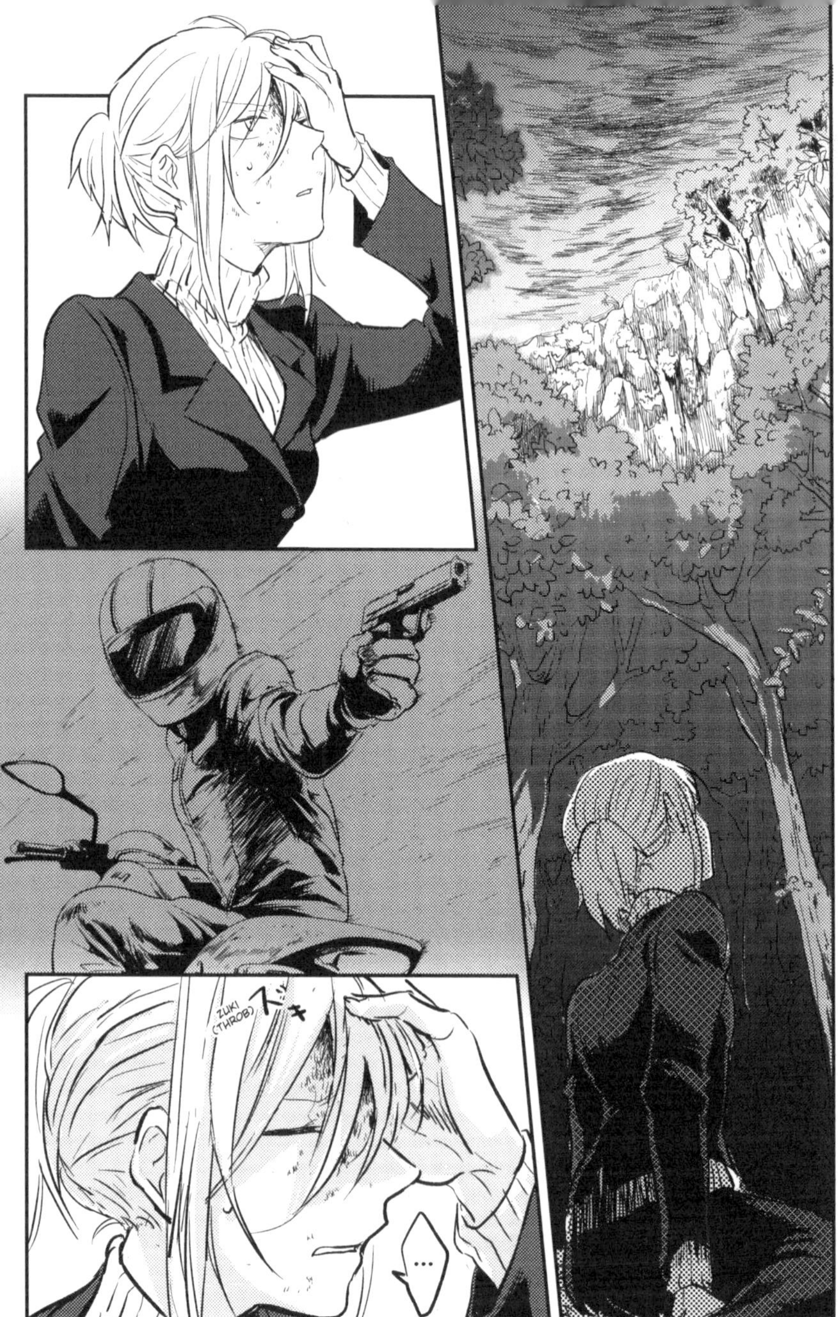
ZUKI (THROB)
...

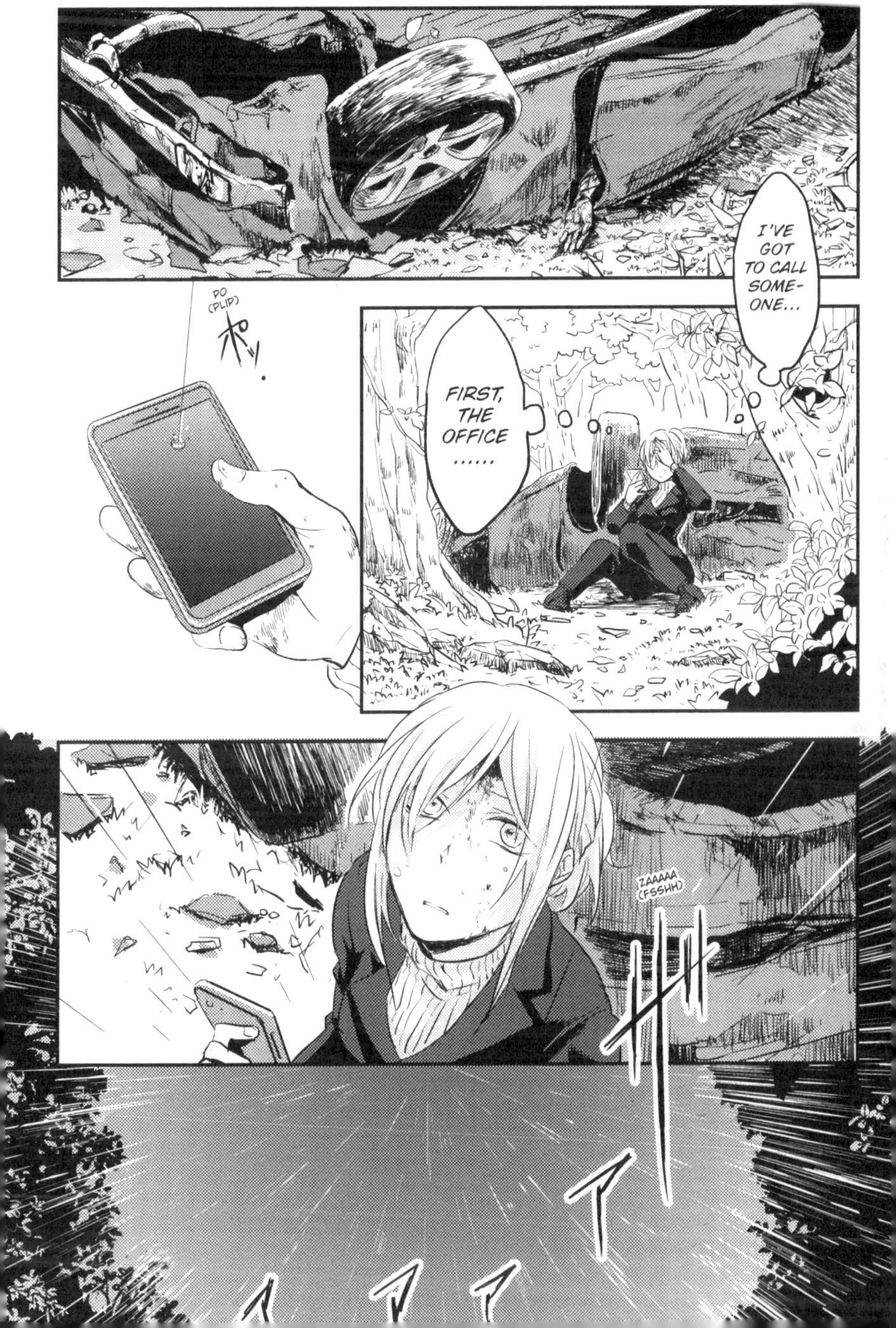
I'VE GOT TO CALL SOME-ONE...
FIRST, THE OFFICE......
PO (PLIP)
ZAAAAA (FSSHH)

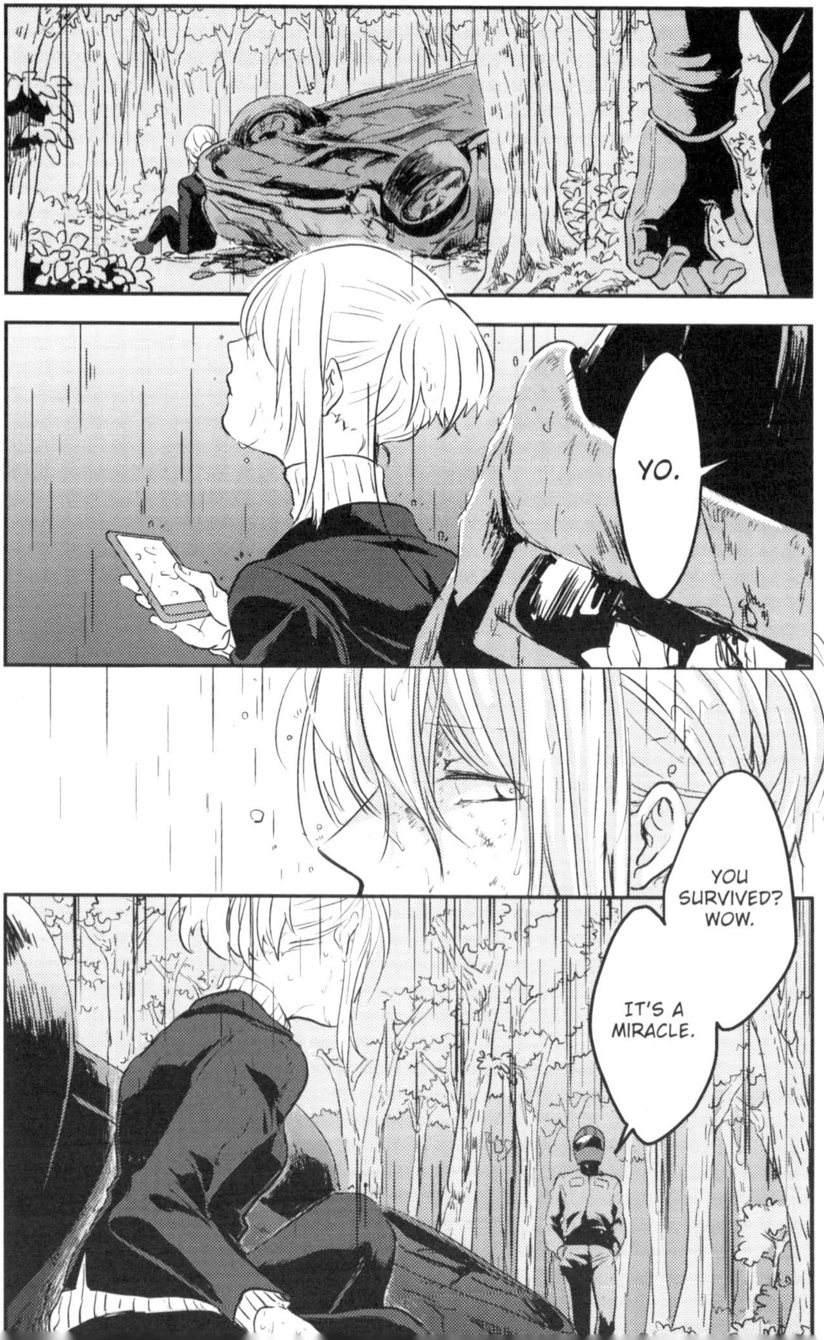
YO.
YOU SURVIVED? WOW.
IT'S A MIRACLE.

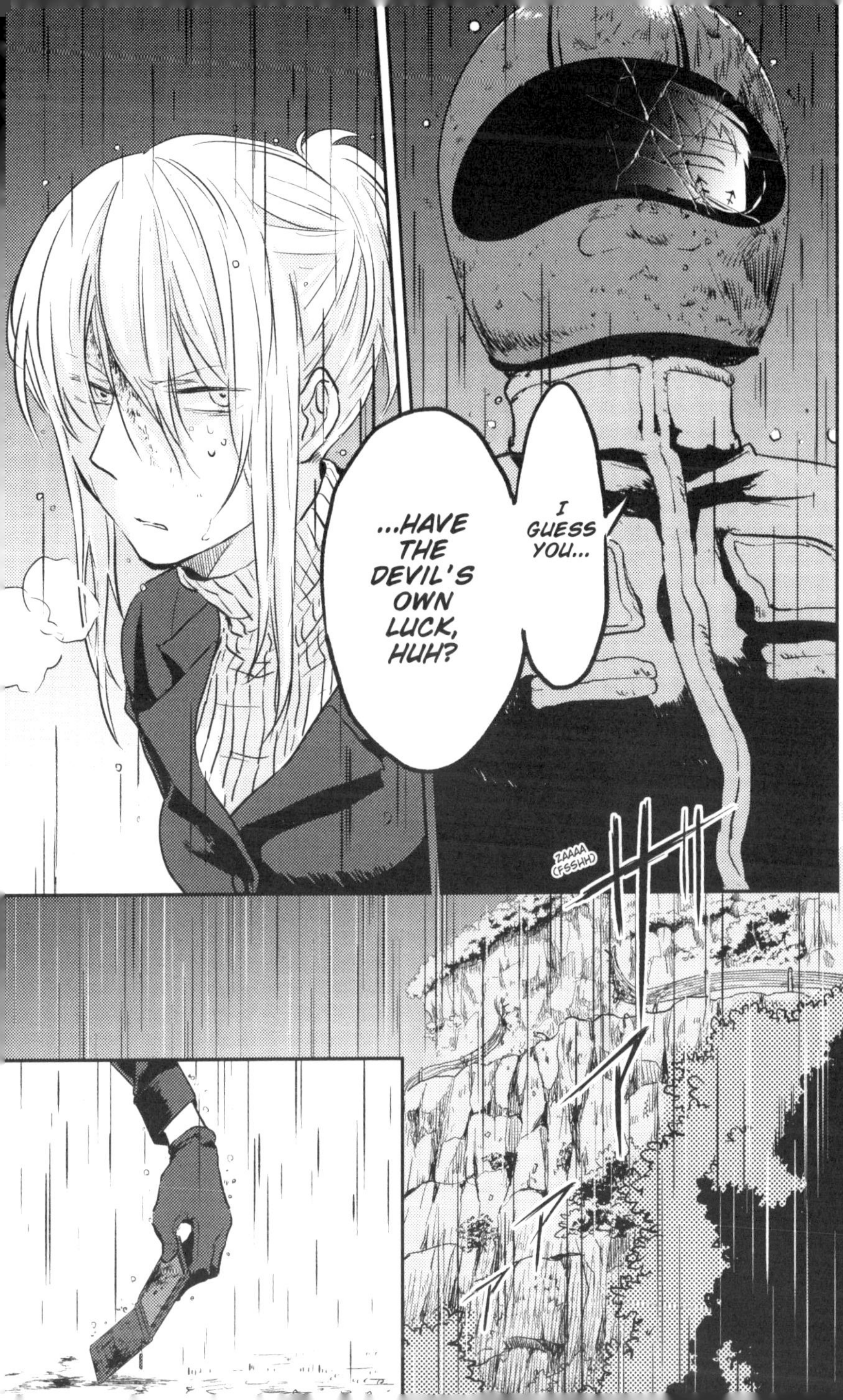
I GUESS YOU...
...HAVE THE DEVIL'S OWN LUCK, HUH?
ZAAAA (FSSHH)

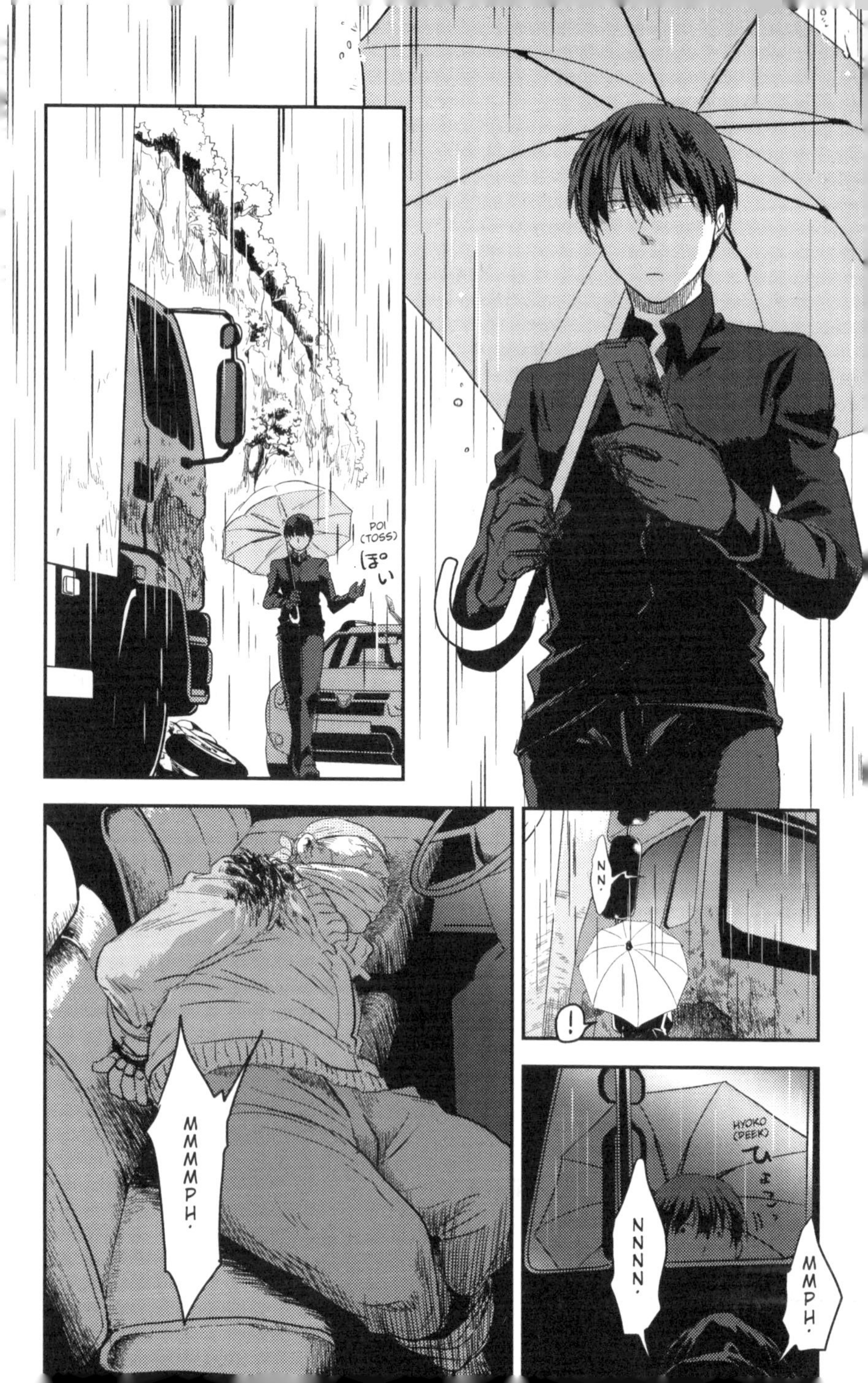
POI
(TOSS)
ぽい
NN.
!
HYOKO
(PEEK)
ひょこっ
MMPH.
NNNN.
MMMMPH.

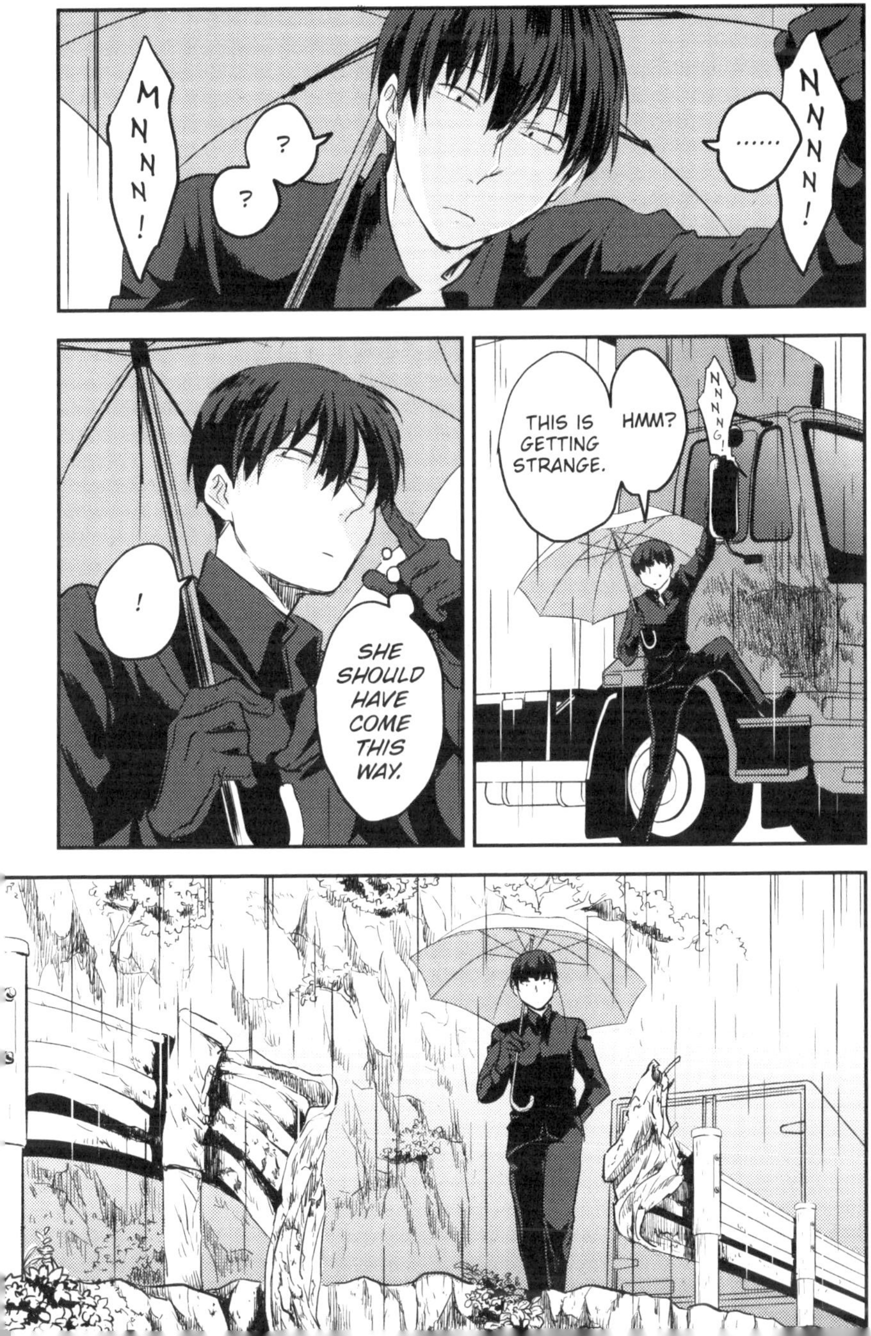
NNNN!
......
??
MNNN!
NNNG!
HMM?
THIS IS GETTING STRANGE.
!
SHE SHOULD HAVE COME THIS WAY.

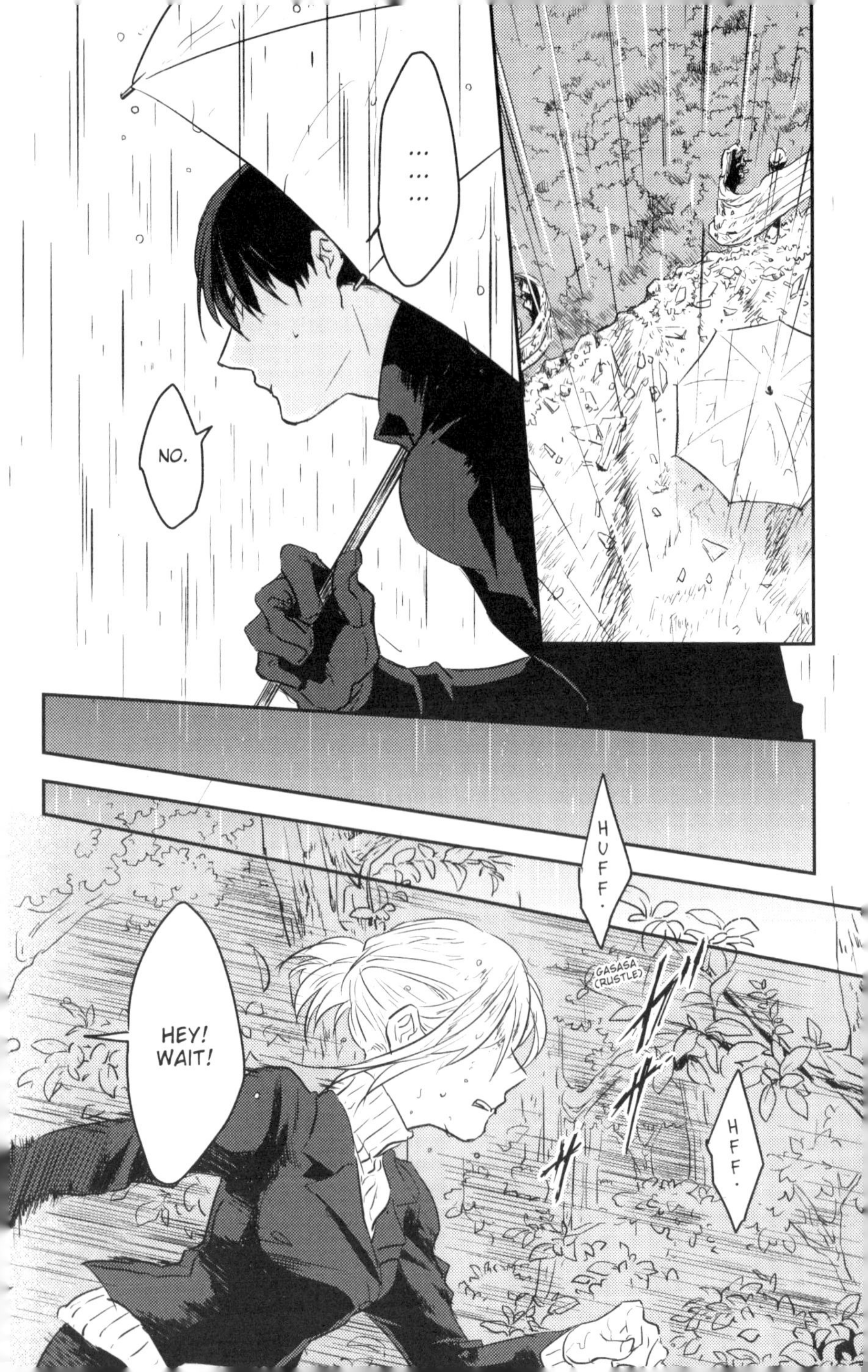
......
NO.
HUFF.
GASASA (RUSTLE)
HFF.
HEY! WAIT!

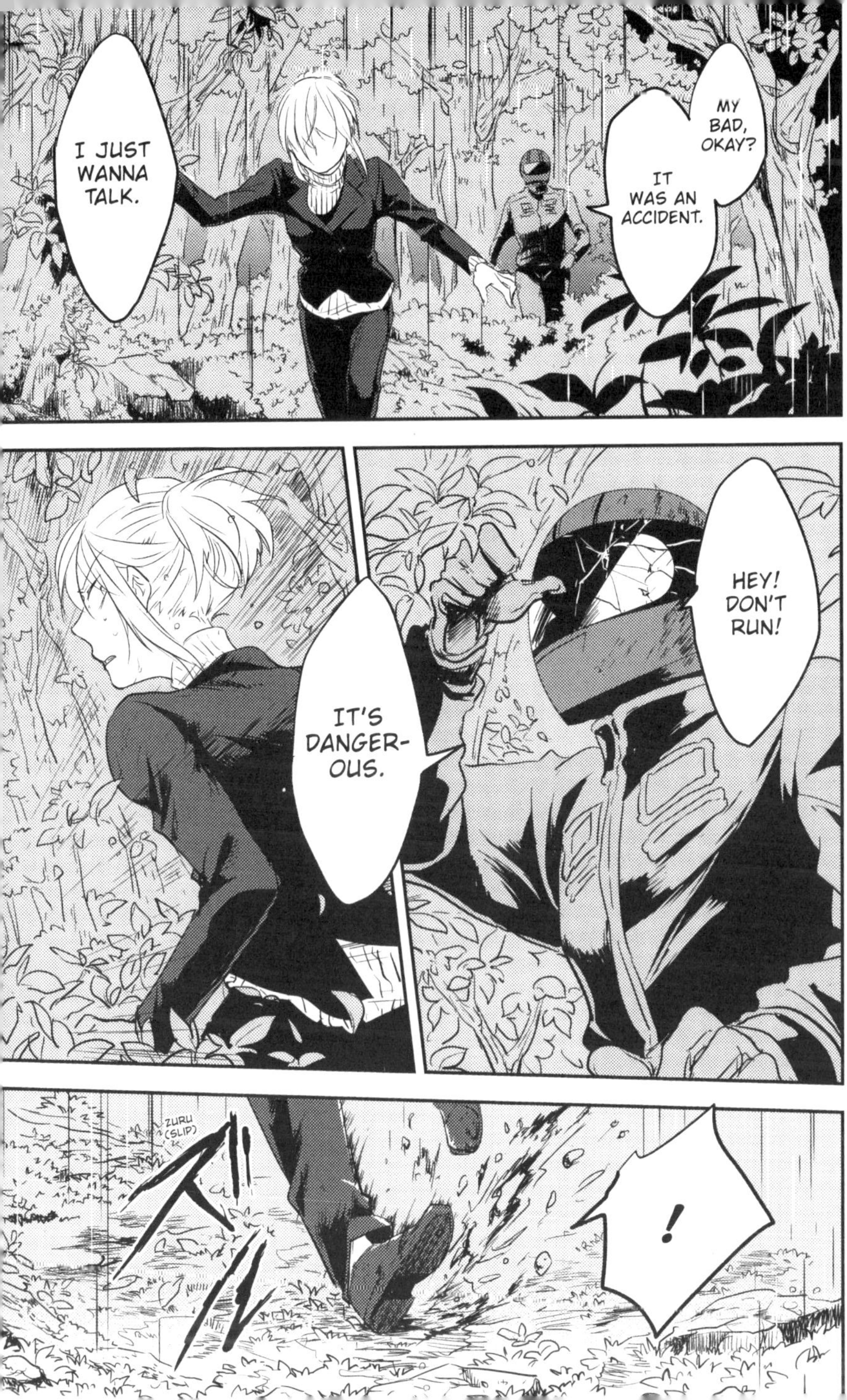
MY BAD, OKAY?
IT WAS AN ACCIDENT.
I JUST WANNA TALK.
HEY! DON'T RUN!
IT'S DANGER-OUS.
!
ZURU (SLIP)

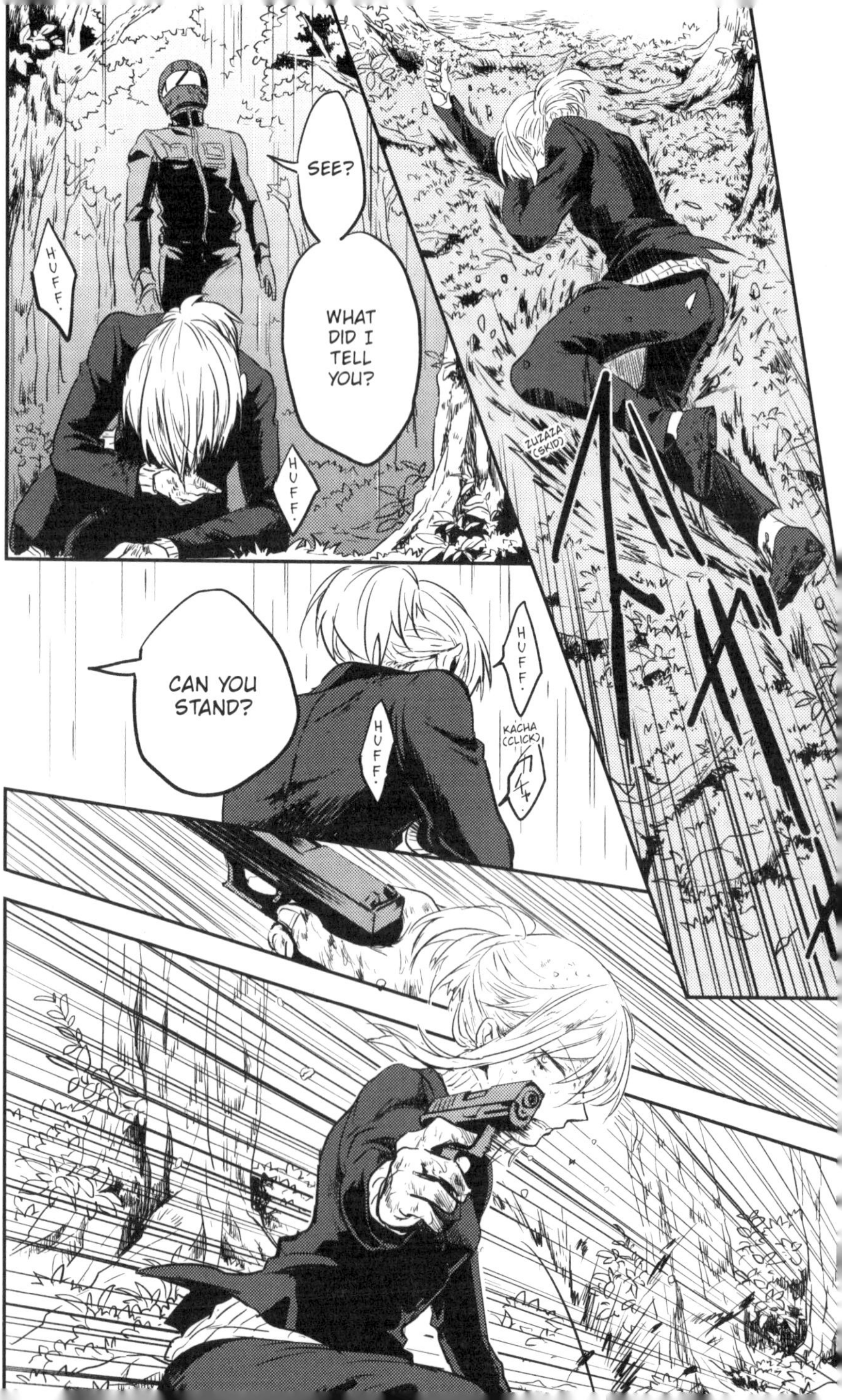
ZUZAZA (SKID)
HUFF.
SEE?
WHAT DID I TELL YOU?
HUFF.
HUFF.
KACHA (CLICK)
HUFF.
CAN YOU STAND?

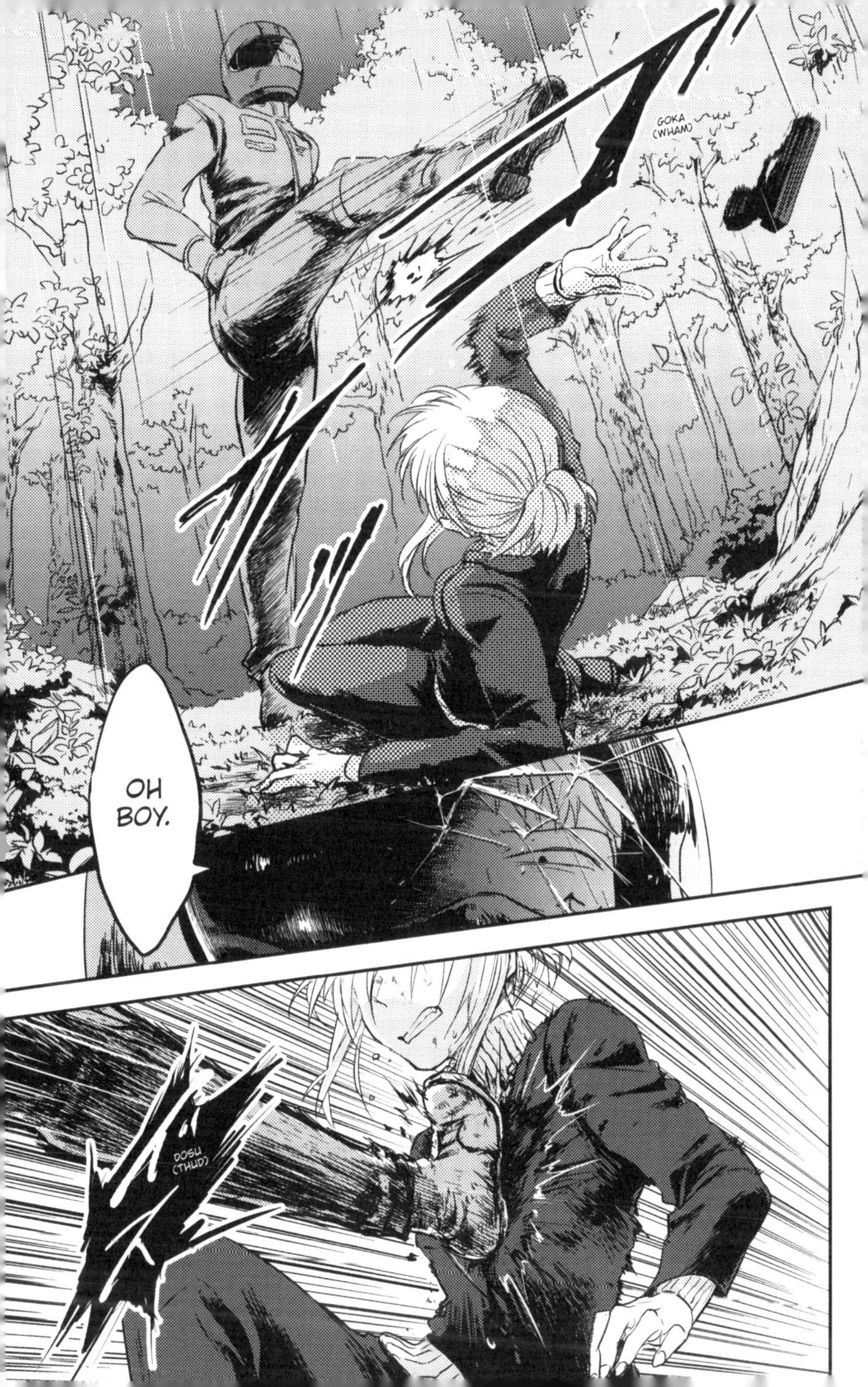
GOKA (WHAM)
OH BOY.
DOSU (THUD)

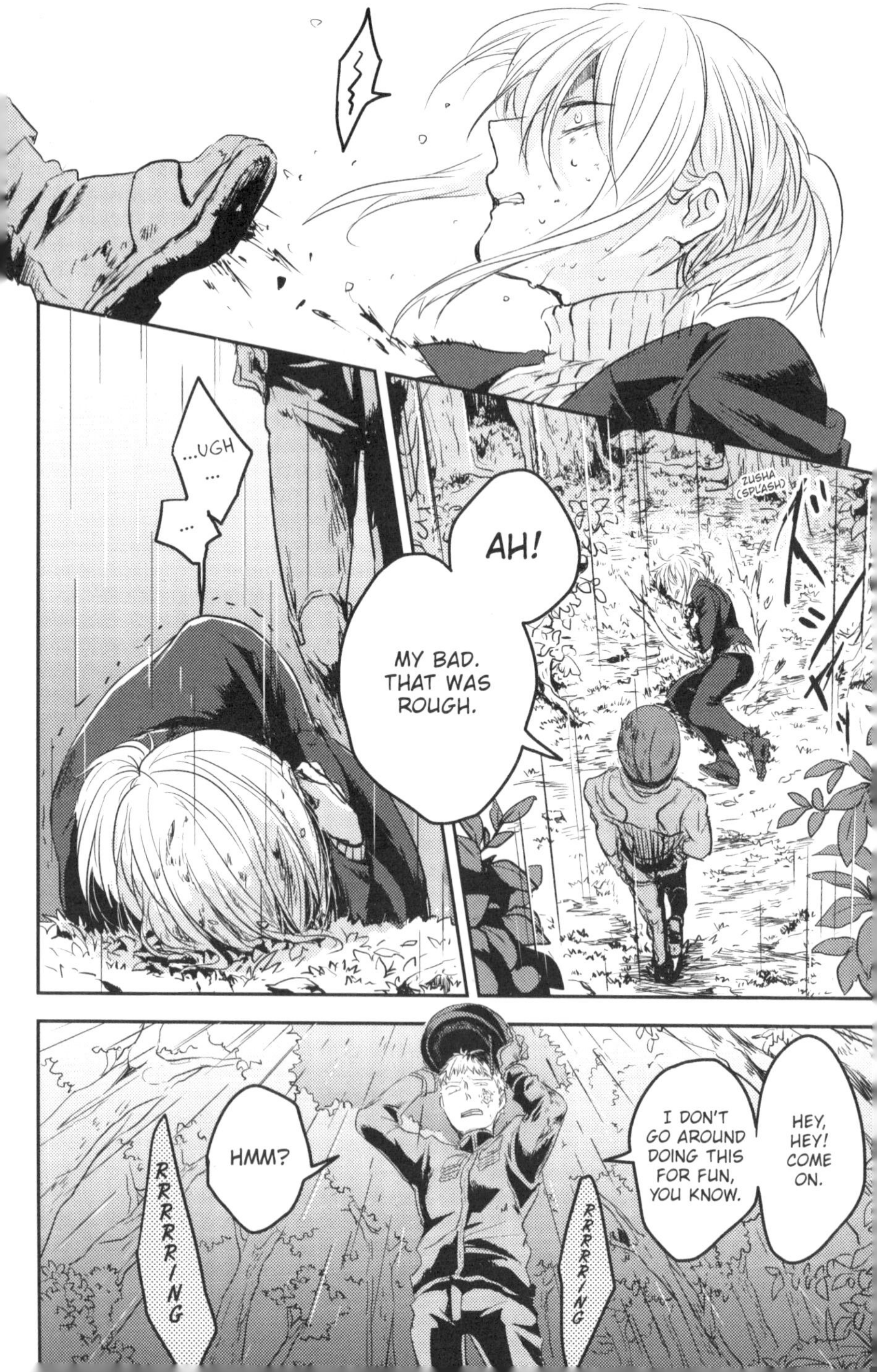

ZUSHA (SPLASH)
AH!
MY BAD. THAT WAS ROUGH.
...UGH
...
...
HEY, HEY! COME ON.
I DON'T GO AROUND DOING THIS FOR FUN, YOU KNOW.
RRRRRING
HMM?
RRRRRING

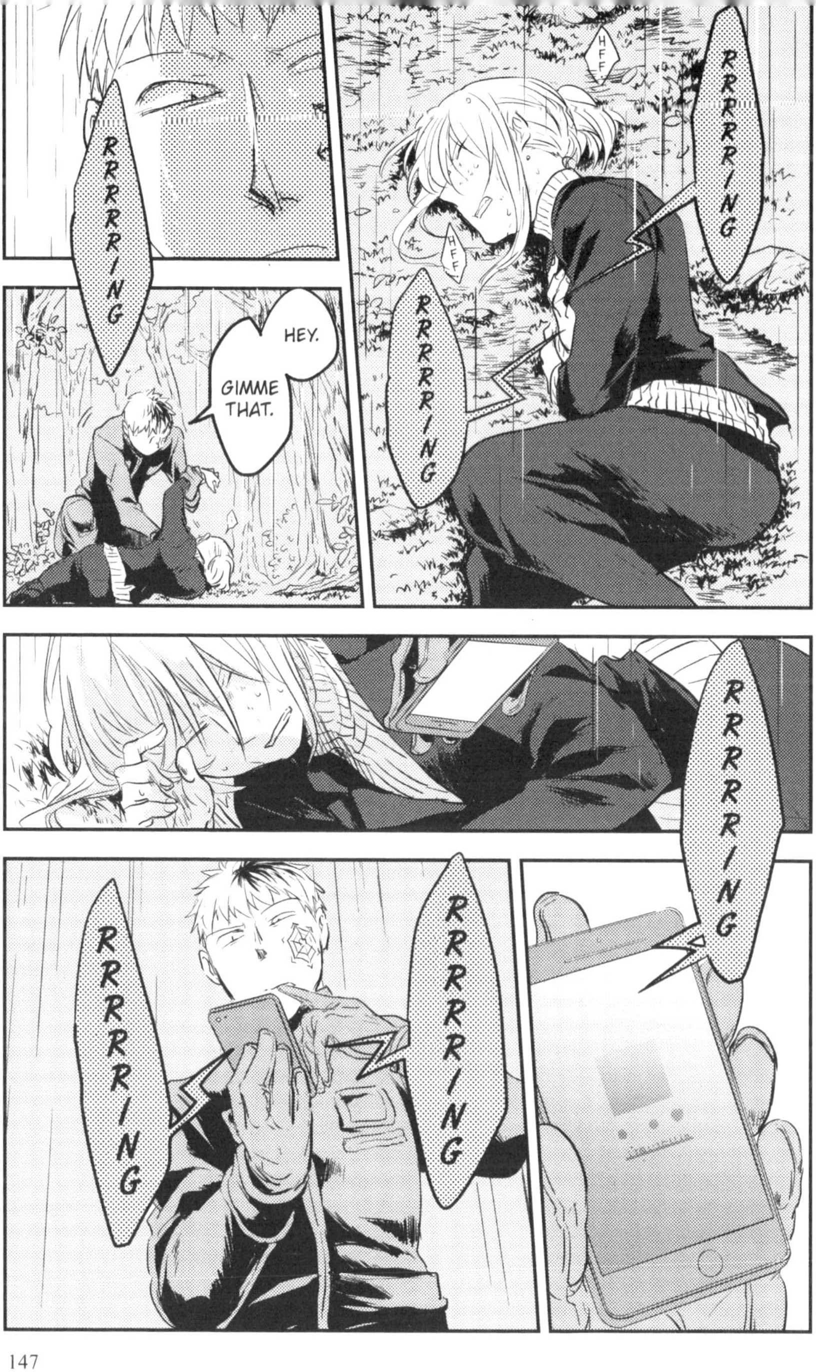
RRRRRING
HFF
HFF
RRRRRING
RRRRRING
HEY.
GIMME THAT.
RRRRRING
RRRRRING
RRRRRING

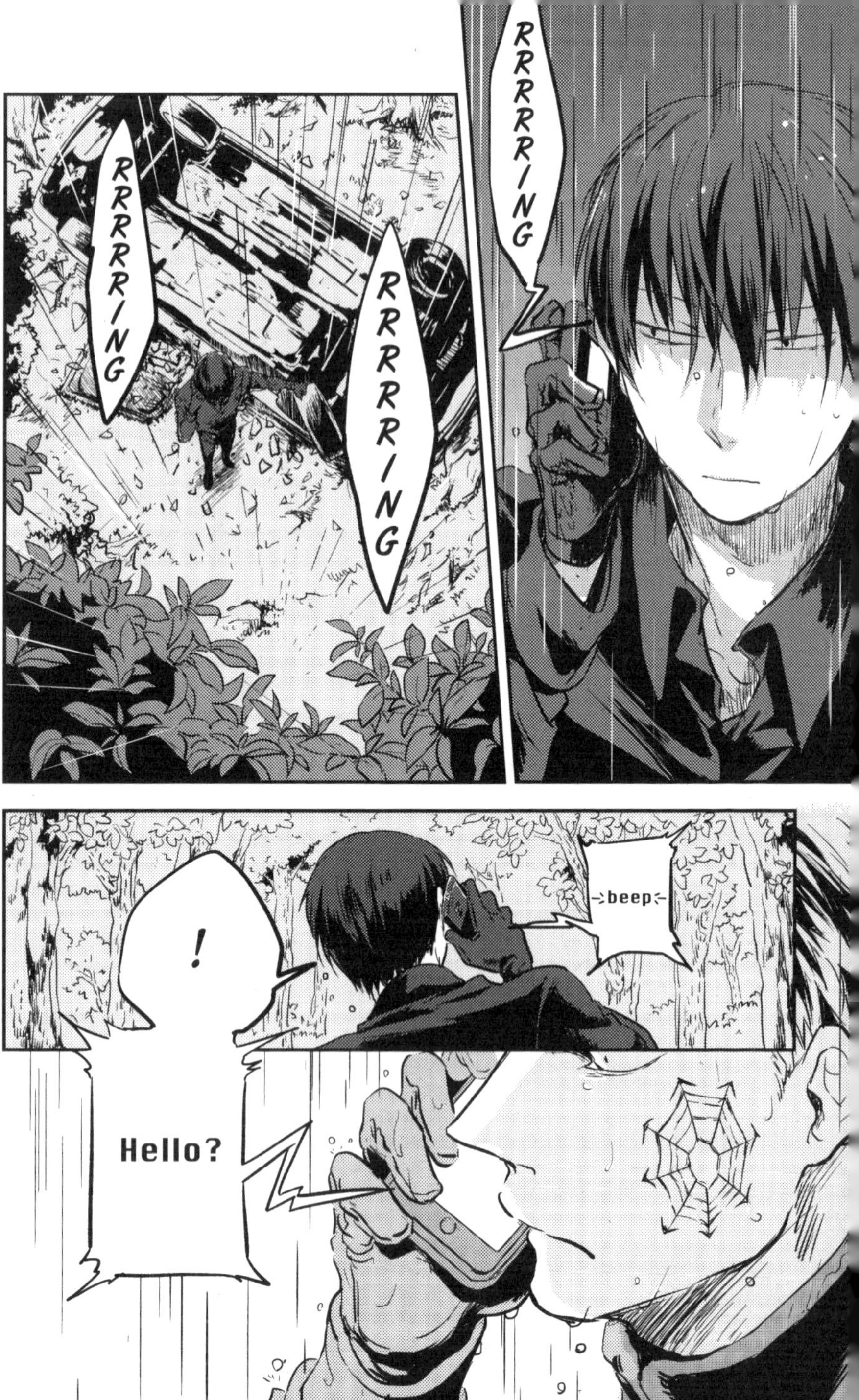
RRRRRING
RRRRRING
RRRRRING
beep
!
Hello?

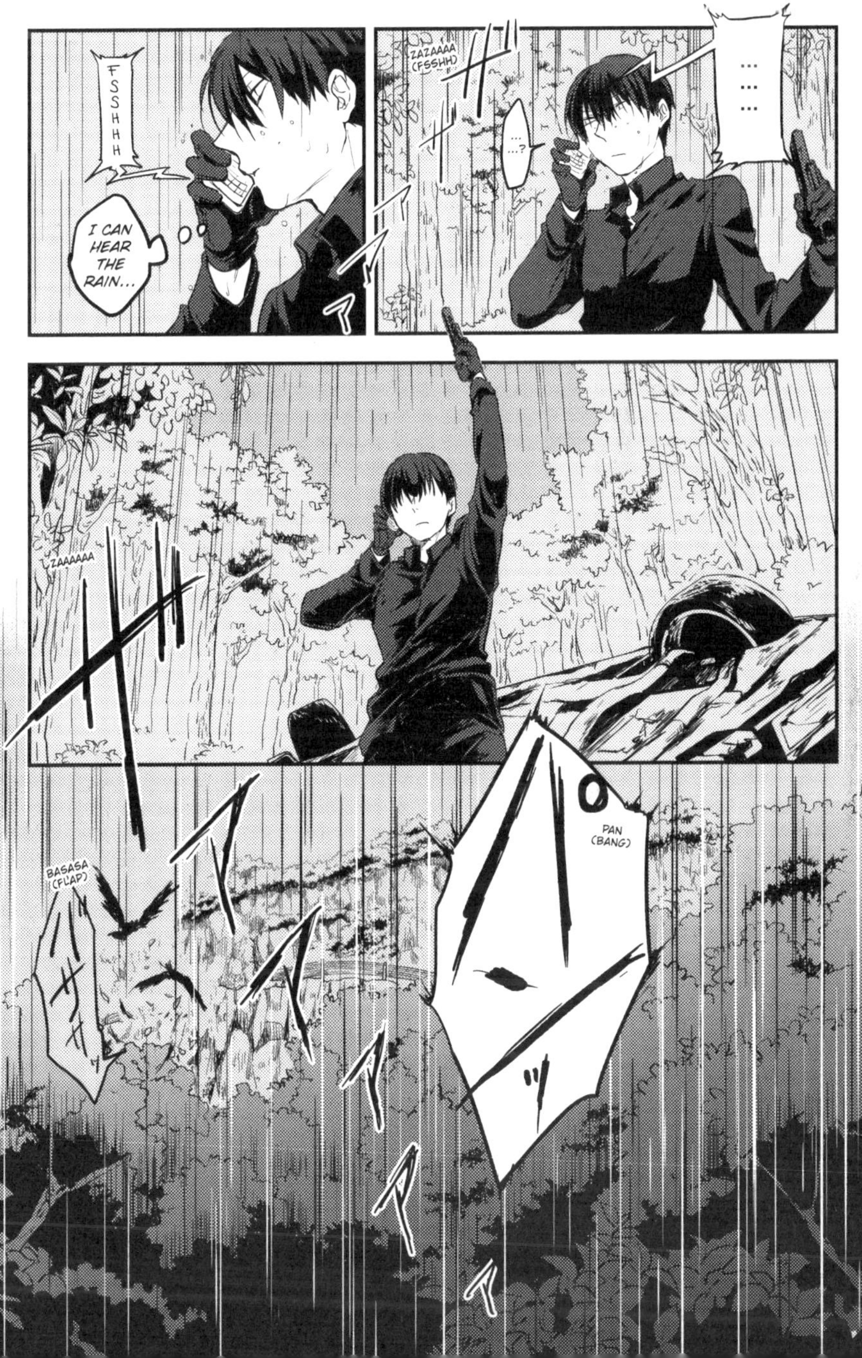
...
...
...
ZAZAAAA (FSSHH)
...
...?
FSSHHH
I CAN HEAR THE RAIN...
ZAAAAAA
PAN (BANG)
BASASA (FLAP)

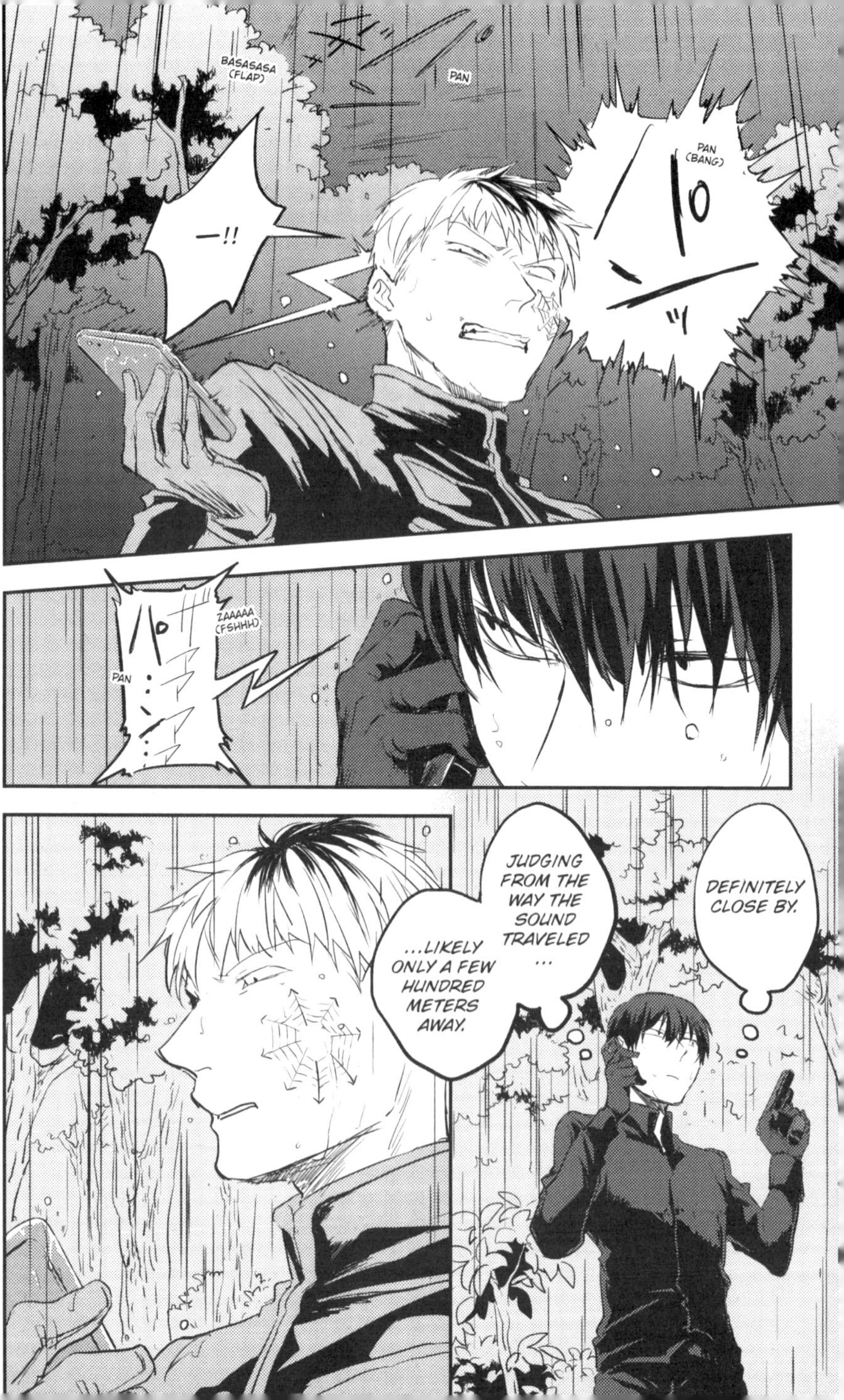
PAN
PAN (BANG)
BASASASA (FLAP)
—!!
ZAAAAA (FSHHH)
PAN
DEFINITELY CLOSE BY.
JUDGING FROM THE WAY THE SOUND TRAVELED...
...LIKELY ONLY A FEW HUNDRED METERS AWAY.

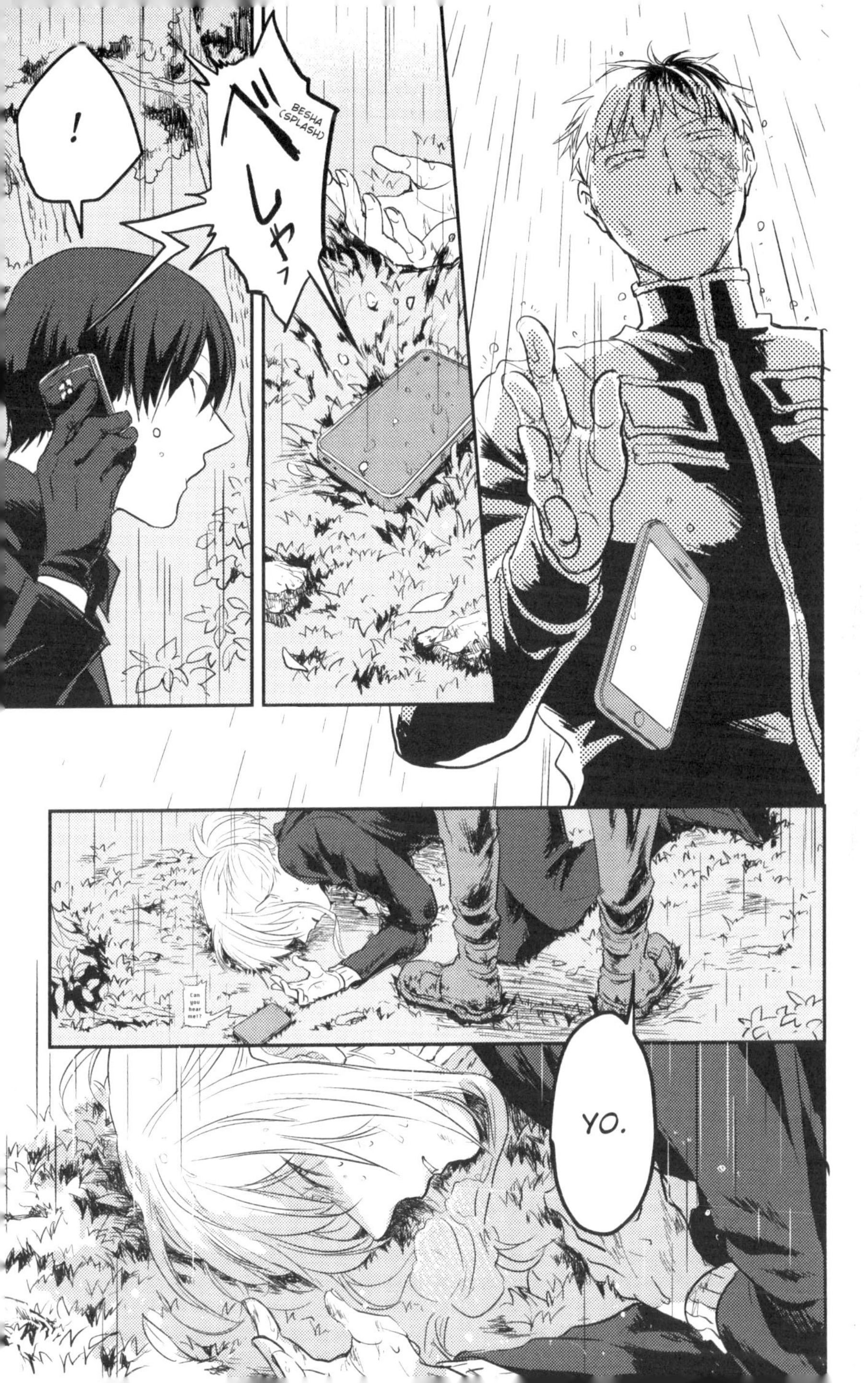
ベしゃっ
BESHA (SPLASH)
!
Can you hear me!?
YO.

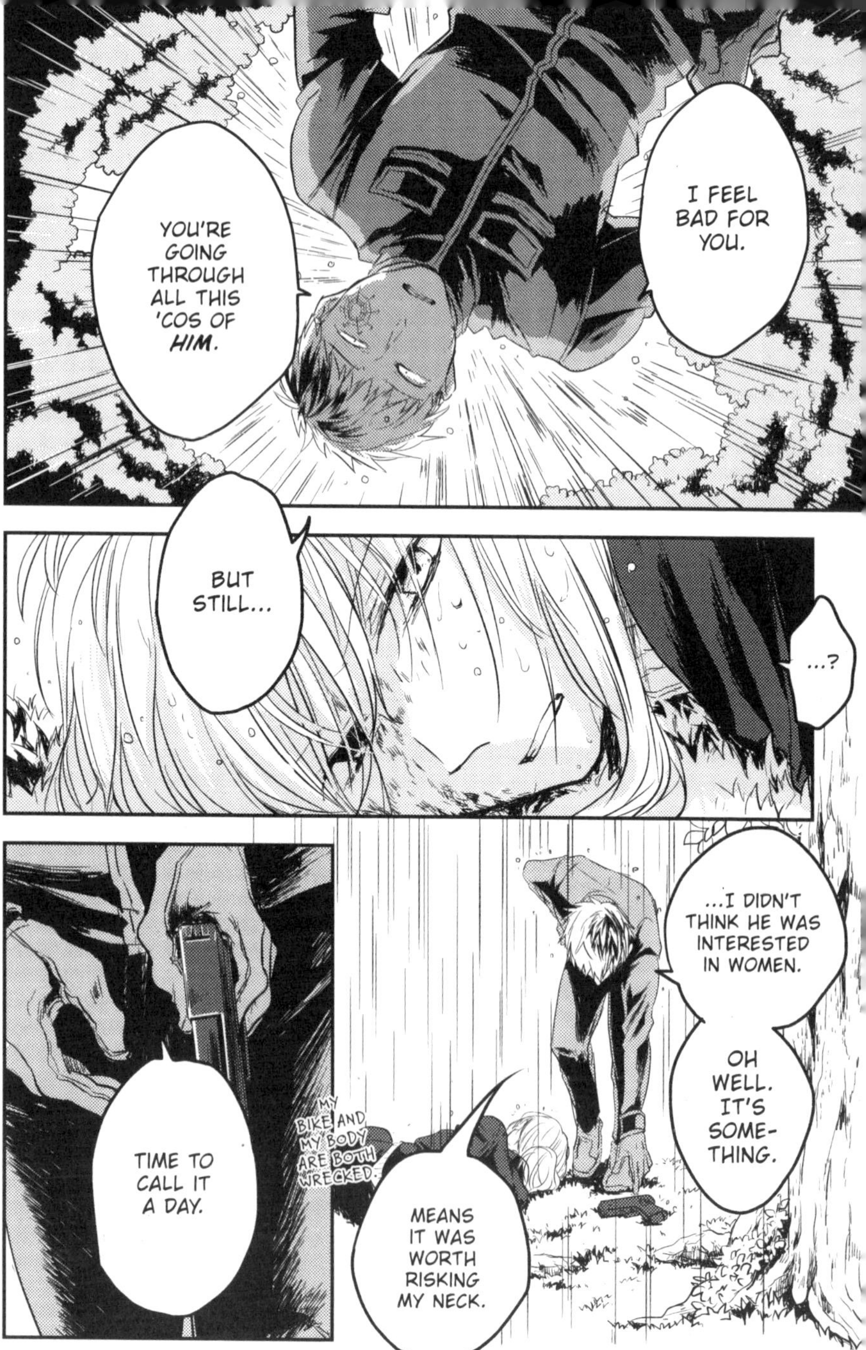
I FEEL BAD FOR YOU.
YOU'RE GOING THROUGH ALL THIS 'COS OF *HIM*.
BUT STILL...
...?
...I DIDN'T THINK HE WAS INTERESTED IN WOMEN.
OH WELL. IT'S SOME-THING.
MEANS IT WAS WORTH RISKING MY NECK.
MY BIKE AND MY BODY ARE BOTH WRECKED.
TIME TO CALL IT A DAY.

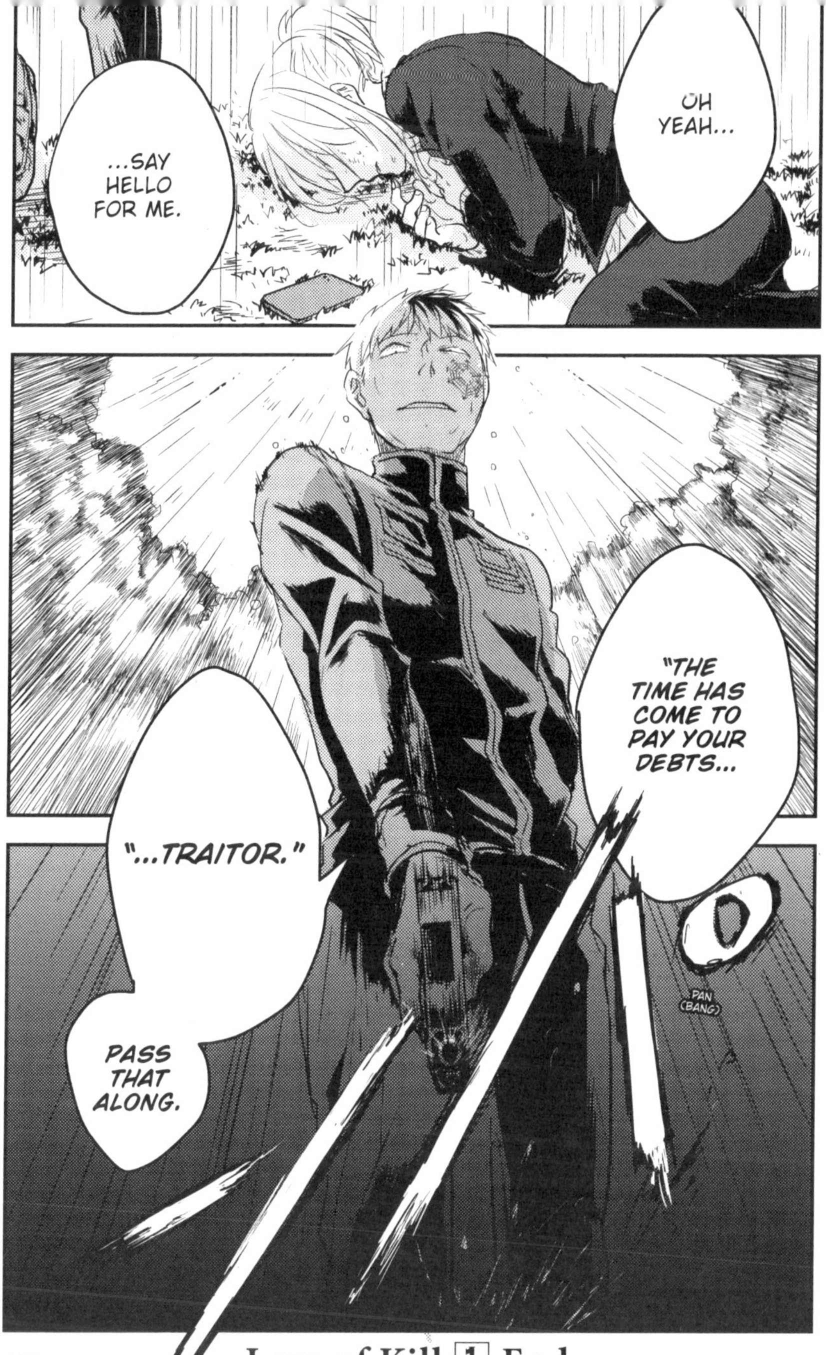
OH YEAH...
...SAY HELLO FOR ME.
"THE TIME HAS COME TO PAY YOUR DEBTS...
"...TRAITOR."
PAN (BANG)
PASS THAT ALONG.

Love of Kill [1] End

THE FOLLOWING IS A SPECIAL COMIC
FOR THE COLLECTED VOLUME.

Special File

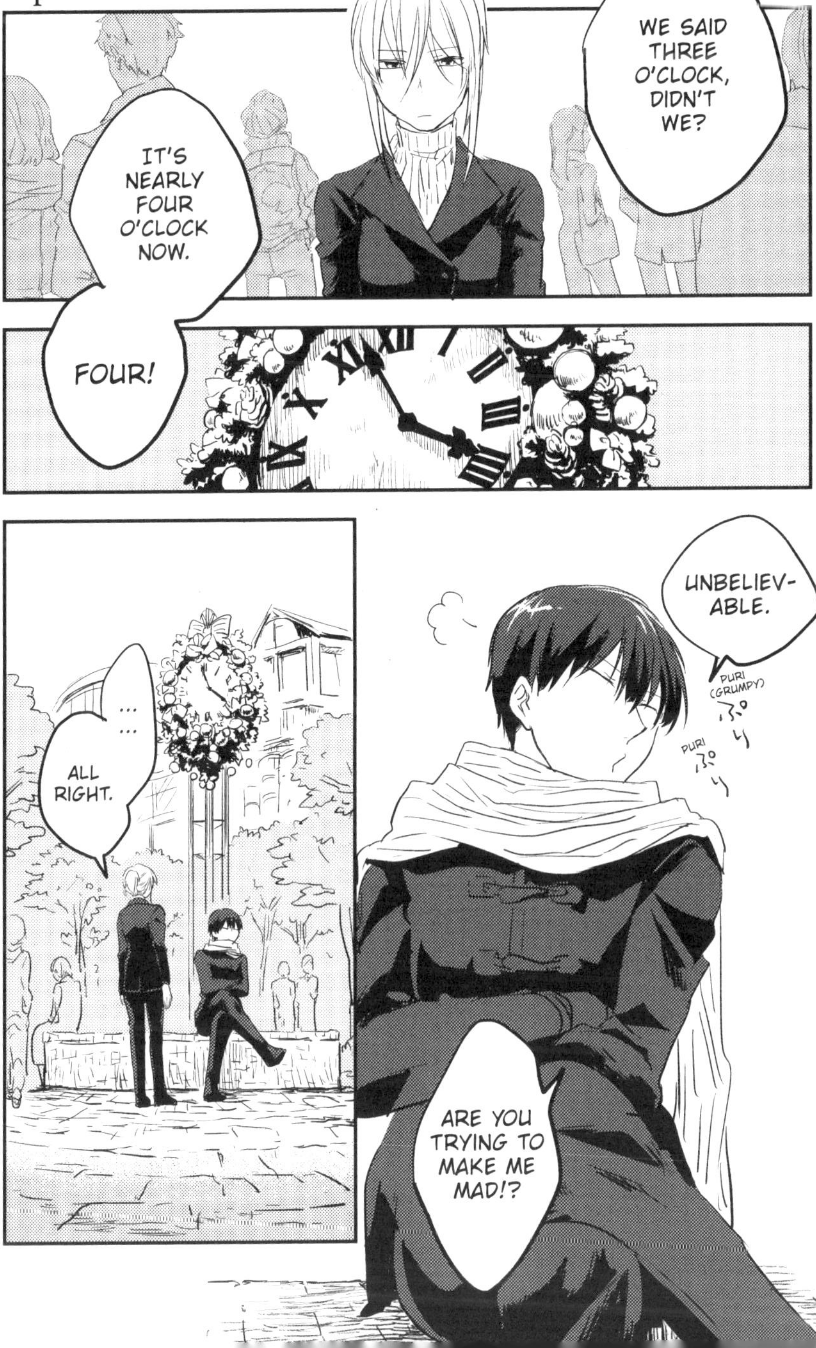
WE SAID THREE O'CLOCK, DIDN'T WE?
IT'S NEARLY FOUR O'CLOCK NOW.
FOUR!
UNBELIEV-ABLE.
PURI (GRUMPY) ぷり
PURI ぷり
ARE YOU TRYING TO MAKE ME MAD!?
... ...
ALL RIGHT.

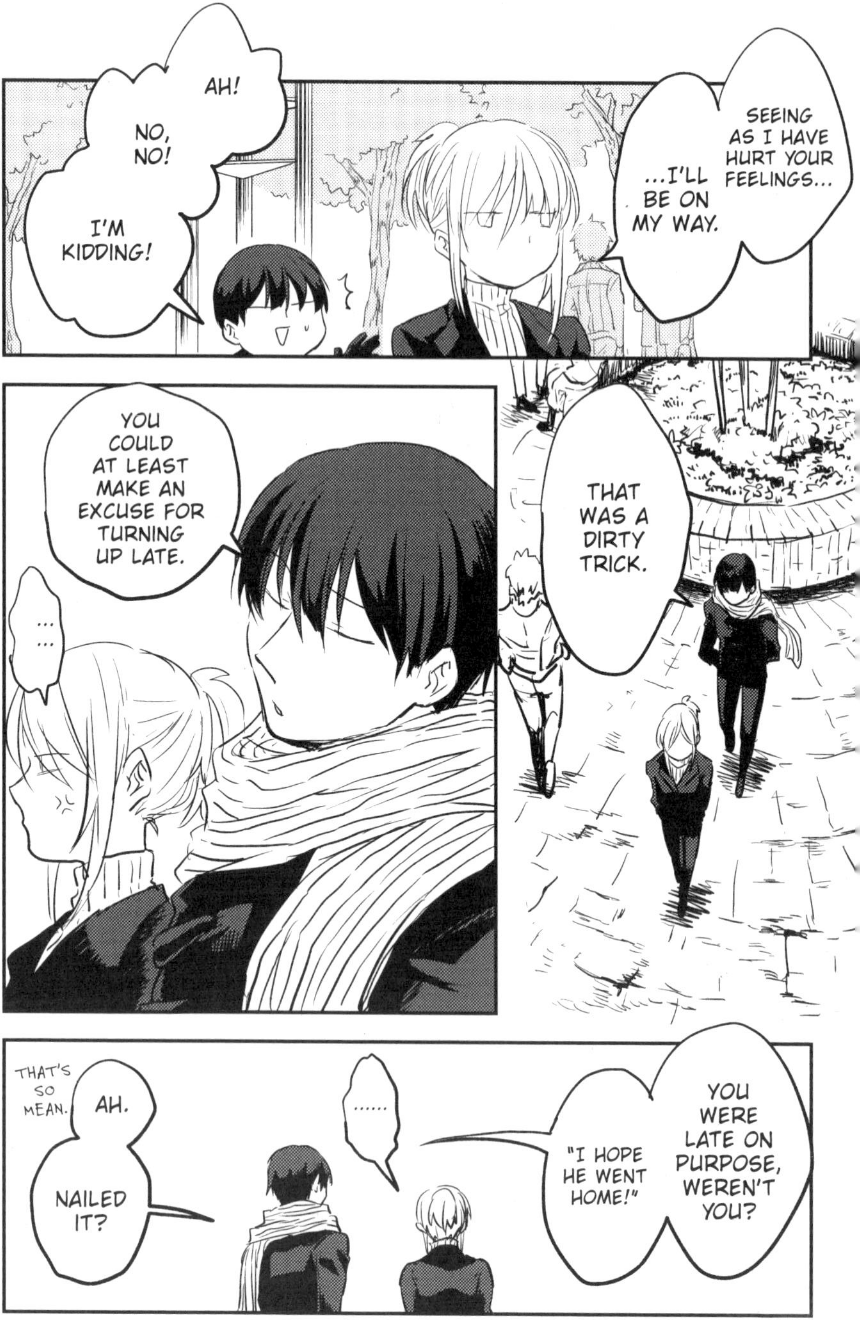
SEEING AS I HAVE HURT YOUR FEELINGS...
...I'LL BE ON MY WAY.
AH! NO, NO! I'M KIDDING!
THAT WAS A DIRTY TRICK.
YOU COULD AT LEAST MAKE AN EXCUSE FOR TURNING UP LATE.
......
YOU WERE LATE ON PURPOSE, WEREN'T YOU?
"I HOPE HE WENT HOME!"
......
AH. NAILED IT?
THAT'S SO MEAN.

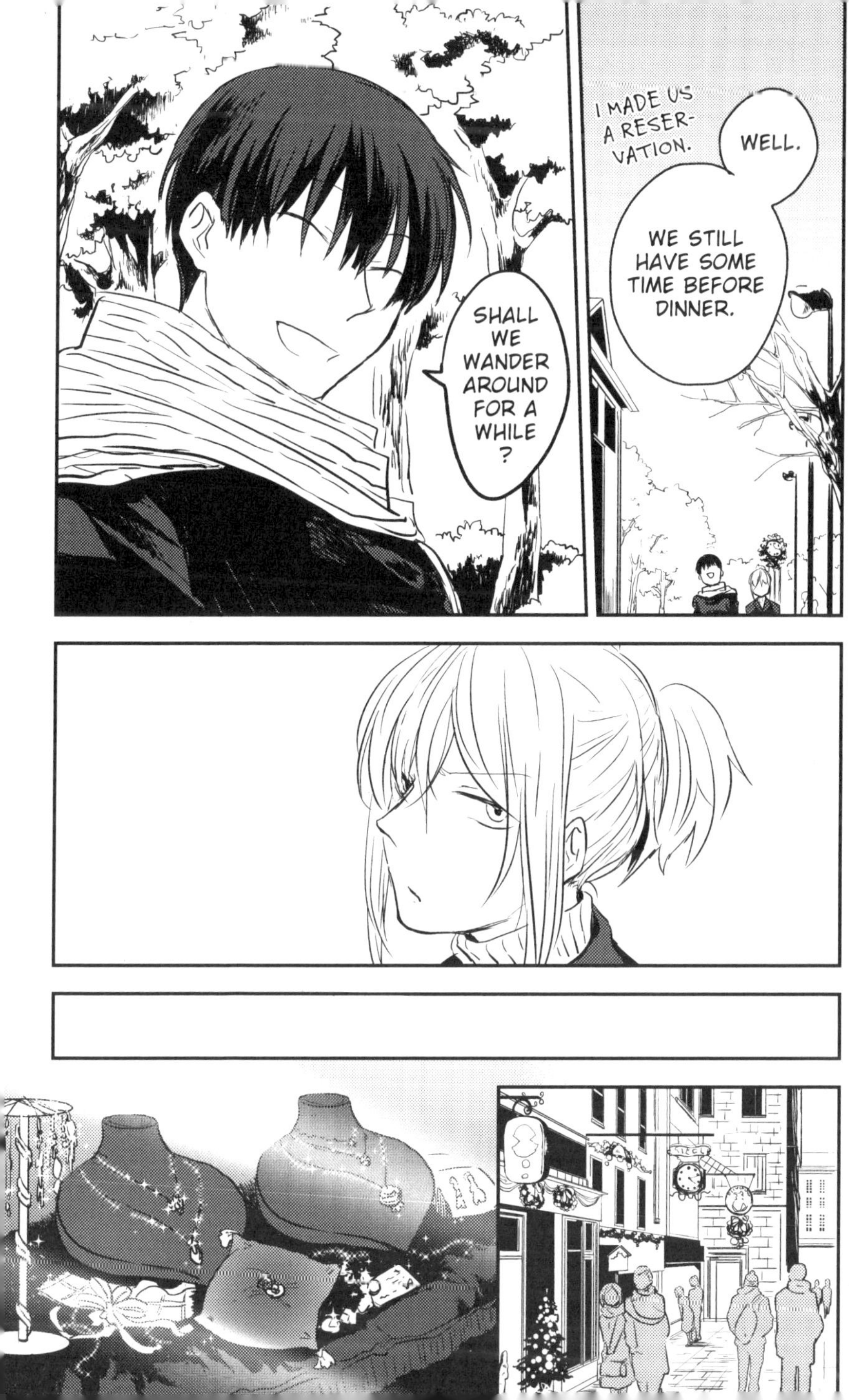
WELL.
WE STILL HAVE SOME TIME BEFORE DINNER.
I MADE US A RESERVATION.
SHALL WE WANDER AROUND FOR A WHILE?

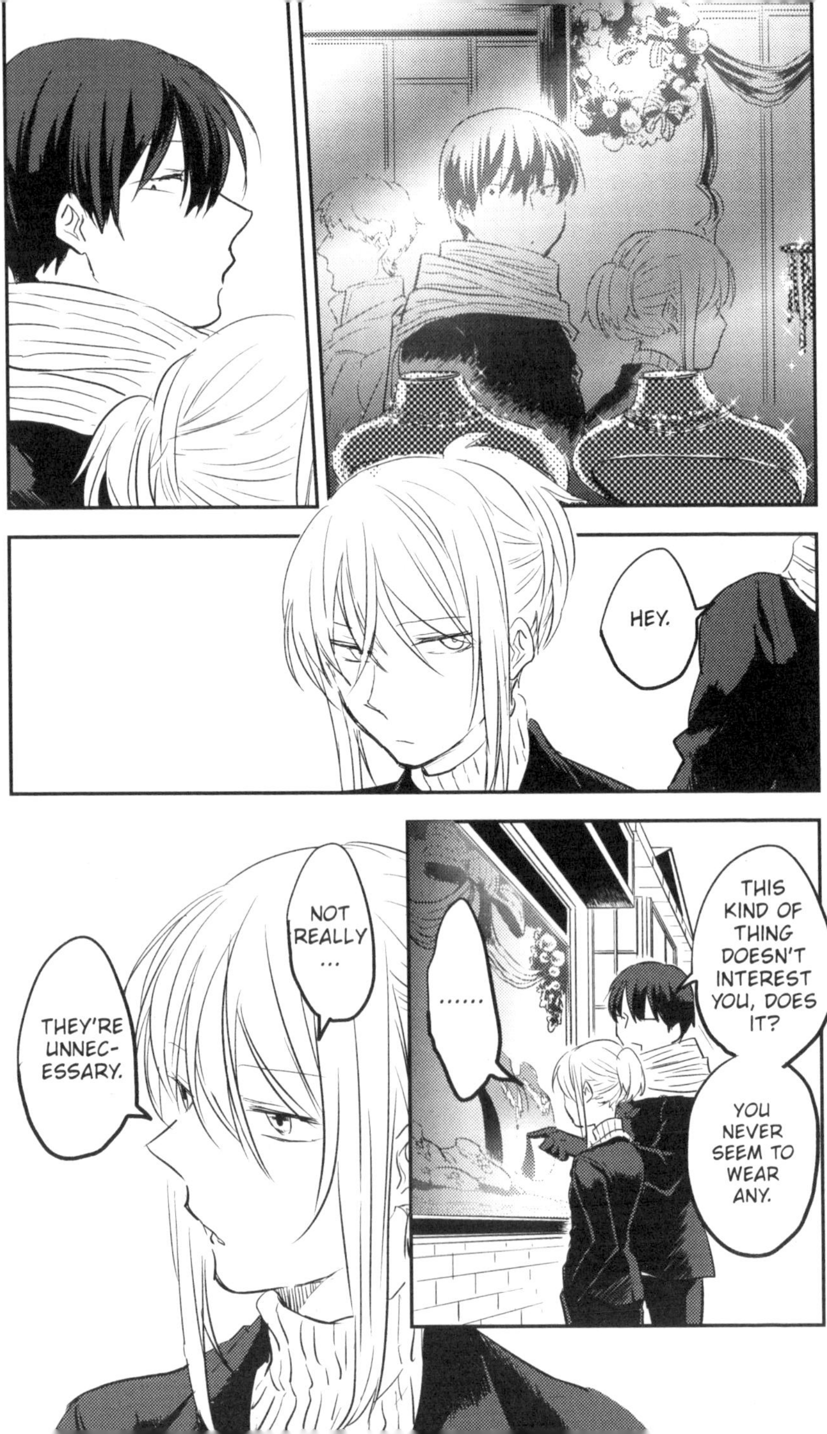
HEY.
THIS KIND OF THING DOESN'T INTEREST YOU, DOES IT?
YOU NEVER SEEM TO WEAR ANY.
......
NOT REALLY ...
THEY'RE UNNEC-ESSARY.

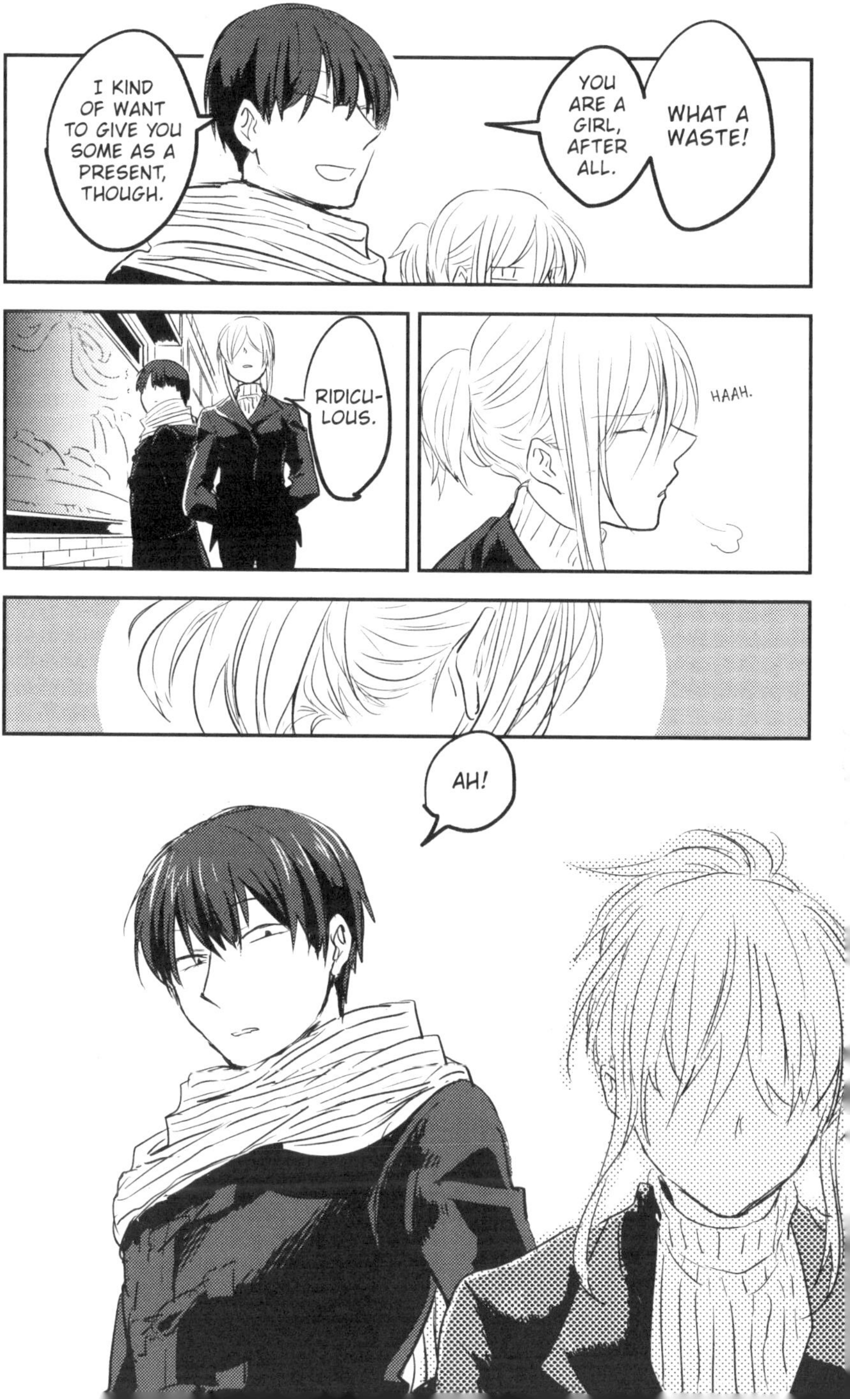
WHAT A WASTE!
YOU ARE A GIRL, AFTER ALL.
I KIND OF WANT TO GIVE YOU SOME AS A PRESENT, THOUGH.
HAAH.
RIDICULOUS.
AH!

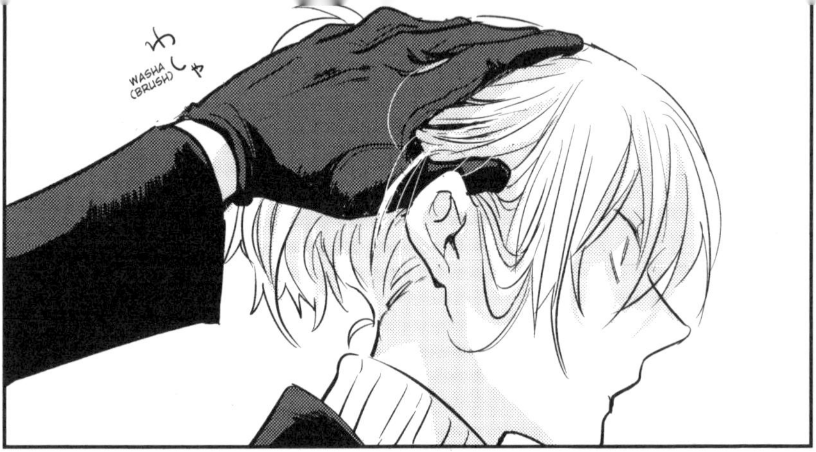
わしゃ
WASHA (BRUSH)

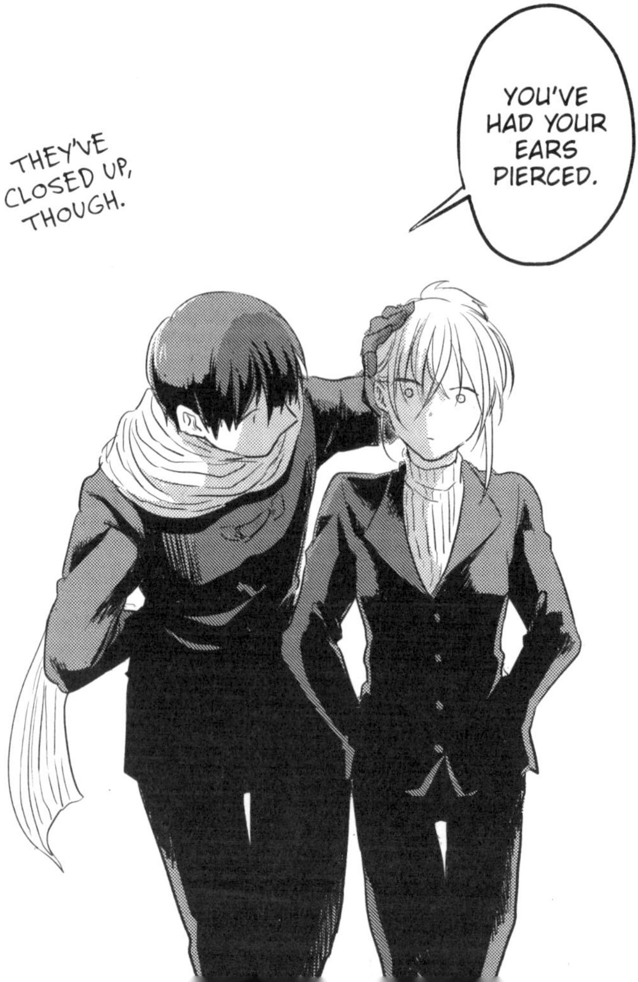
YOU'VE HAD YOUR EARS PIERCED.
THEY'VE CLOSED UP, THOUGH.

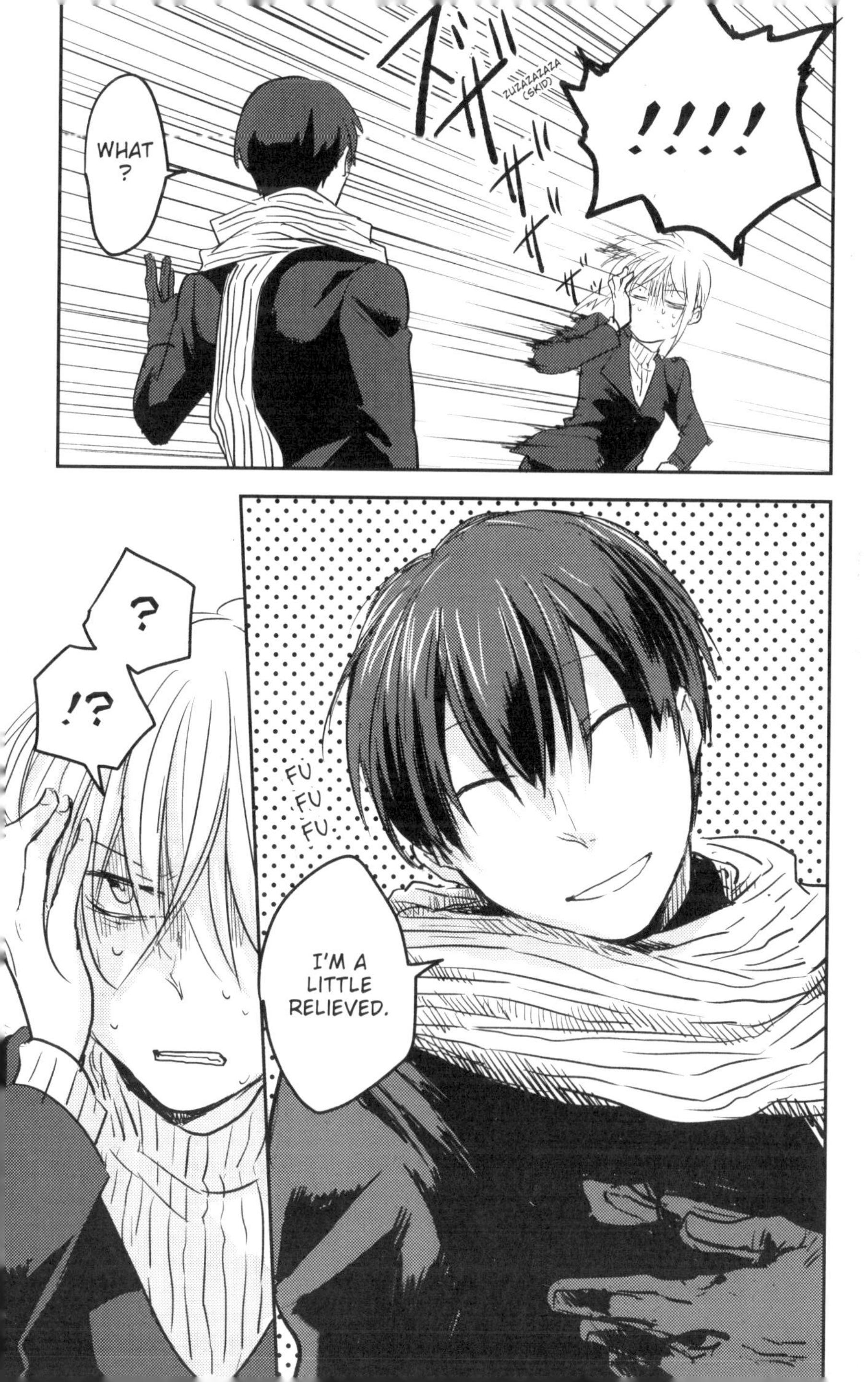
!!!!!
ZUZAZAZAZA (SKID)
WHAT ?
FU FU FU
I'M A LITTLE RELIEVED.
?
!?

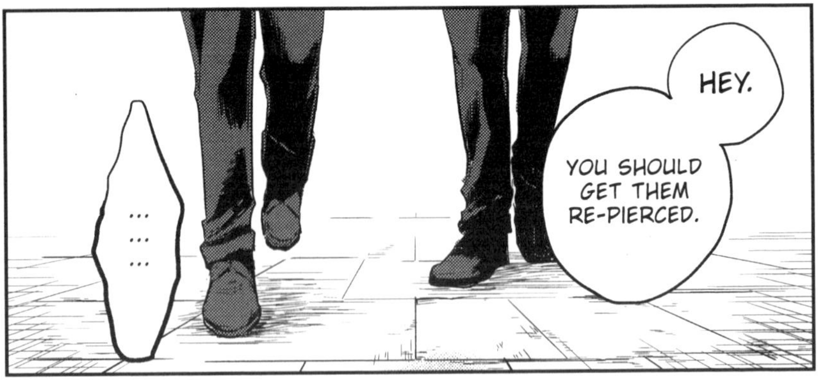
HEY.
YOU SHOULD GET THEM RE-PIERCED.
... ...

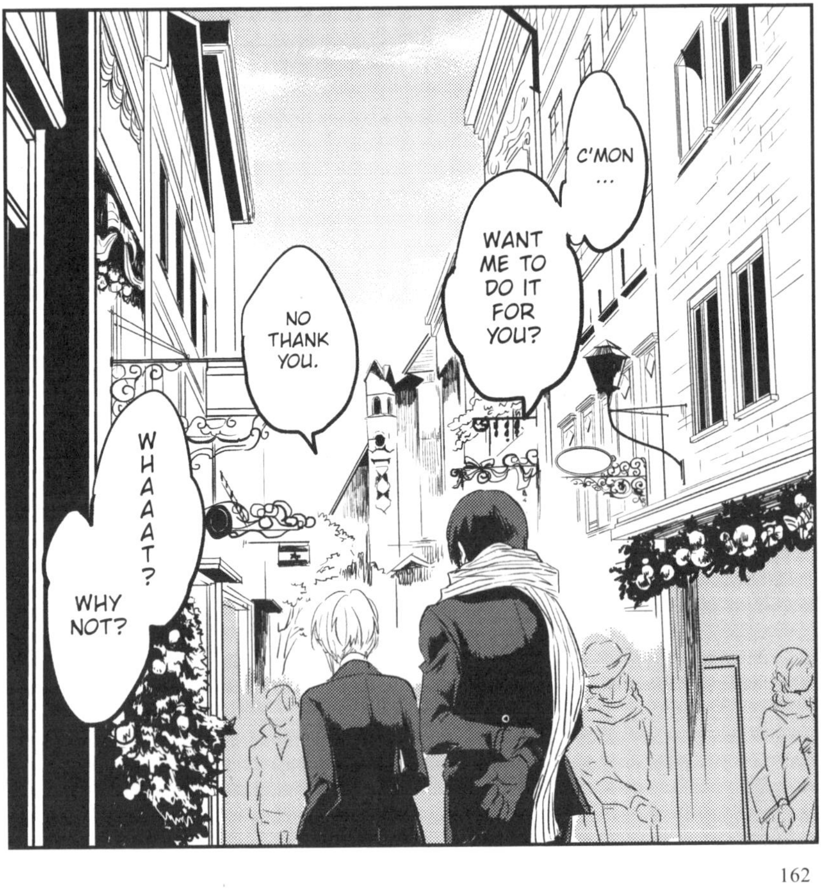
C'MON ...
WANT ME TO DO IT FOR YOU?
NO THANK YOU.
WHAAAAT?
WHY NOT?

AFTERWORD

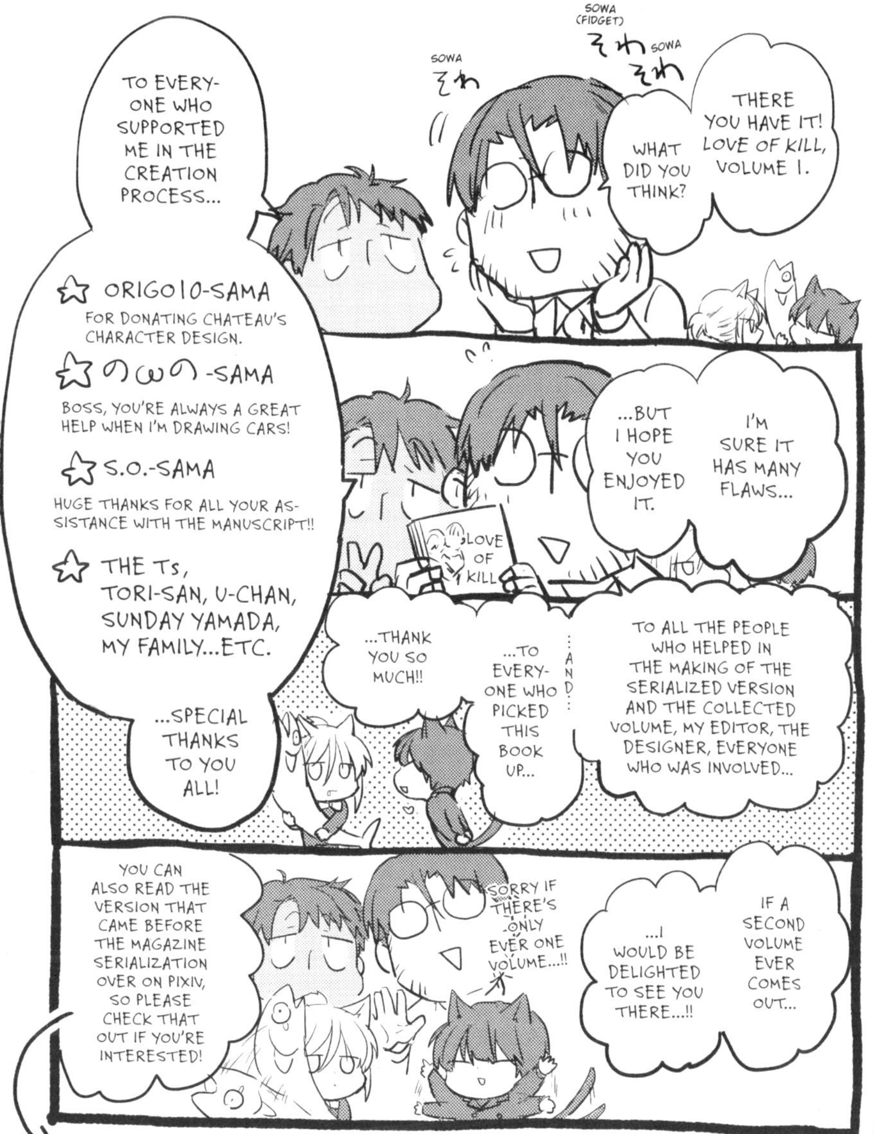
SOWA (FIDGET)
SOWA
SOWA
THERE YOU HAVE IT! LOVE OF KILL, VOLUME 1.
WHAT DID YOU THINK?
TO EVERYONE WHO SUPPORTED ME IN THE CREATION PROCESS...
☆ ORIGO10-SAMA
FOR DONATING CHATEAU'S CHARACTER DESIGN.
☆ のωの-SAMA
BOSS, YOU'RE ALWAYS A GREAT HELP WHEN I'M DRAWING CARS!
☆ S.O.-SAMA
HUGE THANKS FOR ALL YOUR ASSISTANCE WITH THE MANUSCRIPT!!
☆ THE Ts, TORI-SAN, U-CHAN, SUNDAY YAMADA, MY FAMILY...ETC.
I'M SURE IT HAS MANY FLAWS...
...BUT I HOPE YOU ENJOYED IT.
LOVE OF KILL
TO ALL THE PEOPLE WHO HELPED IN THE MAKING OF THE SERIALIZED VERSION AND THE COLLECTED VOLUME, MY EDITOR, THE DESIGNER, EVERYONE WHO WAS INVOLVED...
...AND...
...TO EVERYONE WHO PICKED THIS BOOK UP...
...THANK YOU SO MUCH!!
...SPECIAL THANKS TO YOU ALL!
IF A SECOND VOLUME EVER COMES OUT...
...I WOULD BE DELIGHTED TO SEE YOU THERE...!!
SORRY IF THERE'S ONLY EVER ONE VOLUME...!!
YOU CAN ALSO READ THE VERSION THAT CAME BEFORE THE MAGAZINE SERIALIZATION OVER ON PIXIV, SO PLEASE CHECK THAT OUT IF YOU'RE INTERESTED!

http://www.pixiv.net/member.php?id=874760
(Only available in Japanese)

LOVE -OF KILL 01

Fe

Translation: Eleanor Ruth Summers   **Lettering: Chiho Christie**

KOROSHIAI Vol. 1
© Fe 2016
First published in Japan in 2016 by KADOKAWA CORPORATION, Tokyo.
English translation rights arranged with KADOKAWA CORPORATION, Tokyo, through Tuttle-Mori Agency, Inc., Tokyo.

English translation © 2021 by Yen Press, LLC

Yen Press
150 West 30th Street, 19th Floor
New York, NY 10001

Visit us at yenpress.com
facebook.com/yenpress
twitter.com/yenpress
yenpress.tumblr.com
instagram.com/yenpress

First Yen Press Edition: March 2021

Yen Press is an imprint of Yen Press, LLC.
The Yen Press name and logo are trademarks of Yen Press, LLC.

The publisher is not responsible for websites (or their content) that are not owned by the publisher.

Library of Congress Control Number: 2020951788

ISBNs: 978-1-9753-2281-6 (paperback)
      978-1-9753-2282-3 (ebook)

10 9 8 7 6 5 4 3 2

TPA

Printed in South Korea